Raspberry Pi OS System Administration

The fourth volume in a new series exploring the basics of Raspberry Pi Operating System administration, this installment builds on the insights provided in Volumes 1, 2, and 3 to provide a compendium of easy-to-use and essential Raspberry Pi OS administration for the novice user, with specific focus on ancillary topics that can be used with the Raspberry Pi OS based upon upstream Debian Bookworm release, and the Raspberry Pi 5.

The overriding idea behind system administration of a modern, 21st-century Linux system such as the Raspberry Pi OS is the use of systemd to ensure that the Linux kernel works efficiently and effectively to provide these three foundation stones of computer operation and management: computer system concurrency, virtualization, and secure persistence. This fourth volume includes full-chapter explications, with many examples, of the following:

1) the Zettabyte File System (ZFS),
2) the X Window System, the Wayland protocol, XWayland, the Wayfire window manager, XCB, Qt5, and GTK4 graphics,
3) the Emacs text editor, and
4) a basic introduction to important Raspberry Pi commands for the novice user.

This book is aimed at students and practitioners looking to maximize their use of the Raspberry Pi OS. With plenty of practical examples, projects, and exercises, this volume can also be adopted in a more formal learning environment to supplement and extend the basic knowledge of a Linux operating system.

Robert M. Koretsky is a retired lecturer in Mechanical Engineering at the University of Portland School of Engineering. He previously worked as an automotive engineering designer at the Freightliner Corp. in Portland, Oregon. He's married, and has two kids and two grandkids.

Raspberry Pi OS System Administration with systemd
A Practical Approach
Series Editor: Robert M. Koretsky

Raspberry Pi OS System Administration with systemd: A Practical Approach
Robert M. Koretsky

Raspberry Pi OS System Administration with systemd and Python: A Practical Approach
Robert M. Koretsky

Raspberry Pi OS Text Editors, git, and LXC: A Practical Approach
Robert M. Koretsky

Raspberry Pi OS System Administration: Ancillary Topics
Robert M. Koretsky

www.routledge.com/Raspberry-Pi-OS-System-Administration-with-systemd/book-series/123

Raspberry Pi OS System Administration
Ancillary Topics

Robert M. Koretsky

CRC Press
Taylor & Francis Group
Boca Raton London New York

CRC Press is an imprint of the
Taylor & Francis Group, an **informa** business

A CHAPMAN & HALL BOOK

First edition published 2025
by CRC Press
2385 NW Executive Center Drive, Suite 320, Boca Raton FL 33431

and by CRC Press
4 Park Square, Milton Park, Abingdon, Oxon, OX14 4RN

CRC Press is an imprint of Taylor & Francis Group, LLC

ISBN: 978-1-032-75297-6 (hbk)
ISBN: 978-1-032-75296-9 (pbk)
ISBN: 978-1-003-47326-8 (ebk)

DOI: 10.1201/9781003473268

Typeset in Palatino
by Newgen Publishing UK

To my family.

Bob Koretsky

Contents

Series Preface

This series of books covers the basics of Raspberry Pi Operating System administration, and is geared toward a novice user. Each book is a complete, self-contained introduction to important system administration tasks, and to other useful programs. The foundation of all of them is the systemd super-kernel. They guide the user along a path that gives the "why" and "how to" of those important system administration topics, and they also present the following essential application facilities in four volumes:

1) Raspberry Pi OS System Administration with systemd, Volume 1
2) Raspberry Pi OS System Administration with systemd and Python, Volume 2
3) Raspberry Pi OS Text Editing, git, Virtualization with LXC/LXD, Volume 3
4) Raspberry Pi OS System Administration with systemd: Ancillary Topics, Volume 4

They can be used separately, or together, to fit the learning objectives/pace, and interests of the individual, independent learner, or can be adopted in a more formal learning environment, to supplement and extend the basic knowledge of a Linux operating system in a classroom environment that uses the Raspberry Pi OS.

In addition, each book has In-Chapter Exercises throughout, and a Question, Problems, and Projects addendum to help reinforce the learning goals of the individual student or reader.

An online Github site, with further materials and updates, program source code, solutions to In-Chapter Exercises, plus other supplements, is provided for each volume. It can be found at:

www.github.com/bobk48/RaspberryPiOS

The fundamental prerequisites of each volume are:

(1) knowledge of how to type a syntactically-correct Linux command on the command line,
(2) having access to a dedicated Raspberry Pi computer with the latest Raspberry Pi Operating System already installed and running on it,
(3) in some cases, being a privileged user on the system that is able to execute the **sudo** command to assume superuser status, and
(4) having a basic knowledge of how to edit and save text files in the **nano** text editor.

All instructions in these volumes were tested on either a Raspberry Pi 4B, or a Raspberry Pi 400, both with 4GB of memory, and the latest version of the Raspberry Pi OS at the time, either Debian-Bullseye or Debian-Bookworm.

Volume 4 Preface

Continuing the series of books that cover basic Raspberry Pi Operating System administration, this volume presents important subjects that are now available in the updated version of the Raspberry Pi OS. This new version is based upon the upstream Debian Bookworm release, and is meant to run on the Raspberry Pi 5, as well as on older Raspberry Pi systems, such as the Pi 3, Pi 4b, and Pi 400.

The topics presented in this volume are:

1. A basic introduction to important Raspberry Pi commands for the novice user.

2. A full-chapter explication, with many examples, of the Zettabyte File System (ZFS).

3. A full-chapter description, with many examples, of the X Window System, the Wayland protocol, XWayland, Wayfire, XCB, Qt5, and GTK4 graphics.

4. A full-chapter tutorial on the Emacs text editor, to supplement the text editors presented in Volume 3.

The subjects are geared toward a beginner and are complete, self-contained introductions to these ancillary programs, using the systemd super-kernel. They guide the user along a path that gives the "why" and "how to" of important Raspberry Pi applications. This volume can easily fit the learning objectives, pace, and interests of the individual, independent learner, or can be adopted in a more formal environment to supplement and extend the basic knowledge of a Linux operating system and its applications and programs in a classroom environment that uses the Raspberry Pi OS.

0

"Quick Start" into Sysadmin for the Raspberry Pi Operating System

0.0 Objectives

* To explain how to manage and maintain files and directories
* To show where to get system-wide help for Raspberry Pi OS commands
* To demonstrate the use of a beginner's set of utility commands
* To cover the basic commands and operators

cat, cd, cp, exit, hostname, login, lp, lpr, ls, man, mesg, mkdir, more, mv, passwd, PATH, pwd, rm, rmdir, telnet, unalias, uname, whatis, whereis, who, whoami

0.1 Introduction

To start working productively with system administration on the Raspberry Pi OS, the beginner needs to have some familiarity with these sequential topics, as follows:

1. How to maintain and organize files in the file structure of the operating system. Creating a tree-like structure of folders (also called directories), and storing files in a logical fashion in these folders, is critical to working efficiently in the Raspberry Pi OS.

2. How to get help on text-based commands and their usage. With keyboard entry, in a command-based, Character User Interface (CUI) environment, being able to find out, in a quick and easy way, how to use a command, its options, and arguments by typing it on the keyboard correctly, is imperative to working efficiently.

DOI: 10.1201/9781003473268-1

3. How to execute a small set of essential utility commands to set up or customize your working environment. Once a beginner is familiar with the right way to construct file maintenance commands, adding a set of utility commands makes each session more productive.

To use this chapter successfully as a springboard into the remainder of the book, you should carefully read, follow, and execute the instructions and command line sessions we provide, in the order presented. Each section in this chapter, and every subsequent chapter as well, builds on the information that precedes it. They will give you the concepts, command tools, and methods that will enable you to do system administration using the Raspberry Pi OS.

Throughout this book, we illustrate everything using the following version of the Raspberry Pi OS, on the hardware listed:

System: Host: raspberrypi Kernel: 6.1.0-rpi7-rpi-v8 arch: aarch64 bits: 64
   compiler: gcc v: 12.2.0 Desktop: LXDE v: 0.10.1 Distro: Debian GNU/Linux
   12   (bookworm)
Machine: Type: ARM System: Raspberry Pi 400 Rev 1.0 details: N/A
   rev: c03130   serial: 10000000fdd89bf2

In the chapters, the major commands we want to illustrate are first defined with an abbreviated syntax description, which will clarify general components of those commands. The syntax description format is as follows:

Syntax: The exact syntax of how a command, its options, and its arguments are correctly typed on the command line

Purpose: The specific purpose of the command

Output: A short description of the results of executing the command

Commonly used options/features: A listing of the most popular and useful options and option arguments

In addition, the following web link is to a site that allows you to type-in a single or multiple Raspberry Pi OS commands, and get a verbose explanation of the components of that command:

https://explainshell.com/

In-Chapter Exercises

1. Type the following commands on your Raspberry Pi OS command line, and note the results. Which ones are syntactically incorrect? Why? (The Bash prompt is shown as the $ character in each, and we assume that **file1** and **file2** exist)

    $ **la -ls**

$ **cat**

$ **more -q file1**

$ **more file2**

$ **time**

$ **lsblk-a**

2. How can you differentiate a Raspberry Pi OS command from its options, option arguments, and command arguments?

3. What is the difference between a single Raspberry Pi OS command, and a multiple Raspberry Pi OS command, as typed on the command line before pressing **<Enter>**?

4. If you get no error message after you enter a Raspberry Pi OS command, how do you know that it actually accomplished what you wanted it to?

0.2 File Maintenance Commands and Help On Raspberry Pi OS Command Usage

After your first-time login to a new Raspberry Pi OS, one of your first actions will be to construct and organize your workspace environment, and the files that will be contained in it. The operation of organizing your files according to some logical scheme is known as *file maintenance*. A logical scheme used to organize your files might consist of creating *bins* for storing files according to the subject matter of the contents of the files, or according to the dates of their creation. In the following sections, you will type file creation and maintenance commands that produce a structure similar to what is shown in Figure 0.1. Complete the operations in the following sections in the order they are presented, to get a better overview of what file maintenance really is. Also, it is critical that you review what was presented in the Preface regarding the structure of a Raspberry Pi OS command, so that when you begin to type commands for file maintenance, you understand how the syntax of what you are typing conforms to the general syntax of any Raspberry Pi OS command.

0.2.1 File and Directory Structure

When you first open a terminal, or console, window, you are working in the *home directory*, or folder, of the autonomous user associated with the user-name and password you used to log into the system with. Whatever directory you are presently in is known as the *current working directory*, and there is only one current working directory active at any given time. It is helpful to visualize the structure of your files and directories using a diagram. Figure 0.1

is an example of a home directory and file structure for a user named **bob**. In this figure, directories are represented as parallelograms and plain files (e.g., files that contain text or binary instructions) are represented as rectangles. A *pathname*, or path, is simply a textual way of designating the location of a directory or file in the complete file structure of the Raspberry Pi OS system you are working on. For example, the path to the file **myfile2** in Figure 0.1 is **/home/bob/myfile2**. The designation of the path begins at the root (/) of the entire file system, descends to the folder named **home**, and then descends again to the home directory of the user named **bob**.

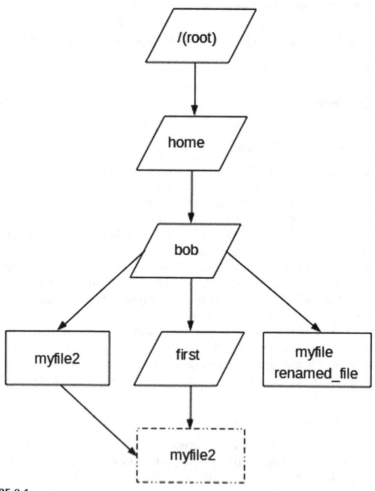

FIGURE 0.1

Example directory structure.

As shown in Figure 0.1, the files named **myfile, myfile2,** and **renamed_file** are stored under or in the directory **bob**. Beneath **bob** is a *subdirectory* named **first**. In the following sections, you will create these files, and the subdirectory structure, in the home directory of the username that you have logged into your Raspberry Pi OS system with.

In-Chapter Exercise

5. Type the following two commands on your Raspberry Pi OS system:

    $ **cd /**
    $ **ls**

Similar to Figure 0.1, sketch a diagram of the directories and files whose names you see listed as the output of the second command. Save this diagram for use later.

0.2.2 Viewing the Contents of Files

To begin working with files, you can easily create a new text file by using the cat command. The syntax of the cat command is as follows:

cat [options] [file-list]

Purpose: Join one or more files sequentially or display them in the console window

Output: Contents of the files in **file-list** displayed on the screen, one file at a time

Commonly used options/features:

+E   Display $ at the end of each line
-n   Put line numbers on the displayed lines
-- help   Display the purpose of the command and a brief explanation of each option

The **cat** command, short for concatenate, allows you to join files. In the example you will join what you type on the keyboard to a new file being created in the current working directory. This is achieved by the redirect character >, which takes what you type at the *standard input* (in this case the keyboard) and directs it into the file named **myfile**. You can consider the keyboard, and the stream of information it provides, as a file. As stated in the Preface, this usage is an example of a command, **cat** with no options, option arguments, or command arguments. It simply uses the command, a redirect character, and a target, or destination, named **myfile**, where the redirection will go.

This is the very simplest example of a *multiple command* typed on the command line, as opposed to a single command, as shown and briefly described in the Preface. In a multiple command, you can string together single Raspberry Pi OS commands in a chain with connecting operators, such as the redirect character shown here.

$ cat > myfile
This is an example of how to use the cat command to add plain text to a file
<Ctrl+D>
$

You can type as many lines of text, pressing **<Enter>** on the keyboard to distinguish between lines in the file, as you want. Then, on a new line, when you hold down **<Ctrl+D>**, the file is created in the current working directory, using the command you typed. You can view the contents of this file, since it is a plain text file that was created using the keyboard, by doing the following:

$ more myfile
This is an example of how to use the cat command to add plain text to a file
$

This is a simple example of the syntax of a single Raspberry Pi OS command.
    The general syntax of the more command is as follows:

more [options] [file-list]
Purpose: Concatenate/display the files in **file-list** on the screen, one
              screen at a time
Output: Contents of the files in **file-list** displayed on the screen, one
              page at a time
Commonly used options/features:
+E/str   Start two lines before the first line containing **str**
-nN   Display N lines per screen/page
+N   Start displaying the contents of the file at line number N

The **more** command shows one screenful of a file at a time by default. If the file is several pages long, you can proceed to view subsequent pages by pressing the **<Space>** key on the keyboard, or by pressing the **Q** key on the keyboard to quit viewing the output.

In-Chapter Exercise

    6. Use the **cat** command to produce another text file named testfile. Then join the contents of myfile and testfile into one text file, named myfile3, with the **cat** command.

0.2.3 Creating, Deleting, and Managing Files

To copy the contents of one file into another file, use the **cp** command. The general syntax of the **cp** command is as follows:

cp [options] file1 file2
Purpose: Copy **file1** to **file2**; if **file2** is a directory, make a copy of **file1** in this directory
Output: Copied files
Commonly used options/features:
-i If destination exists, prompt before overwriting
-p Preserve file access modes and modification times on copied files
-r Recursively copy files and subdirectories

For example, to make an exact duplicate of the file named **myfile**, with the new name **myfile2**, type the following:

```
$ cp myfile myfile2
$
```

This usage of the **cp** command has two required command arguments. The first argument is the source file that already exists and which you want to copy. The second argument is the destination file or the name of the file that will be the copy. Be aware that many Raspberry Pi OS commands can take plain, ordinary, or regular files as arguments, or can take directory files as arguments. This can change the basic task accomplished by the command. It is also worth noting that not only can file names be arguments, but *pathnames* as well. A pathname is the route to any particular place in the file system structure of the operating system. This changes the site or location, in the path structure of the file system, of operation of the command.

In order to change the name of a file or directory, you can use the **mv** command. The general syntax of the **mv** command is as follows:

mv [options] file1 file2
mv [options] file-list directory
Purpose: First syntax: Rename file1 to file2
Second syntax: Move all the files in file-list to directory
Output: Renamed or relocated files
Commonly used options/features:
-f Force the move regardless of the file access modes of the destination file
-i Prompt the user before overwriting the destination

In the following usage, the first argument to the **mv** command is the source file name, and the second argument is the destination name.

```
$ mv myfile2 renamed_file
$
```

It is important at this point to notice the use of spaces in Raspberry Pi OS commands. What if you obtain a file from a Windows system that has one or more spaces in one of the file names? How can you work with this file in Raspberry Pi OS? The answer is simple. Whenever you need to use that file name in a command as an argument, enclose the file name in double quotes ("). For example, you might obtain a file that you have "detached" from an e-mail message from someone on a Windows system, such as **latest revisions october.txt**.

In order to work with this file on a Raspberry Pi OS system—that is, to use the file name as an argument in a Raspberry Pi OS command—enclose the whole name in double quotes. The correct command to rename that file to something shorter would be:

```
$ mv "latest revisions october.txt" laterevs.txt
$
```

In order to delete a file, you can use the **rm** command. The general syntax of the **rm** command is as follows:

rm [options] file-list
Purpose: Removes files in **file-list** from the file structure (and disk)
Output: Deleted files
Commonly used options/features:
-f   Remove regardless of the file access modes of **file-list**
-i   Prompt the user before removing files in **file-list**
-r   Recursively remove the files in **file-list** if **file-list** is a directory; use with caution!

To delete the file **renamed_file** from the current working directory, type:

```
$ rm renamed_file
$
```

In-Chapter Exercise

7.   Use the **rm** command to delete the files testfile and myfile3.

The most important command you will execute to do file maintenance is the **ls** command. The general syntax for the **ls** command is as follows:

ls [options] [pathname-list]

Purpose: Sends the names of the files and directories in the directory speci-
              fied by **pathname-list** to the display screen

Output: Names of the files and directories in the directory specified by
              pathname-list, or the names only if **pathname-list** contains file
              names only

Commonly used options/features:

-F   Display a slash character (/) after directory names, an asterisk (*) after
      binary executables, and an "at" character (@) after symbolic links

-a   Display names of all the files, including hidden files

-i   Display inode numbers

-l   Display long list that includes file access modes, link count, owner, group,
      file size (in bytes), and modification time

The **ls** command will list the names of files or folders in your current working
directory or folder. In addition, as with the other commands we have used so
far, if you include a complete pathname specification for the **pathname-list**
argument to the command, then you can list the names of files and folders
along that pathname list. To see the names of the files now in your current
working directory, type the following:

$ **ls**
Desktop   Documents   Downloads   Dropbox   Music   Pictures
Public   Templates   Videos
$

Please note that you will probably not get a listing of the same file names
as we showed above here, because your system will have placed some files
automatically in your home directory, as in the example we used, aside from
the ones we created together named **myfile** and **myfile2**. Also note that this
file name listing does not include the name **renamed_file**, because we deleted
that file.

The next command you will execute is actually just an alternate or modified way of executing the **ls** command, one that includes the command name
and options. As shown in the Preface, a Raspberry Pi OS command has
options that can be typed on the command line along with the command to
change the behavior of the basic command. In the case of the **ls** command, the
options l and a produce a longer listing of all ordinary and system (dot) files,
as well as providing other attendant information about the files.

Don't forget to put the space character between the **s** and the -(dash).
Remember again that spaces delimit, or partition, the components of a
Raspberry Pi OS command as it is typed on the command line!

Now, type the following command:

$ **ls -la**
total 30408

drwxr-xr-x	25	bob	bob	4096	May 5 07:53	.
drwxr-xr-x	5	root	root	4096	Oct 20 2022	..
drwxr-xr-x	5	bob	bob	4096	Apr 23 16:32	.audacity-data
-rw-------	1	bob	bob	36197	May 5 07:51	.bash_history
-rw-r--r--	1	bob	bob	220	Apr 4 2022	.bash_logout
-rw-r--r--	1	bob	bob	3523	Apr 4 2022	.bashrc
-rw-r--r--	1	bob	bob	47329	Sep 19 2022	Blandemic.txt
drwxr-xr-x	2	bob	bob	4096	Apr 4 2022	Bookshelf
drwxr-xr-x	15	bob	bob	4096	Apr 17 14:05	.cache
drwx------	32	bob	bob	4096	Apr 28 07:08	.config
drwx------	3	root	root	4096	Jun 29 2022	.dbus
drwxr-xr-x	7	bob	bob	4096	Apr 27 05:21	Desktop

Output truncated...

As you see in this screen display (which shows the listing of files in our home directory and will not be the same as the listing of files in your home directory), the information about each file in the current working directory is displayed in eight columns. The first column shows the type of file, where d stands for directory, l stands for symbolic link, and – stands for ordinary or regular file. Also in the first column, the access modes to that file for user, group, and others is shown as r, w, or x. In the second column, the number of links to that file is displayed. In the third column, the username of the owner of that file is displayed. In the fourth column, the name of the group for that file is displayed. In the fifth column, the number of bytes that the file occupies on disk is displayed. In the sixth column, the date that the file was last modified is displayed. In the seventh column, the time that the file was last modified is displayed. In the eighth and final column, the name of the file is displayed. This way of executing the command is a good way to list more complete information about the file. Examples of using the more complete information are (1) so that you can know the byte size and be able to fit the file on some portable storage medium, or (2) to display the access modes, so that you can alter the access modes to a particular file or directory.

In-Chapter Exercise

8. Use the **ls -la** command to list all of the filenames in your home directory on your Raspberry Pi OS system. How does the listing you obtain compare with the listing shown above? Remember that our listing was done on a Raspberry Pi OS system.

You can also get a file listing for a single file in the current working directory by using another variation of the ls command, as follows:

```
$ ls -la myfile
-rw-r--r--        1 bob  bob        797 Jan 16 10:00 myfile
$
```

This variation shows you a long listing with attendant information for the specific file named **myfile**. A breakdown of what you typed on the command line is 1) **ls**, the command name, 2) **-la**, the options, and 3) **myfile**, the command argument.

What if you make a mistake in your typing, and misspell a command name or one of the other parts of a command? Type the following on the command line:

```
$ lx -la myfile
lx: not found
$
```

The lx: not found reply from Raspberry Pi OS is an error message. There is no **lx** command in the Raspberry Pi OS operating system, so an error message is displayed. If you had typed an option that did not exist, you would also get an error message. If you supplied a file name that was not in the current working directory, you would get an error message, too. This makes an important point about the execution of Raspberry Pi OS commands. If no error message is displayed, then the command executed correctly and the results might or might not appear on screen, depending on what the command actually does. If you get an error message displayed, you must correct the error before Raspberry Pi OS will execute the command as you type it.

Note
Typographic mistakes account for a large percentage of the errors that beginners make!

0.2.4 Creating, Deleting, and Managing Directories

Another critical aspect of file maintenance is the set of procedures and the related Raspberry Pi OS commands you use to create, delete, and organize directories in your Raspberry Pi OS account on a computer. When moving through the file system, you are either ascending or descending to reach the directory you want to use. The directory directly above the current working directory is referred to as the *parent* of the current working directory. The directory or directories immediately under the current working directory are referred to as the *children* of the current working directory. The most common mistake for beginners is misplacing files. They cannot find the file names listed with the **ls** command because they have placed or created the files in a directory either above or below the current working directory in the file structure. When you create a file, if you have also created a logically organized set of directories beneath your own home directory, you will know where to store the file. In the following set of commands, we create a directory beneath the home directory and use that new directory to store a file.

To create a new directory beneath the current working directory, you use the **mkdir** command. The general syntax for the **mkdir** command is as follows:

mkdir [options] dirnames
Purpose: Creates directory or directories specified in **dirnames**
Output: New directory or directories
Commonly used options/features:
-m MODE   Create a directory with given access modes
-p   Create parent directories that don't exist in the pathnames
              specified in **dirnames**

To create a child, or subdirectory, named **first** under the current working directory, type the following:

$ mkdir first
$

This command has now created a new subdirectory named **first** under, or as a child of, the current working directory. Refer back to Figure 0.1 for a graphical description of the directory location of this new subdirectory.

In order to change the current working directory to this new subdirectory, you use the **cd** command. The general syntax for the **cd** command is as follows:

cd [directory]
Purpose: Change the current working directory to **directory** or return to the
              home directory when **directory** is omitted
Output: New current working directory

To change the current working directory to **first** by descending down the path structure to the specified directory named **first**, type the following:

$ cd first
$

You can always verify what the current working directory is by using the **pwd** command. The general syntax of the **pwd** command is as follows:

pwd
Purpose: Displays the current working directory on screen
Output: Pathname of current working directory

You can verify that **first** is now the current working directory by typing the following:

```
$ pwd
/home/bob/first
$
```

The output from the Raspberry Pi OS on the command line shows the path-name to the current working directory or folder. As previously stated, this path is a textual route through the complete file structure of the computer that Raspberry Pi OS is running on, ending in the current working directory. In this example of the output, the path starts at /, the root of the file system. Then it descends to the directory **home**, a major branch of the file system on the computer running Raspberry Pi OS. Then it descends to the directory **bob**, another branch, which is the home directory name for the user. Finally, it descends to the branch named **first**, the current working directory.

On some systems, depending on the default settings, another way of deter-mining what the current working directory is can be done by simply looking at the command line prompt. This prompt may be prefaced with the complete path to the current working directory, ending in the current working directory.

You can ascend back up to the home directory, or the parent of the subdir-ectory **first**, by typing the following:

```
$ cd
$
```

An alternate way of doing this is to type the following, where the tilde char-acter (~) resolves to, or is a substitute for, the specification of the complete path to the home directory:

```
$ cd ~
$
```

To verify that you have now ascended up to the home directory, type the following:

```
$ pwd
/home/bob
$
```

You can also ascend to a directory above your home directory, sometimes called the parent of your current working directory, by typing the following:

```
$ cd ..
$
```

In this command, the two periods (..), represent the parent, or branch above the current working directory. Don't forget to type a space character between the **d** and the first period. To verify that you have ascended to the parent of your home directory, type the following:

```
$ pwd
/home
$
```

To descend to your home directory, type the following:

```
$ cd
$
```

To verify that there are two files in the home directory that begin with the letters my, type the following command:

```
$ ls my*
myfile myfile2
$
```

The asterisk following the y on the command line is known as a *metacharacter*, or a character that represents a pattern; in this case, the pattern is any set of characters. When Raspberry Pi OS interprets the command after you press the **<Enter>** key on the keyboard, it searches for all files in the current working directory that begin with the letters my and end in anything else.

In-Chapter Exercise

9. Use the **cd** command to ascend to the root (/) of your Raspberry Pi OS file system, and then use it to descend down each subdirectory from the root recursively to a depth of two subdirectories, sketching a diagram of the component files found on your system. Make the named entries in the diagram as complete as possible, listing as many files as you think necessary. Retain this diagram as a useful map of your particular Raspberry Pi OS distribution's file system.

Another aspect of organizing your directories is movement of files between directories, or changing the location of files in your directories. For example, you now have the file **myfile2** in your home directory, but you would like to move it into the subdirectory named **first**. See Figure 0.1 for a graphic description to change the organization of your files at this point. To accomplish this, you can use the second syntax method illustrated for the **mv file-list directory** command to move the file **myfile2** down into the subdirectory named **first**. To achieve this, type the following:

```
$ mv myfile2 first
$
```

To verify that **myfile2** is indeed in the subdirectory named first, type the following:

```
$ cd first
$ ls
myfile2
$
```

You will now ascend to the home directory, and attempt to remove or delete a file with the **rm** command.

Caution: you should be very careful when using this command, because once a file has been deleted, the only way to recover it is from archival backups that you or the system administrator have made of the file system.

```
$ cd
$ rm myfile2
rm: myfile2: No such file or directory
$
```

You get the error message because in the home directory, the file named **myfile2** does not exist. It was moved down into the subdirectory named first.

Directory organization also includes the ability to delete empty or non-empty directories. The command that accomplishes the removal of empty directories is **rmdir**. The general syntax of the **rmdir** command is as follows:

rmdir [options] dirnames
Purpose: Removes the empty directories specified in **dirnames**
Output: Removes directories
Commonly used options/features:
-p   Remove empty parent directories as well
-r   Recursively delete files and subdirectories beneath the current directory

To delete an entire directory below the current working directory, type the following:

```
$ rmdir first
rmdir: first: Directory not empty
$
```

Since the file **myfile2** is still in the subdirectory named **first**, **first** is not an empty directory, and you get the error message that the **rmdir** command will not delete the directory. If the directory was empty, **rmdir** would have accomplished the deletion. One way to delete a nonempty directory is by using the **rm** command with the **-r** option. The **-r** option recursively descends down into the subdirectory and deletes any files in it before actually deleting the directory itself. Be cautious with this command, since you may inadvertently delete directories and files with it. To see how this command deletes a nonempty directory, type the following:

$ rm -r first
$

The directory **first** and the file **myfile2** are now removed from the file structure.
$$$$

0.2.5 Obtaining Help with the Man Command

A very convenient utility available on Raspberry Pi OSs is the online help feature, achieved via the use of the **man** command. The general syntax of the **man** command is as follows:

man [options][-s section] command-list
man -k keyword-list

Purpose: First syntax: Display Raspberry Pi OS Reference Manual pages for commands in **command-list** one screen at a time

Second syntax: Display summaries of commands related to keywords in **keyword-list**

Output: Manual pages one screen at a time
Commonly used options/features:
-k keyword-list   Search for summaries of keywords in **keyword-list** in a database and display them
-s sec-num   Search section number **sec-num** for manual pages and display them

To get help by using the **man** command, on usage and options of the **ls** command, for example, type the following:

$ man ls

LS(1)   User Commands   LS(1)

NAME
        ls - list directory contents

SYNOPSIS
        ls [OPTION]   [FILE]

DESCRIPTION

> List information about the FILEs (the current directory
> by default).
>
> Sort entries alphabetically if none of -cftuvSUX nor –sort
> is specified.
>
> Mandatory arguments to long options are mandatory for
> short options too.
>
> -a, --all
>
> > do not ignore entries starting with .
>
> -A, --almost-all
>
> > do not list implied . and ..
>
> --author

Manual page ls(1) line 1 (press h for help or q to quit)

This output from Raspberry Pi OS is a Raspberry Pi OS *manual page*, or *man page*, which gives a synopsis of the command usage showing the options, and a brief description that helps you understand how the command should be used. Typing **q** after one page has been displayed, as seen in the example, returns you to the command line prompt. Pressing the space key on the keyboard would have shown you more of the content of the manual pages, one screen at a time, related to the **ls** command.

To get help in using all the Raspberry Pi OS commands and their options, use the **man man** command to go to the Raspberry Pi OS reference manual pages.

The pages themselves are organized into eight sections, depending on the topic described, and the topics that are applicable to the particular system. Table 0.1 lists the sections of the manual and what they contain. Most users

TABLE 0.1

Sections of the Raspberry Pi OS Manual

Section	What It Describes
1	Executable programs or shell commands
2	System calls (functions provided by the kernel)
3	Library calls (functions within program libraries)
4	Special files (usually found in /dev)
5	File formats and conventions, e.g. /etc/passwd
6	Games
7	Miscellaneous (including macro packages and conventions), e.g. man(7), groff(7), man-pages(7)
8	System administration commands (usually only for root)
9	Kernel routines [Non standard]

find the pages they need in Section 1. Software developers mostly use library and system calls and thus find the pages they need in Sections 2 and 3. Users who work on document preparation get the most help from Section 7. Administrators mostly need to refer to pages in Sections 1, 4, 5, and 8.

The manual pages comprise multi-page, specially formatted, descriptive documentation for every command, system call, and library call in Raspberry Pi OS. This format consists of nine general parts:

1   Executable programs or shell commands

2   System calls (functions provided by the kernel)

3   Library calls (functions within program libraries)

4   Special files (usually found in /dev)

5   File formats and conventions, e.g. /etc/passwd

6   Games

7   Miscellaneous (including macro packages and conventions),
    e.g. man(7), groff(7), man-pages(7)

8   System administration commands (usually only for root)

9   Kernel routines [Non standard]

You can use the **man** command to view the manual page for a command. Because of the name of this command, the manual pages are normally referred to as Raspberry Pi OS man pages. When you display a manual page on the screen, the top-left corner of the page has the command name with the section it belongs to in parentheses, as with LS(1), seen at the top of the output manual page.

The command used to display the manual page for the **passwd** command is:

$ **man passwd**

The manual page for the **passwd** command now appears on the screen, but we do not show its output. Because they are multi-page text documents, the manual pages for each topic take up more than one screen of text to display their entire contents. To see one screen of the manual page at a time, press the space bar on the keyboard. To quit viewing the manual page, press the **Q** key on the keyboard.

Now type this command:

$ **man pwd**

If more than one section of the man pages has information on the same word and you are interested in the man page for a particular section, you can use the **-S** option. The following command line therefore displays the man page for the read system call, and not the man page for the shell command read.

$ **man -S2 read**

The command **man -S3 fopen fread strcmp** sequentially displays man pages for three C library calls: **fopen**, **fread**, and **strcmp**.

To exit from the display of these system calls, type <Ctrl-C>.

Using the **man** command and typing the command with the **-k** option, allows specifying a keyword that limits the search. It is equivalent to using the **apropos** command. The search then yields useful man page headers from all the man pages on the system that contain just the keyword reference. For example, the following command yields the on-screen output on our Raspberry Pi OS system:

$ **man -k passwd**

chgpasswd (8)	- update group passwords in batch mode
chpasswd (8)	- update passwords in batch mode
fgetpwent_r (3)	- get passwd file entry reentrantly
getpwent_r (3)	- get passwd file entry reentrantly
gpasswd (1)	- administer /etc/group and /etc/gshadow
openssl-passwd (1ssl)	- compute password hashes
pam_localuser (8)	- require users to be listed in /etc/passwd
passwd (1)	- change user password
exim4_passwd (5)	- Files in use by the Debian exim4 packages
exim4_passwd_client (5)	- Files in use by the Debian exim4 packages
passwd (1ssl)	- compute password hashes
passwd (5)	- the password file
passwd2des (3)	- RFS password encryption
update-passwd (8)	- safely update /etc/passwd, /etc/shadow and /etc/group
vncpasswd (1)	- VNC Server password utility

Output truncated...

0.2.6 Other Methods of Obtaining Help

To get a short description of what any particular Raspberry Pi OS command does, you can use the **whatis** command. This is similar to the command **man -f**. The general syntax of the **whatis** command is as follows:

$ **whatis keywords**

Purpose: Search the whatis database for abbreviated descriptions of each keyword

Output: Prints a one-line description of each keyword to the screen

The following is an illustration of how to use **whatis:**

The output of the two commands are truncated.

$ **whatis man**
man (7)   - macros to format man pages
man (1)   - an interface to the on-line
                   reference manuals
$

You can also obtain short descriptions of more than one command by entering multiple arguments to the **whatis** command on the same command line, with spaces between each argument. The following is an illustration of this method:

$ **whatis login set setenv**
login (1)   - begin session on the system
login (3)   - write utmp and wtmp entries
setenv (3)   - change or add an environment variable
set: nothing appropriate.
$

The following in-chapter exercises ask you to use the **man** and **whatis** commands to find information about the **passwd** command. After completing the exercises, you can use what you have learned to change your login password on the Raspberry Pi OS system that you use.

In-Chapter Exercises

10. Use the **man** command with the **-k** option to display abbreviated help on the **passwd** command. Doing so will give you a screen display similar to that obtained with the **whatis** command, but it will show all apropos command names that contain the characters passwd.

11. Use the **whatis** command to get a brief description of the **passwd** command shown above, and then note the difference between the commands **whatis passwd** and **man -k passwd**.

0.3 Utility Commands

There are several major commands that allow the beginner to be more productive when using a Raspberry Pi OS. A sampling of these kinds of utility commands is given in the following sections, and is organized as system setups, general utilities, and communications commands.

0.3.1 Examining System Setups

The **whereis** command allows you to search along certain prescribed paths to locate utility programs and commands, such as shell programs. The general syntax of the **whereis** command is as follows:

whereis [options] filename

Purpose: Locate the binary, source, and man page files for a command

Output: The supplied names are first stripped of leading pathname components and extensions, then pathnames are displayed on screen

Commonly used options/features:

-b Search only for binaries

-s Search only for source code

For example, if you type the command **whereis bash** on the command line, you will see a list of the paths to the Bash shell program files themselves, as follows:

$ **whereis bash**
bash: /bin/bash /etc/bash.bashrc /usr/share/man/man1/bash.1.gz

Note that the paths to a "built-in", or internal, command cannot be found with the **whereis** command.

When you first log on, it is useful to be able to view a display of information about your **userid**, the computer or system you have logged on to, and the operating system on that computer. These tasks can be accomplished with the **whoami** command, which displays your **userid** on the screen. The general syntax of the **whoami** command is as follows:

whoami

Purpose: Displays the effective user id

Output: Displays your effective user id as a name on standard

The following shows how our system responded to this command when we typed it on the command line.

$ **whoami**
bob
$

The following in-chapter exercises give you the chance to use **whereis**, **whoami**, and two other important utility commands, **who** and **hostname** to obtain important information about your system.

In-Chapter Exercises

12. Use the **whereis** command to locate binary files for the Korn shell, the Bourne shell, the Bourne Again shell, the C shell, and the Z shell. Are any of these shell programs not available on your system?

13. Use the **whoami** command to find your username on the system that you're using. Then use the **who** command to see how your username is listed, along with other users of the same system. What is the on-screen format of each user's listing that you obtained with the **who** command? Try to identify the information in each field on the same line as your username.

14. Use the **hostname** command to find out what host computer you are logged on to. Can you determine from this list whether you are using a stand-alone computer or a networked computer system? Explain how you can know the difference from the list that the **hostname** command gives you.

0.4 Printing Commands

A very useful and common task performed by every user of a computer system is the printing of text files at a printer. This is accomplished using the configured printer(s) on the local, or a remote, system. Printers are controlled and managed with the Common UNIX Printing System (CUPS). We show this utility in detail in Chapter 1.

The common commands that perform printing on a Raspberry Pi OS system are **lpr** and **lp**. The general syntax of the **lpr** command is as follows:

lpr [options] filename
Purpose: Send files to the printer
Output: Files sent to the printer queue as print jobs
Commonly used options/features:
-P printer Send output to the named printer
-# copies   Produce the number of copies indicated for each named file

The following **lpr** command accomplishes the printing of the file named **order.pdf** at the printer designated on our system as **spr**. Remember that no space is necessary between the option (in this case **-P**) and the option argument (in this case **spr**).

$ **lpr -Pspr order.pdf**
$

The following **lpr** command accomplishes the printing of the file named **memo1** at the default printer.

$ **lpr memo1**
$

The following multiple command combines the **man** command and the **lpr** command, and ties them together with the Raspberry Pi OS pipe (|) redirection character, to print the man pages describing the **ls** command at the printer named **hp1200**.

$ **man ls | lpr -Php1200**
$

The following shows how to perform printing tasks using the **lp** command. The general syntax of the **lp** command is as follows:

lp [options][option arguments] file(s)
Purpose: Submit files for printing on a designated system printer, or alter pending print jobs

Output: Printed files or altered print queue

Commonly used options/features:
-d destination Print to the specified destination

-n copies Sets the number of copies to print.

In the first command, the file to be printed is named **file1**. In the second command, the files to be printed are named **sample** and **phones**. Note that the **-d** option is used to specify which printer to use. The option to specify the number of copies is **-n** for the **lp** command.

$ **lp -d spr file1**
request id is spr-983 (1 file(s))
$ **lp -d spr -n 3 sample phones**
request id is spr-984 (2 file(s))
$

1

ZFS Administration and Use

1.0 Objectives

* To describe and give an overview of the Zettabyte File System (ZFS)
* To illustrate the use of the **zpool** and **zfs** commands in the context of system administration
* To give a brief ZFS commands and operations reference encyclopedia
* To give a complete example of file system backups using the **zfs snap-shot** command in a Bash Shell script
* To cover the commands and primitives

    zpool, zfs

1.1 Introduction

This chapter will detail the hands-on mechanics of a modern file system commonly known as the Zettabyte File System (ZFS). ZFS has the following attributes: it corrects itself at the bit level, it is very secure, it is a volume manager, and it provides its own real-time file backup system procedures. It is sometimes called a "user" file system, because ordinary privileged users of the system have control over ZFS operations through the use of typed-in commands. We show examples of using the two most important ZFS commands, **zpool** and **zfs**.

At the time of the writing of this book, ZFS was easily installed on the Debian Bookworm-based Raspberry Pi OS.

DOI: 10.1201/9781003473268-2

Note
ZFS could not easily or reliably be made the root file system at either initial installation, or using some post-installation procedure. Additionally, ZFS installation could not be easily or reliably installed on the previous, Bullseye-based Raspberry Pi OS.
To download and install ZFS on the Debian Bookworm-based Raspberry Pi OS, we used the following command as root:

```
# sed -r -i'.BAK' 's/^deb(.*)$/deb\1 contrib/g' /etc/apt/sources.list
# apt update
# apt install linux-headers-arm64 zfsutils-linux zfs-dkms zfs-zed
```
Output truncated...

In order to do anything in this chapter, you must first use these three commands to download and install ZFS on your Debian Bookworm-based Raspberry Pi system.
To test that the installation worked properly, use the following commands (we got the output shown):

```
# modprobe zfs
# zfs version
```

zfs-2.1.11-1
zfs-kmod-2.1.11-1

Warning
This warning applies at the time of the writing of this book. It is important to realize that if you want to create and use ZFS on your Raspberry Pi system other than for practice Examples 1.1 and 1.2 in Section 1.2, you must have an additional storage device, or devices, attached to your hardware. This means additional externally mounted media, regardless of which bus that media is communicating through. We have found that if you attempt to create zpools on your boot/system medium, such as an internally mounted microSD card, this will render that medium unbootable! See the specific advisory we provide at the beginning of Section 1.2.
A drawback of the following practical worked examples in this chapter is that ideally, in a commercial production situation where you would use ZFS to full advantage on Raspberry Pi systems, the hardware would have Error Correction Code (ECC) system memory only. That type of memory is available almost exclusively on server-class machines, but is also available for some commercial desktop systems. For learning purposes, we do not assume you are using ECC memory, simply because the Raspberry

Pi hardware doesn't have that class of memory available! But if you're running your Raspberry Pi system from an externally mounted SSD for instance, that type of media generally has the equivalent of ECC memory capability.

We highly recommend a disk storage model that puts the operating system on a single medium (microSD card or SSD), and user data files on a second, larger capacity medium. What that storage model allows you to accomplish is to keep the system operable, maintained, and upgradable on its own discrete storage medium; user data are securely archived on another, possibly redundant, device or devices. That model implementation, and its effectiveness for archiving user data files, is made possible by what we show in this chapter. We also show techniques for implementing this storage model when your Raspberry Pi has a single external, non-boot/ system medium mounted. This model strictly conforms to the warning we previously gave you, and must accommodate the ECC memory drawback also mentioned.

1.1.1 zpool and zfs Command Syntax

The following are the general syntax forms for the **zpool** and **zfs** commands. For a more complete description of these two important commands, see the man pages for **zfs** and **zpool** on your Raspberry Pi system (after you have installed ZFS according to the instructions given above!)

****

zpool SYNTAX
zpool sub-command [options] [option arguments] [command arguments]

Purpose: To create and manage storage pools of virtual devices such as disk drives

Commonly used options/features:

zpool create name vdev	Creates a new pool with name on the specified vdev
zpool create –o copies=2 name	Creates a new pool name with the property copies set to 2
zpool destroy name	Destroys, or removes, a pool name
zpool list name	Lists storage space and health of pool name
zpool scrub name	Verifies that the checksums on pool name are correct
zpool status name	Displays the status of pool name

****

****

zfs SYNTAX

zfs sub-command [options] [option arguments] [command arguments]

Purpose: To create and manage datasets or file systems mapped to devices such as disk drives

Commonly used options/features:

zfs create name	Creates a dataset with name
zfs create –o copies=2 name	Creates a dataset name with the property copies set to 2
zfs destroy name	Destroys, or removes, a dataset name
zfs list	Lists all datasets
zfs rollback name	Returns dataset name to a previous snapshot state

****

1.1.2 ZFS Terminology

The following describes the basic terminology used throughout this chapter, and as it applies to ZFS practice in general as well:

Boot environment: A boot environment is a bootable environment consisting of a ZFS root file system and, optionally, other file systems mounted underneath it. Exactly one boot environment can be active at a time. Heed the Warning given in Section 1.1!

Checksum: A 256-bit hash of the data in a file system block. The checksum capability can range from the simple and fast fletcher4 (the default) to cryptographically strong hashes such as SHA256.

Clone: A file system whose initial contents are identical to the contents of a ZFS snapshot.

Dataset: A generic name for the following ZFS components: clones, file systems, snapshots, and volumes. Each dataset is identified by a unique name in the ZFS name space. Datasets are identified using the following format:

pool/path[@snapshot]

pool   Identifies the name of the storage pool that contains the dataset

path   A slash-delimited pathname for the dataset component

snapshot   An optional component that identifies a snapshot of a dataset

Deduplication: Data deduplication is a method of reducing storage capacity needs by eliminating redundant data. Only one unique instance of the data is actually retained on storage media. Redundant data are replaced with a pointer to the unique data copy.

Filesystem: A ZFS dataset of type file system that is mounted within the standard system namespace, and behaves like other file systems.

Mirror: A vdev that stores identical copies of data on two or more media, in a variety of ways defined by Redundant Array of Independent Disks (RAID) specifications. If any disk in a mirror fails, any other disk in that mirror can provide the same data, according to those RAID specifications.

Pool: A logical group of devices describing the layout and physical characteristics of the available storage. Disk space for datasets is allocated from a pool.

RAID-Z: A virtual device that stores data and parity on multiple disks, using the RAID specifications.

Resilvering: The process of copying data from one device to another device is known as resilvering. For example, if a mirror device is replaced or taken offline, the data from an up-to-date mirror device are copied to the newly restored mirror device. This process is referred to as mirror resynchronization in traditional volume management.

Slice: A disk partition created with partitioning software.

Snapshot: A read-only copy of a file system or volume at a given point in time.

Vdev (virtual device): A whole disk, a disk partition, a file, or a collection of the previous, usually all of the same type. There is no performance penalty for using disk partitions rather than entire disks. The write cache is disabled for partitions, thus incurring a performance penalty. Using files as vdevs is discouraged, except for experimenting and testing purposes as we do in this chapter for beginners! A collection of vdevs is a mirror.

Volume: A dataset that represents a block device. For example, you can create a ZFS volume as a swap device.

1.1.3 How ZFS Works

Create zpool mapped to vdev >
Create ZFS file system(s) on zpool >
Add files to filesystem(s)>
Manage the files, file systems, zpools, and vdevs.
Simply stated, you create a named zpool first, which at the time it is created is mapped or associated with a vdev, such as an external medium physically

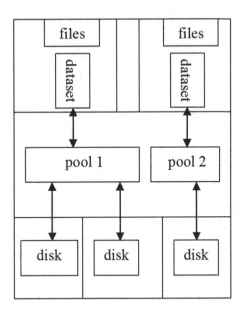

FIGURE 1.1
ZFS components.

attached to your Raspberry Pi. Then you create one or more file systems in that zpool. Then you add files to the file system(s). Finally, you manage the files, file systems, zpools, and vdevs using the appropriate ZFS commands.

Working with ZFS on a Raspberry Pi system is a matter of efficiently and easily managing zpools that have vdevs "mapped" to them, and then managing file systems, and their files, in those zpools.

Figure 1.1 shows this relationship between files, datasets (file systems), pools, and disks. **pool 1** has two disks mapped to it, and a dataset with a number of files in it. **pool 2** has a single disk mapped to it, and has a dataset in it. This layering of files and datasets, pools, and disks is the basic structure of ZFS.

1.1.4 Important ZFS Concepts

Some very important points have to be made here:

1. Only one zpool can be mapped or associated with any vdev. So if you want to create a zpool on a physical medium, like a hard disk, or one of its slices, no other existing active zpool can be mapped to that vdev!

2. There are seven types of vdev in ZFS:
   - Disk (default): The physical hard drives in your system, usually the whole drive or primary slice

- File: The absolute path of preallocated files/images, similar to the Section 1.2.2, Example 1.1
- Mirror: Standard software RAID1 mirror
- RAID-Z1/2/3: Nonstandard distributed parity-based software RAID levels
- Spare: Hard drives marked as a *hot spare* for ZFS software RAID
- Cache: Device used for a level-2 adaptive read cache (L2ARC)
- Log: A separate log (SLOG) called the ZFS intent log (ZIL)

3. Unlike a traditional file system, where the mount point of the file system begins at a particular logical drive letter, the default mount point for a zpool is root (/).

This is how the path to a file named **test.txt** appears when it is in the zpool named **data1** on the file system **bob**:

/data1/bob/test.txt

Here's how the path to a file named **test.txt** appears on a traditional file system:

C:\Users\Robert\Desktop\test.txt

When you want a ZFS file system to expand onto more than one disk, for example, you add more disks to the zpool.

4. A zpool can be enlarged by adding more devices, but it cannot be shrunk (at least not at this time)!

1.2 Example ZFS Pools and File Systems: Using the **zpool** and **zfs** Commands

Advisory

As stated in Section 1.1, it is important to realize that if you want to create and use ZFS on a system other than for the practice Examples 1.1 and 1.2 we show in this section, you must have an additional storage media, or devices, attached to your hardware. On a Raspberry Pi system, this could be an additional, externally mounted USB3 SATA hard drive, PCIe NVMe media on the USB3 bus, or USB flashdrives.

Per the Warning given in Section 1.1, we have found that if you attempt to create zpools on your Raspberry Pi system/boot medium, this will render that medium unbootable!

For example, the following command line session illustrates what you should NOT do:

$ **sudo zpool create test /dev/mmcblk0p1**
invalid vdev specification
use '-f' to override the following errors:
/dev/mmcblk0p1 does not contain an EFI label but it may contain partition information in the MBR.
$ **sudo zpool create test /dev/sda1**
invalid vdev specification
use '-f' to override the following errors:
/dev/sda1 contains a filesystem of type 'ext4'
$

If you force the override in either of the above two commands, you will render your Raspberry Pi OS boot/system medium unbootable. The second command assumes that /dev/sda is your system boot medium.

In this section, you are allowed to quickly determine the logical device names of disks attached to your Raspberry Pi system. We then present you with five examples that will give you some basic experience in using the **zpool** and **zfs** commands.

1.2.1 A Quick and Easy Way to Find the Logical Device Names of Media Actually Installed on Your System

It's important to know how to determine, in a very quick and easy manner, what the currently installed logical device names of media actually attached and usable on your system are. What we mean by "attached and usable" is that the medium is properly connected, is recognized by the Raspberry Pi OS, and has a device driver that the OS can use to communicate with it.

The simple method that follows shows how to determine what media are attached and usable on your system, and what the logical device names of those and any others you might want to add to your system are.

Change your current working directory to **/dev**. Type **ls**. If you're running your system from a microSD card, it shows up as something like **mmcbblk0**, and partitions on it appear as **mmcblk0p1**, etc. Externally mounted USB media, such as USB3-mounted SSD drives, for example, show up in the **ls** listing as **sda**, **sdb**, and so on. The full path to the first slice, or partition, on one of these is specified as **/dev/sda1**.

You can use the Gparted Partition Editor, a GUI app available if you've installed it on your Raspberry Pi system, to view all usable media, and their logical device names. In the examples in this chapter, we use Gparted to partition, and put file systems on physical media that we are going to use as vdevs for ZFS.

1.2.2 Basic ZFS Examples

In this section we present six instructive, introductory examples of how to work with ZFS. It is expected that for you to get the full benefit from them, you do them and their attendant In-Chapter Exercises in the order presented.

Example 1.1: The zpool Command: Using Files Instead of Disks as Vdevs

Objective: To introduce the **zpool** command, implemented on files instead of disks, and to show forms of ZFS pool creation and mirroring.

Introduction: A vdev, as defined previously, can be a physical device such as a disk drive, a file, a single slice on a hard disk drive, or a collection of devices. Before beginning to use ZFS on physical devices, and to practice using ZFS on an existing file system instead of deploying ZFS on actual SATA hard disk drives, we will create and manipulate files with the important ZFS commands.

To repeat the warning and advisory given above in Section 1.1, you can create the zpools here in this, and the following example, on the boot/system medium, because you're using files to simulate vdevs.

Also, if you do not have a second medium attached to your Raspberry Pi, you can do this example to gain an appreciation of what ZFS is.

In case you want to use four real disks, for example, mounted and partitioned in this preliminary introductory example, make a note of the full path to their device names (e.g./dev/sdb1). You will be destroying all the partition information and data on these disks, so be sure they're not needed during the time you're doing the example!

Note
If you make a mistake anywhere along the way, you can always start over by executing the cleanup steps shown at the end of the example and begin again.

Prerequisites:

1. Installation of ZFS on your Raspberry Pi system, as shown in Section 1.1.

2. Having root access, and knowing root's password on your Raspberry Pi.

Procedures: Follow the steps in the order shown to complete this example.

1. Become root, and then create four 128 MB files as follows (the files must be a minimum of 64 MB in size):

   $ **sudo su** -
   root@raspberrypi:~# **truncate --size 128m /home/bob/disk1**
   root@raspberrypi:~# **truncate --size 128m /home/bob/disk2**

root@raspberrypi:~# **truncate --size 128m /home/bob/disk3**
root@raspberrypi:~# **truncate --size 128m /home/bob/disk4**
root@raspberrypi:~#

Check the /home/bob directory with the following command:

root@raspberrypi:~# **ls -lh /home/bob**
total 48K
...
-rw-r--r-- 1 root root 128M Nov 22 12:36 disk1
-rw-r--r-- 1 root root 128M Nov 22 12:37 disk2
-rw-r--r-- 1 root root 128M Nov 22 12:37 disk3
-rw-r--r-- 1 root root 128M Nov 22 12:37 disk4
Output truncated...

In this example, we initially create and use files to simulate disks on an already existing file system, and we named them **disk1**, **disk2**, **disk3**, and **disk4** to enhance that "illusion".

2. Before creating new pools you should check for existing pools to avoid confusing them with the example pools we create here. You can check what pools exist with **zpool list**:

    root@raspberrypi:~# **zpool list**
    no pools available
    root@raspberrypi:~#

3. Pools are created using the **zpool create** command. We can create a single disk pool using a file as follows (you must use the absolute path to the file), and check the zpools that now exist:

    root@raspberrypi:~# **zpool create data /home/bob/disk1**
    root@raspberrypi:~# **zpool list**
    NAME   SIZE   ALLO   FREE   EXPANDSZ   FRAG   CAP
    DEDUP HEALTH   ALTROOT
    data   112M   104K   112M   -   2%   0 %
    1.00x ONLINE   -

4. Now we will create an actual file in the new pool, check its size, and get a zpool listing of it:

    root@raspberrypi:~# **truncate --size 32m /data/data20file**
    root@raspberrypi:~# **ls -lh /data/data20file**
    -rw-r--r-- 1 root root 32M Nov 22 12:43 /data/data20file

```
root@raspberrypi:~# zpool list
NAME   SIZE   ALLOC   FREE   EXPANDSZ   FRAG   CAP
DEDUP   HEALTH        ALTROOT
data   112M   108K    112M   -          2%     0 %
1.00x  ONLINE        -
```

5. We will now destroy the pool data with **zpool destroy**, and check on
    the zpools now available:

```
root@raspberrypi:~# zpool destroy data
root@raspberrypi:~# sudo zpool list
No pools available
root@raspberrypi:~#
```

6. Creating a Mirrored Pool with Files

    A pool composed of a single medium doesn't really offer any redun-
    dancy, especially if that medium fails! One way of providing protec-
    tion against physical media failure is to use a mirrored pair of disks in
    a pool, with the following commands:

```
root@raspberrypi:~# zpool create data2 mirror /home/bob/disk1 /\
home/bob/disk2
root@raspberrypi:~# zpool list
NAME   SIZE   ALLOC   FREE   CKPOINT   EXPANDSZ
FRAG   CAP   DEDUP        HEALTH   ALTROOT
data2  112M   105K    112M   -         -
2%     0%    1.00x        ONLINE   -
root@raspberrypi:~#
```

7. To get more information about the pool **data2**, we use **zpool status**:

```
root@raspberrypi:~# zpool status data2
pool: data2
state: ONLINE
config:

        NAME                STATE    READ   WRITE   CKSUM
        data2               ONLINE   0      0       0
          mirror-0          ONLINE   0      0       0
            /home/bob/disk1 ONLINE   0      0       0
            /home/bob/disk2 ONLINE   0      0       0

errors: No known data errors
```

8. Now you can create a file in the **data2** pool.

    root@raspberrypi:~# **truncate --size 32m /data2/data2file**
    root@raspberrypi:~#

    Note the change in the pool after we have added a file to it, using the
    following command:

    root@raspberrypi:~# **zpool list**
    NAME   SIZE   ALLOC   FREE   CKPOINT   EXPANDSZ
    FRAG   CAP   DEDUP   HEALTH   ALTROOT
    data2   112M   152K   112M   -   -
    2%   0%   1.00x   ONLINE   -
    root@raspberrypi:~#

    A fraction of the disk has been used, but more importantly the data are
    now stored redundantly over two disks.

9. Let's test that redundancy by overwriting the first "disk" label with
    random data. If you are using real hard disks, you could physically
    remove the disk from the computer.

    root@raspberrypi:~# **dd if=/dev/random of=/home/bob/disk1 bs=\
    512 count=1**
    1+0 records in
    1+0 records out
    512 bytes copied, 0.000477905 s, 1.1 MB/s
    root@raspberrypi:~#

10. ZFS automatically checks for errors when it reads/writes files, but we
    can force a check with the **zfs scrub** command.

    root@raspberrypi:~# **zpool scrub data2**
    root@raspberrypi:~#

11. Let's check the status of the pool:

    root@raspberrypi:~# **zpool status**
    pool: data2
    state: DEGRADED
    status: One or more devices could not be used because the label is
                missing or invalid. Sufficient replicas exist for the pool to
                continue functioning in a degraded state.
    action: Replace the device using 'zpool replace'.

```
see:      https://openzfs.github.io/openzfs-docs/msg/ZFS-8000-4J
scan:     scrub repaired 0B in 00:00:00 with 0 errors on Sun Nov 19
          09:30:34 2023
config:
```

NAME	STATE	READ	WRITE	CKSUM
data2	DEGRADED	0	0	0
mirror-0	DEGRADED	0	0	0
/home/bob/disk1	UNAVAIL	0	0	0 corrupted data
/home/bob/disk2	ONLINE	0	0	0

```
errors: No known data errors
root@raspberrypi:~#
```

12. The disk we used **dd** on is showing as UNAVAIL (unavailable) with corrupted data, but no data errors are reported for the pool as a whole, and we can still read and write to the pool:

```
root@raspberrypi:~# truncate --size 32m /data2/data2file2
root@raspberrypi:~# ls -l /data2/
total 1
-rw-r--r-- 1 root root 33554432 Nov 19 09:25 data2file
-rw-r--r-- 1 root root 33554432 Nov 19 09:34 data2file2
root@raspberrypi:~#
```

13. To maintain redundancy we should replace the broken disk with another. If you are using a physical disk you can use the **zpool replace** command (the zpool man page has details). However, in this file-based example we will just remove the disk file from the mirror and recreate it.

    Devices are detached with **zpool detach**:

```
root@raspberrypi:~# zpool detach data2 /home/bob/disk1
root@raspberrypi:~#
```

14. Let's check the status of the pool:

```
root@raspberrypi:~# zpool status data2
pool:     data2
state:    ONLINE
scan:     scrub repaired 0B in 00:00:00 with 0 errors on Sun Nov 19
          09:30:34 2023
config:
```

NAME	STATE	READ	WRITE	CKSUM
data2	ONLINE	0	0	0
/home/bob/disk2	ONLINE	0	0	0

errors: No known data errors
root@raspberrypi:~#

15. Let's remove the disk, and then try to replace it, to simulate a failure:

    root@raspberrypi:~# **rm /home/bob/disk1**
    root@raspberrypi:~# **truncate --size 128m /home/bob/disk1**
    root@raspberrypi:~#

16. In order to replace it in the mirror, we need to do the following. To attach another device we specify an existing device in the mirror to attach it to with **zpool attach**:

    root@raspberrypi:~# **zpool attach data2 /home/bob/disk2 /home/\\
    bob/disk1**
    root@raspberrypi:~#

17. Check the status of the pool:

    root@raspberrypi:~# **zpool status data2**
    pool: data2
    state: ONLINE
    scan: resilvered 167K in 00:00:00 with 0 errors on Sun Nov 19
             11:26:47 2023
    config:

NAME	STATE	READ	WRITE	CKSUM
data2	ONLINE	0	0	0
mirror-0	ONLINE	0	0	0
/home/bob/disk2	ONLINE	0	0	0
/home/bob/disk1	ONLINE	0	0	0

    errors: No known data errors
    root@raspberrypi:~#

18. Adding to a Mirrored Pool

    A very critical and extremely useful systems administration procedure that you can accomplish with ZFS is to add disks to a pool without taking it offline. Let's double the size of our **data2** pool:

root@raspberrypi:~# **zpool list**

NAME   SIZE   ALLOC   FREE   CKPOINT   EXPANDSZ
FRAG   CAP   DEDUP   HEALTH   ALTROOT
data2   112M   130K   112M   -   -
4%   0%   1.00x   ONLINE   -
root@raspberrypi:~#

19. We can use the **zpool add** command to add disks to the existing pool.

root@raspberrypi:~# **zpool add data2 mirror /home/bob/disk3 /\\
home/bob/disk4**
root@raspberrypi:~# **zpool list**
NAME   SIZE   ALLOC   FREE   CKPOINT   EXPANDSZ
FRAG   CAP   DEDUP   HEALTH   ALTROOT
data2   224M   139K   224M   -   -
2%   0%   1.00x   ONLINE   -
root@raspberrypi:~#

20. The file systems within the pool are always available. If we look at the status now, it shows the pool consists of two mirrors:

root@raspberrypi:~# **zpool status data2**
pool: data2
state: ONLINE
scan: resilvered 167K in 00:00:00 with 0 errors on Sun Nov 19
11:26:47 2023
config:

NAME	STATE	READ	WRITE	CKSUM
data2	ONLINE	0	0	0
mirror-0	ONLINE	0	0	0
/home/bob/disk2	ONLINE	0	0	0
/home/bob/disk1	ONLINE	0	0	0
mirror-1	ONLINE	0	0	0
/home/bob/disk3	ONLINE	0	0	0
/home/bob/disk4	ONLINE	0	0	0

errors: No known data errors
root@raspberrypi:~#

21. We can see where the data is currently written in our pool using **zpool iostat -v**:

root@raspberrypi:~# **zpool iostat -v data2**

pool	capacity		operations		bandwidth	
	alloc	free	read	write	read	write
data2	139K	224M	0	0	127	1.74K
mirror-0	125K	112M	0	1	1.11K	10.9K
/home/bob/disk2	-	-	0	0	118	749
/home/bob/disk1	-	-	0	0	27	4.04K
mirror-1	14K	112M	0	0	156	15.4K
/home/bob/disk3	-	-	0	0	78	7.69K
/home/bob/disk4	-	-	0	0	78	7.69K

root@raspberrypi:~#

22. All the data are currently written on the first mirror pair and none on the second. This makes sense, as the second pair of disks was added after the data were written. If we write some new data to the pool, the new mirror will be used:

root@raspberrypi:~# **truncate --size 64m /data2/data2file3**
root@raspberrypi:~# **zpool iostat -v data2**

pool	capacity		operations		bandwidth	
	alloc	free	read	write	read	write
data2	138K	224M	0	0	121	1.68K
mirror-0	116K	112M	0	1	798	7.73K
/home/bob/disk2	-	-	0	0	113	723
/home/bob/disk1	-	-	0	0	19	2.87K
mirror-1	22.5K	112M	0	0	70	7.02K
/home/bob/disk3	-	-	0	0	35	3.51K
/home/bob/disk4	-	-	0	0	35	3.51K

23. We see how a little more of the data has been written to the new mirror than to the old: ZFS tries to make the best use of all the resources in the pool. Now do these in-chapter exercises, and then continue onto the next step.

In-Chapter Exercises

  1.1 If you have not already done so, execute all of the steps so far of
      Example 1.1, using proper commands and pathnames.
  1.2 In Example 1.1, step4, what is the pathname to **datafile20**?
  1.3 If you were to use a text editor like emacs to create a text file named
      text1.txt in the file system named **data**, how would you designate
      the complete pathname to that text file?
  1.4 In Example 1.1, after step 6 was executed correctly, and you
      created a text file with emacs in the **data2** file system, would
      the pathnames to the two mirrored versions of that text file be
      different? In other words, could you edit each one of them separ-
      ately by designating different pathnames to them?
  1.5 In Example 1.1, step 19, could you add a single disk into the
      mirrored **data2** zpool, instead of the two disks specified?
  1.6 In Example 1.1, step 20., are the mirrors named **mirror-0** and
      mirror-1 mirrors of each other?

24. Cleanup

    To clean up after doing our work, let's delete everything we created
    in this example.

    From the root directory, destroy the **data2** file system and its files.

    root@raspberrypi:~# **zfs destroy -r data2**
    root@raspberrypi:~#

25. Next, destroy the **data2** zpool.

    root@raspberrypi:~# **zpool destroy data2**

26. Finally, destroy the disk simulation files, and leave root.

    root@raspberrypi:~# **rm /home/bob/disk***
    root@raspberrypi:~# **exit**
    logout
    bob@raspberrypi:~ $

Conclusion: We can use the **zpool** command and its **create** sub-command to
associate or map file systems to vdevs, whether the vdev is a file itself or an
actual physical medium.

Example 1.2: The zfs Command, Send and Receive, Snapshot

Objectives: The following is a complete example of using the command
                zfs, with the sub-commands **send** and **receive**. Its primary
                objective is to show how to create a file system with the **zfs**
                command, and work with ZFS file systems.

Introduction: In this example, we backup a file system with an incremental
                update, from one file system to another, on the same zpool
                and vdev. As with Example 1.1, this example creates a file
                in your home directory that *simulates* a vdev, so you don't
                have to have a second hard disk available! This is the easiest,
                most cost-effective technique, and the best way to practice
                and develop your basic skills with ZFS.

Background: Here, you back up a file system named **data** in the zpool
                named **sender** to another file system named **backup** in the
                same pool, on the same vdev. The **data** file system contains
                a file we create named **test.txt**. It uses the **snapshot** sub-
                command of the **zfs** command to achieve this. ZFS snapshots
                are frozen-in-time "pictures" of the state of the filesystem
                they are taken of.

Two critical operations that involve taking snapshots of a ZFS filesystem
are rolling back a snaphot, and using the **zfs promote** command. A brief
description of those follows, with more examples provided in Section 1.3.3,
items 8 through 10, and Section 1.4.

Rolling back a ZFS filesystem
This important procedure allow you to revert a ZFS file system to a previous
snapshot. Simply stated, it's a builtin means for ZFS to backup and restore
files. ZFS snapshots capture the state of the file system at a specific point
in time, allowing you to roll back to that state if needed. Here's a detailed
example of rolling back a ZFS filesystem:

1.   List Snapshots

First, list the available snapshots for the ZFS filesystem you want to roll back.
You can use the **zfs list** command for this:

zfs list -t snapshot -r pool/filesystem

In the above command, replace **pool/filesystem** with the actual name of your
ZFS pool and filesystem. This command will display a list of snapshots, along
with their creation times.

2.   Choose the Snapshot

Identify the snapshot to which you want to roll back. Note the name and creation time of the snapshot. For example, let's say you want to roll back to a snapshot named **@backup_20230101**. Notice the name is descriptive of the date that the snapshot is taken.

3.   Perform the Roll Back

To roll back the ZFS filesystem to the chosen snapshot, use the **zfs rollback** command:

zfs rollback pool/filesystem@backup_20230101

Replace **pool/filesystem** with the actual name of your ZFS pool and filesystem, and **backup_20230101** with the name of the snapshot you want to roll back to.

4.   Verify the Rollback

Verify that the rollback was successful by listing the contents of the ZFS filesystem:

ls /path/to/mount/point

Replace **/path/to/mount/point** with the actual mount point of your ZFS filesystem. Check if the files and directories match the state captured by the chosen snapshot.

5.   Set the Mountpoint (if necessary!)

If your ZFS filesystem has a different mount point and you want to persist it after a reboot, set the mount point:

zfs set mountpoint=/new/mount/point pool/filesystem

Replace **/new/mount/point** with the desired mount point.

Notes

a)   Rolling back a ZFS filesystem will destroy all changes made since the chosen snapshot. Be careful and ensure you have a backup or understand the implications.

b)   The filesystem must be unmounted, or not in use during the rollback.

c)   It's a good practice to take a new snapshot before performing a rollback, to provide a secure and quick way to revert to the original if necessary.

zfs promote command

The **zfs promote** command, in the context of ZFS, is used to make a clone file system the parent of its originating snapshot. This essentially "promotes" the clone to become the new source file system, and the original file system becomes the clone. This can be useful in scenarios where you want to roll back to an earlier snapshot, or make changes to a clone, and then promote it to the main file system. Here is a detailed explanation:

1. Creating the Snapshot

    First, you need to create a snapshot of the original file system. This snapshot serves as a point-in-time, "immutable picture" reference.

    zfs snapshot tank/source@snapshot1

2. Creating a Clone

    Next, you create a clone of the snapshot of the original file system, which initially shares the data with the source file system.

    zfs clone tank/source@snapshot1 tank/clone

3. Make Changes to the Clone

    You can make changes to the clone without affecting the original file system.

    echo "New data" > /tank/clone/somefile.txt

4. Promote the Clone

    Now, if you want to make the clone the new source file system, you use the **zfs promote** command.

    zfs promote tank/clone

    Note
    After this command, tank/clone becomes the new source file system, and tank/source becomes the clone.
    Again, in the Procedures below, if you make a mistake anywhere along the way, you can always start over by executing the cleanup steps shown at the end of the example, and begin again.

Prerequisites: Installation of ZFS on your Raspberry Pi system, as shown in Section 1.1, and having completed Example 1.1.

Procedures:

To accomplish the objectives of this example, do the following steps in the order presented.

1. Become root and then list the zpools that exist currently on the system. On your Raspberry Pi system, this can be done with the **sudo su -** command.

    bob@raspberrypi:~ $ **sudo su -**
    root@raspberrypi:~# **zpool list**
    no pools available
    root@raspberrypi:~#

2. Create the vdev as a file.

    root@raspberrypi:~# **truncate --size 100m /home/bob/master**
    root@raspberrypi:~#

3. Create a zpool in that vdev named **sender**.

    root@raspberrypi:~# **zpool create sender /home/bob/master**
    root@raspberrypi:~#

4. Create a ZFS file system, named data, in the sender zpool.

    root@raspberrypi:~# **zfs create sender/data**
    root@raspberrypi:~#

5. Create a test file in the sender/data ZFS file system.

    root@raspberrypi:~# **echo "created: 09:58" > /sender/data/test.txt**
    root@raspberrypi:~#

6. Create a snapshot of the ZFS file system named sender/data.

    root@raspberrypi:~# **zfs snapshot sender/data@1**
    root@raspberrypi:~#

7. Examine the location where the snapshot has been saved. First, use the **zfs list** command with the **snapshot** command argument as follows:

Note

This is a very common procedure we use throughout the rest of this chapter, to check on the disposition of ZFS file systems.

```
root@raspberrypi:~# zfs list -t snapshot
NAME                  USED  AVAIL  REFER  MOUNTPOINT
sender/data@1         0B    -      24.5K  -
root@raspberrypi:~#
```

8. By default the snapshot location is hidden. To unhide it, use the **zfs set** command.

```
root@raspberrypi:~# zfs set snapdir=visible sender/data
root@raspberrypi:~#
```

9. See what the contents of the data file system are, using the **ls -la** command as follows:

```
root@raspberrypi:~# ls -la /sender/data
total 2
drwxr-xr-x    3    root root    3 Nov 21 14:49 .
drwxr-xr-x    3    root root    3 Nov 21 14:49 ..
-rw-r--r--    1    root root    15 Nov 21 14:49 test.txt
drwxrwxrwx    1    root root    0 Nov 21 14:49 .zfs
root@raspberrypi:~#
```

10. The snapshot directory that contains the first snapshot is under **.zfs**, as shown. So let's change to the directory that contains it, and use **ls -la** to see what is in that directory.

```
root@raspberrypi:~# cd /sender/data/.zfs/snapshot/1
root@raspberrypi:/sender/data/.zfs/snapshot/1# ls -la
total 2
drwxr-xr-x    2    root root    3 Nov 21 14:49 .
drwxrwxrwx    2    root root    2 Nov 21 14:49 ..
-rw-r--r--    1    root root    15 Nov 21 14:49 test.txt
root@raspberrypi:/sender/data/.zfs/snapshot/1#
```

The file **test.txt** in this directory is a "frozen" picture of what was contained in the **/sender/data** file system at the time we did step 6.

11. Return to your home directory.

    root@raspberrypi:/sender/data/.zfs/snapshot/1# **cd**
    root@raspberrypi:~#

12. Create a ZFS file system named **backup** in the **sender** zpool.

    root@raspberrypi:~# **zfs create sender/backup**
    root@raspberrypi:~#

13. Send the snapshot to the backup file system.

    root@raspberrypi:~# **zfs send sender/data@1 | zfs receive -F sender/**
    backup
    root@raspberrypi:~#
    After the above command executes, the file **test.txt** is in the backup
    file system.

14. Set the sender/backup file system to read only to prevent data
    corruption. Make sure to do this before accessing anything in the
    sender/backup file system.

    root@raspberrypi:~# **zfs set readonly=on sender/backup**
    root@raspberrypi:~#

15. Now we will make some changes in the original file. Use the echo
    command to update the original **test.txt** file to simulate changes in the
    data file system.

    root@raspberrypi:~# **echo "`date`" >> /sender/data/test.txt**
    root@raspberrypi:~#

16. Create a second snapshot of **sender/data**.

    root@raspberrypi:~# **zfs snapshot sender/data@2**
    root@raspberrypi:~#

17. Send the differences. You may get an error message saying that the
    destination has been modified if you did not set the **sender/data** file
    system to read only three commands previously in step 14.

    root@raspberrypi:~# **zfs send -i sender/data@1 sender/data@2 | zfs**
    receive \\ sender/backup
    root@raspberrypi:~#

18. *Optional Step:* At this point you could use ssh to send the file system to another zpool on another machine, such as **backup_server** (where you need to supply the IP address and have root privileges on that system), as follows:

    root@raspberrypi:~# **zfs send sender/data@1 | ssh backup_server zfs **
    receive backup/data@1
    root@raspberrypi:~#

19. Now let's take a look at what is in the second snapshot directory.

    root@raspberrypi:~# **cd /sender/data/.zfs/snapshot/2**
    # **ls -la**
    total 2
    drwxr-xr-x   2   root root   3 Nov 22 10:52 .
    dr-xr-xr-x   2   root root   2 Nov 22 11:02 ..
    -rw-r--r--   1   root root   44 Nov 22 11:01 test.txt
    root@raspberrypi:/sender/data/.zfs/snapshot/2#

20. Let's look at the contents of the **test.txt** file.

    root@raspberrypi:/sender/data/.zfs/snapshot/2# **more test.txt**
    created: 09:58
    Tue 21 Nov 2023 03:00:37 PM PST
    root@raspberrypi:/sender/data/.zfs/snapshot/2#

21. Now let's compare what is in the second snapshot directory to the **sender** and **backup** file systems.

    root@raspberrypi:/sender/data/.zfs/snapshot/2# **cd**
    root@raspberrypi:~# **cd /sender/data**
    root@raspberrypi:/sender/data# **ls**
    test.txt
    root@raspberrypi:/sender/data# **more test.txt**
    created: 09:58
    Tue 21 Nov 2023 03:00:37 PM PST
    root@raspberrypi:/sender/data# **cd ..**
    root@raspberrypi:/sender# **cd backup**
    root@raspberrypi:/sender/backup# **ls**
    test.txt
    root@raspberrypi:/sender/backup# **more test.txt**
    created: 09:58
    Tue 21 Nov 2023 03:00:37 PM PST
    root@raspberrypi:/sender/backup#

22. Return to your home directory.

    root@raspberrypi:/sender/backup# **cd**
    root@raspberrypi:~#

Now do these In-Chapter Exercises, and then continue onto the next step.

In-Chapter Exercises

    1.7   If you have not already done so, execute all the steps of Example 1.2 using proper commands and pathnames.

    1.8   What commands would you use to make the current working directory the one that contains the second snapshot?

    1.9   What are the contents of the first snapshot file, **test.txt**? Can you use the nano text editor to edit the contents of test.txt in the snapshot directory root@raspberrypi:/sender/data/.zfs/snapshot/1? What results do you get if you do this, and why?

    1.10 Redo Example 1.2 using two different zpools named **source** and **target**. Create a file system on the zpool **source** named **origin**, and create a file system on the zpool **target** named **destination**. Instead of using the **echo** command to create the file **test.txt** in the **source/origin** file system, use your favorite text editor, like nano. Then create a couple of sequential snapshots of **origin** and **destination**, making some changes in **test.txt** with nano in between taking the snapshots. Finally, use the techniques shown in Example 1.2 to verify that the snapshots indeed contain the changes you made with nano in **test.txt**.

23. To clean up after doing our work, let's delete everything we created in this example.

Note
Destroying the datasets destroys the snapshots!
From the root directory, destroy the **backup** file system and its data.

root@raspberrypi:~# **zfs destroy -r sender/backup**

1. Next, destroy the data file system and its data.
   root@raspberrypi:~# **zfs destroy -r sender/data**

25. Next, destroy the **sender** zpool.
    root@raspberrypi:~# **zpool destroy sender**

26. Finally, delete the disk simulation file and exit root.

    root@raspberrypi:~# **rm /home/bob/master**
    root@raspberrypi:~# **exit**
    logout
    bob@raspberrypi:~ $

Conclusion: You can use **zfs send/receive** as a backup mechanism, either locally between two hard disks attached to the system, or between systems over a network.

Example 1.3: Mirroring of USB3 Flashdrives

Objectives: To create a mirror of a pair of USB3 flashdrives that have been added to the system sometime after the initial build of the system.

Introduction: The following example illustrates two of the most important storage model and disk maintenance procedures a user can operate under and perform: the maintenance of user files on media other than the boot/system medium that the Raspberry Pi OS is installed on, and the *mirroring* of a physical device using the **zpool attach** command. In the example, we mirror a ZFS vdev user flashdrive onto another flashdrive of equal size. This is a very important system administration maintenance task, because if one of the flashdrives fails, you have an exact duplicate of it attached to your machine, which contains and archives the user data redundantly.

The *resilvering* operation for a 256 GB flashdrive in this example, with very little data on it, takes about five minutes, depending on the USB ports you have inserted the flashdrives in.

You can operate in a redundant way with the two mirrored flashdrives. You will not lose service if only one of them fails. The original flashdrive can have all of your user datasets on it. If for some reason, you do have a media failure, you can then replace the failed flashdrive if necessary, and in a few simple ZFS command steps, restore the integrity and redundancy of the user data on your system without taking the mirrored zpool offline! This is an operation that a commercial system administrator would perform, as well as an ordinary, single-user of a desktop Raspberry Pi system.

Note
This example does not archive the boot/system medium, stored perhaps on a microSD card. The ZFS **zpool attach** command applied to a mirrored pair creates a constantly mirrored "clone" of the user data media, and all

datasets on them. This is critical, because you never know when your user data medium is going to fail! You can have any number of backup schemes in place, to save user datasets with full, rolling, or incremental backups using **rsync** or **zfs snapshot**. But this example's methodology allows you to constantly have an exact clone of your user data medium available as long as it is running and active.

Of course, a more advanced and necessarily complex technique for doing what is shown here would involve multiple media, including higher levels of RAID-Z datasets on media, and even the medium that holds the ZIL.

If you make a mistake anywhere along the way, you can always start over by executing the cleanup step shown at the end of the example, and begin again. Depending on how far you go in the procedure, you can also reformat the flashdrives with the Gparted program (which is what we recommend you use to format them in the first place) and restart from the beginning.

Prerequisites:

1. Installation of ZFS on your Raspberry Pi system, as shown in Section 1.1.

2. That you have previously completed Examples 1.1, and 1.2.

3. That you have previously determined the logical device names, and the full paths to the flashdrives using the methods "A Quick and Easy Way to Find Out the Logical Device Names of Disks Actually Installed on Your System" we've shown previously. The complete logical device names of our flashdrives (not our boot/system, disk!), that we want to create a mirrored pair of are **/dev/sda1** and **/dev/sdb1**. On your system they may not be exactly the same, but they will be very similar.

4. That you have correctly connected, and put a single primary partition on the flashdrives, using Gparted, or a similar facility such as **fdisk**. Additionally, we have found that unmounting these flashdrives, with the **umount** command, as follows, is a critical first step to creating the zpools on them:

    root@raspberrypi:~# **umount /dev/sda1**
    root@raspberrypi:~# **umount /dev/sdb1**

    This is necessary before executing the steps of the procedures below. The pair will still show up in a listing of /dev, even though they're unmounted!

5. The size in bytes of **rpool,** the name of the original user data flashdrive zpool, is smaller than or equal to the size of the primary partition on the second flashdrive you will mirror **rpool** to.

Procedures:
Do the following steps in the order shown to meet the objectives.

1. List the zpools currently on the system with the **zpool list** command.

    ```
    root@raspberrypi:~# zpool list
    no pools available
    root@raspberrypi:~#
    ```

2. Create a zpool named **rpool** with the **zpool create** command.

    ```
    root@raspberrypi:~# zpool create -f rpool /dev/sda1
    ```

    On our 256GB flashdrive, this took a few minutes on our Raspberry Pi 400 running the Debian-Bookworm based Raspberry Pi OS.

3. Use the **attach** sub-command of **zpool** to create a mirror of your original user data disk. Be sure to specify the complete pathname to the devices, as shown.

    ```
    root@raspberrypi:~# zpool attach -f rpool /dev/sda1 /dev/sdb1
    ```

4. This initiates and executes a resilvering of the zpool. While the resilvering is happening (a few minutes on our Raspberry Pi 400), check the status of the pool.

    ```
    root@raspberrypi:~# sudo zpool status
    pool:   rpool
    state:  ONLINE
    status: One or more devices is currently being resilvered.
            The pool will
    continue to function, possibly in a degraded state.
    action: Wait for the resilver to complete.
    scan:   resilver in progress since Mon Nov 20 14:23:15 2023
            112K scanned at 327B/s, 112K issued at 327B/s, 112K total
            183K resilvered, 100.00% done, no estimated completion time
    config:
    ```

NAME	STATE	READ	WRITE	CKSUM
rpool	ONLINE	0	0	0
mirror-0	ONLINE	0	0	0
sda1	ONLINE	0	0	0
sdb1	ONLINE	0	0	0 (resilvering)

```
errors: No known data errors
root@raspberrypi:~#
```

The resilver took a while longer on our Raspberry Pi 400.

Check it again.

```
root@raspberrypi:~# zpool status
pool: rpool
state: ONLINE
scan: resilvered 183K in 00:07:01 with 0 errors on Mon Nov 20
14:30:16 2023
config:

NAME            STATE       READ   WRITE  CKSUM
rpool           ONLINE      0      0      0
  mirror-0      ONLINE      0      0      0
    sda1        ONLINE      0      0      0
    sdb1        ONLINE      0      0      0

errors: No known data errors
root@raspberrypi:~#
```

5. It's interesting to note that the size of the pool **rpool** is only the size of one of the flashdrives in the mirror.

```
root@raspberrypi:~# zpool list

NAME    SIZE   ALLOC   FREE   CKPOINT   EXPANDSZ
FRAG    CAP    DEDUP   HEALTH  ALTROOT
rpool   230G   135K    230G   -                   -
0%      0%     1.00x   ONLINE  -
root@raspberrypi:~#
```

In-Chapter Exercise

1.11 To test the usability of the flashdrives as a ZFS mirrored pair, shut down your machine gracefully. Then disconnect and remove the first disk from the machine. Finally, reboot the machine with only the root, or system disk, and one of the mirrored pair flashdrives on the system. What is the status of the pool you attached the second hard disk to as a mirror, after you do a successful reboot? After completion of this exercise, you may replace the original disks and boot into it normally. Do the remaining step at your discretion.

6. If you want to retain this two-disk mirror, stop. If you want to detach the second hard disk from the pool, thus destroying the mirror, do the following:

```
root@raspberrypi:~# zpool detach rpool /dev/sdb1
$
```

Conclusion: You have created a post-installation two-flashdrive mirror, containing user data on them. In addition, you have used the Gparted program, or a similar program, to prepare those flashdrives for ZFS mirroring.

This example has also shown that to get maximum control over the whole range of sub-commands and options of the **zpool** command, and to be able to integrate that control with other ZFS commands, the command line is the most inclusive, efficient, and reliable method of working with ZFS. As far as we know, there is no reliable graphical interface to ZFS for the Raspberry Pi OS.

Example 1.4: ZFS Filesystems with NFSv4

Objectives:
To illustrate how to set up a Network File System, version 4 (NFSv4) "share" on a Raspberry Pi system, so that you can attach additional media containing your ZFS pools and filesystems to access them from remote computers on your intranet.

Introduction:
To follow up on and extend the objectives and procedures of Example 1.3, you might want to be able to attach additional, and varied, media to your Raspberry Pi, via bus architectures other than the available USB-mounted variety. This could be your objective, in conformance with our recommended data storage, to maintain the boot/system disk for your Raspberry Pi OS on one discrete medium, and your user data files on other media. Currently, even with the introduction of a single-lane PCI Express 2.0 interface on the Raspberry Pi 5, the attachment of external media that doesn't have its own power supply is limited to the four USB connectors mounted on the Raspberry Pi board. Of course, you could always extend that complement of connectors with various hubs, powered or not. But instead of relying on the RPi's media connectivity complement, in this example we mount a ZFS filesystem as a "share" from another computer on our intranet that can accommodate a larger number of additional media, using SATA bus architecture.

Note
There's no reason why the NFSv4 share can't be done using two Raspberry Pi OS computers. So client and server can both be Raspberry Pi systems. In our case here, in terms of operating systems, the second computer that is offering the "share" is running the latest release of Ubuntu software at the time this book was written, Ubuntu 23.10. That second computer becomes the "server", and our Raspberry Pi 400 becomes the "client". The two reasons we used a X86 architecture system running Ubuntu 23.10 are 1) that it could easily have ZFS installed on it, and 2) it had four SATA bus "bays" that could be loaded with large-capacity SSD drives.

In NFSv4, a "share" refers to a directory or file system that is made available to network clients for remote access. It allows multiple clients to access and interact with the shared resources residing on a server over the network, using the NFSv4 protocol. This sharing mechanism is commonly used in networked environments for efficient file access and management. We accomplish that here with the sharing of a ZFS pool and a filesystem on that pool, where the pool and filesystem are resident on the server which can accommodate four SATA bus devices. Some key ideas related to an NFSv4 share:

1. Exporting Directory/File System: The directory or file system that you want to make accessible to remote clients needs to be "exported". This means configuring the NFS server to allow remote clients to access the specified directory or file system.

2. NFS Exports File: In the NFS server configuration, there is often a file called /etc/exports (on Unix/Linux systems) where administrators define which directories or file systems are exported, along with the access permissions and options for each export.

3. Mounting on Client: On the client side, the exported directory or file system can be mounted as if it were a local resource. This allows users on the client machine to interact with the remote files as if they were part of their local file system.

4. Access Control: NFSv4 introduces improved security features compared to earlier versions, including better support for access control lists (ACLs) and stronger authentication mechanisms.

5. Locking Mechanisms: NFSv4 supports advanced locking mechanisms to coordinate access to files between different clients to prevent conflicts and ensure data consistency.

Note
In fact, in Volume 1 of this series, Chapter 1, Section 1.15.2, we give complete procedures for installation and configuration of sharing files between an NFSv4 server and client, both of which are Raspberry Pi systems.

Prerequisites:

1. Completion of Examples 1.1 through 1.3.

2. Having another networked computer attached to your intranet that can use the appropriate network protocols to communicate with a Raspberry Pi system.

In this sharing relationship, the Ubuntu 23.10 server's IP address on our local intranet is 192.168.1.27, and the Raspberry Pi 400 client's IP address is 192.168.1.2. Those IP addresses will be different on your network.

Procedures:
A summary of the Procedures is as follows:

I.   *Installing the NFSv4 Server Package*

In order for you to share files between server and client, you must have the NFSv4 server package installed on the computer from where you want to share your ZFS pools/filesystems via NFSv4 (Figure 1.2). This is called the *server*.

If you're using Ubuntu 23.10 as we are on our HP Proliant Microserver, you can install the NFSv4 server package on your computer as follows:

bob@bob-ProLiant-MicroServer:~$ **sudo apt install nfs-kernel-server -y**

Once the NFSv4 server package is installed, the nfs-server systemd service will be active.

bob@bob-ProLiant-MicroServer:~$ **sudo systemctl status nfs-server. service**

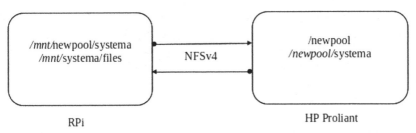

FIGURE 1.2
NFSv4 server and client connected via NFSv4.

● nfs-server.service - NFS server and services
Loaded: loaded (/lib/systemd/system/nfs-server.service; enabled;
preset: enabled)
Drop-In: /run/systemd/generator/nfs-server.service.d
    └─order-with-mounts.conf
Active: active (exited) since Wed 2023-11-22 18:50:01 PST; 15h ago
Main PID: 1353 (code=exited, status=0/SUCCESS)
CPU: 14ms

Nov 22 18:50:01 bob-ProLiant-MicroServer systemd[1]: Starting nfs-
server.service - NFS server and service>
Nov 22 18:50:01 bob-ProLiant-MicroServer systemd[1]: Finished nfs-
server.service - NFS server and service>
lines 1-10/10 (END)
Output truncated...

II. *Installing the NFSv4 Client Package*

On the client Raspberry Pi system, you need to have the NFSv4 client
package installed.

On a Raspberry Pi system, you can run the following command to
install the NFSv4 client package:

bob@raspberrypi:~ $ **sudo apt install nfs-common -y**
Reading package lists... Done
Building dependency tree... Done
Reading state information... Done
nfs-common is already the newest version (1:1.3.4-6).
0 upgraded, 0 newly installed, 0 to remove and 5 not upgraded.
bob@raspberrypi:~ $

Notice that on our Raspberry Pi 400 the package was already installed.
If it wasn't pre-installed on your Raspberry Pi system, you'd have to
continue with the installation in a normal way with APT, using the
command above.

On the Server

III. *Creating ZFS Pools and Filesystems*

To create a ZFS pool, named **newpool**, using a vdev storage device,
check what devices are available with the following command:

```
bob@bob-ProLiant-MicroServer:~$ sudo lsblk -e7 -d
NAME
      MAJ:MIN  RM    SIZE    RO   TYPE   MOUNTPOINTS
sda   8:0      0     447.1G  0    disk
sdb   8:16     0     931.5G  0    disk
sr0   11:0     1     1024M   0    rom

bob@bob-ProLiant-MicroServer:~$
```

In the output, sda is the SATA boot/system disk we're running Ubuntu 23.10 on, and sdb is an unused SATA 1 TB disk. Sdb is the vdev we want to use.

To create a new ZFS pool named newpool, using the vdev device device /*dev*/sdb1, use the following commands:

```
bob@bob-ProLiant-MicroServer:~$ sudo umount /dev/sdb1
bob@bob-ProLiant-MicroServer:~$ sudo zpool create -f newpool /dev/\
                                 sdb1
bob@bob-ProLiant-MicroServer:~$
```

A new ZFS pool named newpool is created, and that ZFS pool newpool will be automatically mounted in the *newpool* directory. All ZFS pools are mounted in a similar manner, starting at root (/). Check the status of the pool named newpool with the following command:

```
bob@bob-ProLiant-MicroServer:~$ sudo zfs list
NAME    USED  AVAIL  REFER  MOUNTPOINT
newpool 360K  899G   96K    /newpool
bob@bob-ProLiant-MicroServer:~$
```

Create a ZFS filesystem named systema in the ZFS pool newpool as follows:

```
bob@bob-ProLiant-MicroServer:~$ sudo zfs create newpool/systema
bob@bob-ProLiant-MicroServer:~$
```

A new ZFS filesystem named systema is created, and automatically mounted in the /*newpool*/systema directory. Use the following command to check this:

```
bob@bob-ProLiant-MicroServer:~$ sudo zfs list
NAME              USED    AVAIL   REFER   MOUNTPOINT
newpool           504K    899G    96K     /newpool
newpool/systema   96K     899G    96K     /newpool/systema

bob@bob-ProLiant-MicroServer:~$
```

IV. Sharing ZFS Pools with NFSv4

This is the critical aspect of your operations on the server. To share the ZFS pool named newpool via NFSv4, you have to set the sharenfs property of your ZFS pool accordingly.

The sharenfs property in the context of the ZFS command is used to control the NFSv4 sharing behavior for a ZFS file system. NFSv4 is a distributed file system protocol that allows remote systems to mount file systems over a network and interact with them as though they are local.

The sharenfs property is specific to ZFS and determines whether a ZFS file system is shared via NFS and, if so, with what options. It has the following syntax:

zfs set sharenfs=value filesystem
Common NFS options include:

ro:	Read-only access.
rw:	Read and write access.
root=client:	Allows the specified client to have superuser (root) access.

To allow everyone on your network read/write access to the ZFS pool newpool, you can set the sharenfs property of the ZFS pool newpool as follows:

bob@bob-ProLiant-MicroServer:~$ **sudo zfs set sharenfs='rw' newpool**
bob@bob-ProLiant-MicroServer:~$

or-

bob@bob-ProLiant-MicroServer:~$ **sudo zfs set sharenfs='rw=*'**
newpool

You can verify whether the sharenfs property is correctly set on the ZFS pool newpool as follows:

bob@bob-ProLiant-MicroServer:~$ **sudo zfs get sharenfs newpool**

NAME	PROPERTY	VALUE	SOURCE
newpool	sharenfs	rw	local

bob@bob-ProLiant-MicroServer:~$

V. Sharing ZFS Filesystems with NFSv4

To share the ZFS filesystem named systema via NFSv4, you have to set the sharenfs property of that ZFS filesystem accordingly. To allow everyone on the network read/write access to the ZFS filesystem systema, you can set the sharenfs property of that ZFS filesystem as follows:

bob@bob-ProLiant-MicroServer:~$ **sudo zfs set sharenfs='rw'**
newpool/systema
bob@bob-ProLiant-MicroServer:~$

or-
bob@bob-ProLiant-MicroServer:~$ **sudo zfs set sharenfs='rw=*'**
newpool/systema

You can verify whether the sharenfs property is correctly set on the ZFS filesystem newpool/systema as follows:

bob@bob-ProLiant-MicroServer:~$ **sudo zfs get sharenfs newpool/**
systema

NAME	PROPERTY	VALUE	SOURCE
newpool/systema	sharenfs	rw	local

bob@bob-ProLiant-MicroServer:~$

VI. Mounting NFSv4 Shared ZFS Pools and Filesystems

To mount the ZFS pools and filesystems that you want to share via NFSv4 with client Raspberry Pi OS machines, you need to know the IP address of your NFS server.

You can run the **hostname -I** command on your NFSv4 server to find the IP address of your NFSv4 server.

bob@bob-ProLiant-MicroServer:~$ **hostname -I**
192.168.1.27
bob@bob-ProLiant-MicroServer:~$

Once you know the IP address of the NFSv4 server, you can list all the available NFSv4 shares on that server as follows:

bob@bob-ProLiant-MicroServer:~$ **showmount -e 192.168.1.27**
Export list for 192.168.1.27:
/newpool/systema *
/newpool   *
bob@bob-ProLiant-MicroServer:~$

As you can see, the ZFS pool name newpool and the ZFS filesystem systema are listed as NFSv4 shares /newpool and /newpool/systema.

On the Raspberry Pi Client

Now you switch your attention to the Raspberry Pi client(s). Create a directory /mnt/newpool for mounting the server NFSv4 share /newpool as follows:

```
bob@raspberrypi:~ $ sudo mkdir -v /mnt/newpool
mkdir: created directory '/mnt/newpool'
bob@raspberrypi:~ $
```

You can mount the NFSv4 share /newpool from the NFSv4 server 192.168.1.27 on the /mnt/newpool directory of your Raspberry Pi client with this command:

```
bob@raspberrypi:~ $ sudo mount -t nfs 192.168.1.27:/newpool /mnt/\
    newpool
bob@raspberrypi:~ $
```

The NFSv4 share /newpool is now mounted on the /mnt/newpool directory of your Raspberry Pi client. To check this, type this command on the client command line:

```
bob@raspberrypi:~ $ df -hT /mnt/newpool
Filesystem    Type    Size    Used    Avail   Use%   Mounted on
192.168.1.27:
/newpool      nfs4    900G    0       900G    0%     /mnt/newpool
bob@raspberrypi:~ $
```

Similarly, create a new directory /mnt/systema for mounting the server NFSv4 share of the ZFS filesystem /newpool/systema on your Raspberry Pi with the following command:

```
bob@raspberrypi:~ $ sudo mkdir -v /mnt/systema
mkdir: created directory '/mnt/systema'

bob@raspberrypi:~ $
```

Then, mount the server NFSv4 share /newpool/systema from the NFS server 192.168.1.27 on the /mnt/systema directory of your Raspberry Pi client as follows:

```
bob@raspberrypi:~$ sudo mount -t nfs 192.168.1.27:/newpool/\
systema /mnt/systema
```

The server NFS share /newpool/systema ZFS filesystem is now mounted on the /mnt/systema directory of your Raspberry Pi client. To check this, type the following command:

bob@raspberrypi:~ $ **df -hT /mnt/systema**
Filesystem   Type   Size   Used   Avail   Use%   Mounted on
192.168.1.27:
/newpool/systema nfs4   900G   0   900G   0%   /mnt/systema

bob@raspberrypi:~ $

VII. Automatically Mounting NFSv4 Shared ZFS Pools and Filesystems

You can mount the server NFSv4 shares ZFS /newpool and /newpool/
systema ZFS filesystem on your Raspberry Pi client automatically at boot
time. To do that, open the Raspberry Pi client /etc/fstab file with the nano
text editor as follows:

bob@raspberrypi:~$ **sudo nano /etc/fstab**
Add the following lines at the end of the /etc/fstab file.

Mount NFS shares
192.168.1.27:/newpool   /mnt/newpool nfsdefaults   0   0
192.168.1.27:/newpool/systema   /mnt/systema nfs   defaults   0   0

Once you're done, in nano press **<Ctrl> + X** followed by **Y** and **<Enter>**
to save the /etc/fstab file.

For the changes to take effect, restart your computer (NFSv4 client) as
follows:
bob@raspberrypi:~$ **sudo reboot**

The next time your Raspberry Pi client machine boots, the NFSv4 shares /
newpool and /newpool/systema will be mounted in the /mnt/newpool and
/mnt/systema directories. To illustrate this, type the following command on
the Raspberry Pi client command line:

bob@raspberrypi:~ $ **df -hT**

Filesystem	Type	Size	Used	Avail	Use%	Mounted on
/dev/root	ext4	439G	19G	398G	5%	/
devtmpfs	devtmpfs	1.7G	0	1.7G	0%	/dev
tmpfs	tmpfs	1.9G	0	1.9G	0%	/dev/shm
tmpfs	tmpfs	759M	1.3M	758M	1%	/run
tmpfs	tmpfs	5.0M	4.0K	5.0M	1%	/run/lock
/dev/sda1	vfat	253M	31M	222M	13%	/boot
192.168.1.27:/newpool	nfs4	900G	0	900G	0%	/mnt/newpool
192.168.1.27: /newpool/systema	nfs4	900G	0	900G	0%	/mnt/systema
tmpfs	tmpfs	380M	32K	380M	1%	/run/user/1000

bob@raspberrypi:~ $

Both Server and Raspberry Pi Client

VIII. How to Allow Writing to the NFSv4 Shared ZFS Pools and Filesystems on both Server and Client

At this point, if you attempt to write to the NFS shares /newpool or /newpool/systema from either your Raspberry Pi client, or the server, you get a permission denied message! To alleviate this problem, you can do the following:

Set 0777 permission on the /newpool and /newpool/systema directories of the NFSv4, server so that everyone can write to the ZFS newpool and NFS filesystem systema. For our purposes here in this example and tutorial for beginners, this is OK.

bob@bob-ProLiant-MicroServer:~$ **sudo chmod 0777 /newpool**
bob@bob-ProLiant-MicroServer:~$ **sudo chmod 0777 /newpool/systema**
bob@bob-ProLiant-MicroServer:~$

There are other more secure techniques, strategies, and tactics you can deploy to give permissions. Here, we only outline one of them for you:

You can construct special group-specific permissions that allow only members belonging to those groups to write or read from the server pools and files.

Note
NFSv4 maps the UID (User ID) and GID (Group ID) of the specified NFSv4 clients with the UID and GID of the NFSv4 server. So, if a user/group has permission to write to an NFSv4 share on the NFSv4 server, then the same user/group with the same UID/GID will be able to write to that NFS share from the NFSv4 client computer.

IX. Unsharing ZFS Pools and Filesystems

If you want to stop sharing the ZFS pool named newpool, you have to "reset" the sharenfs property of the ZFS pool newpool to **off** on the server as follows:

bob@bob-ProLiant-MicroServer:~$ **sudo zfs set sharenfs=off newpool**
bob@bob-ProLiant-MicroServer:~$

NFS sharing will then be disabled for the ZFS pool newpool. You can check this with the following command:

bob@bob-ProLiant-MicroServer:~$ **sudo zfs get sharenfs newpool**

NAME	PROPERTY	VALUE	SOURCE
newpool	sharenfs	off	local

bob@bob-ProLiant-MicroServer:~$

In the same way, you can stop sharing the ZFS filesystem systema by setting the sharenfs property of the ZFS filesystem systema to **off** as follows:

> bob@bob-ProLiant-MicroServer:~$ **sudo   zfs   set   sharenfs=off**
> **newpool/systema**
> bob@bob-ProLiant-MicroServer:~$

NFSv4 sharing will be disabled for the ZFS filesystem systema. You can check this with the following command:

> bob@bob-ProLiant-MicroServer:~$ **sudo zfs get sharenfs newpool/**
> **systema**

NAME	PROPERTY	VALUE	SOURCE
newpool/systema	sharenfs	off	local

> bob@bob-ProLiant-MicroServer:~$

Conclusion

This example has illustrated a simple method of sharing ZFS pools and filesystems, and how to access them remotely using the NFSv4 file-sharing protocol. It also gave instructions for automatically mounting remote ZFS pools and filesystems on a Raspberry Pi system, entities that you've shared with NFSv4 on NFS v4 client computers at boot time from an X86 architecture server on your intranet, and how to manage access permissions for the NFSv4 shares, to allow write access to the NFSv4 shared files from the NFSv4 client Raspberry Pi system as well.

In-Chapter Exercises

1.12 How would you mirror the single ZFS vdev used in the Example above in any RAID-1 or RAID-Z* configuration you desire on whatever server you are using to complete the Example? Be sure to include the exact ZFS command, and its syntax, that you need to use to accomplish creation of this multi-disk configuration.

1.13 You've purchased an exterior unpowered mounting enclosure for a single SATA SSD, that can be attached to your Raspberry Pi system on one of the USB3 connectors (or if you're working on a Raspberry Pi 5, on the PCIe 2.0 port connector using an approved and   viable HAT). How would you now transfer the SATA drive containing the zpool newpool, and the filesystem systema from the X86 architecture machine used in the Example, in our case an HP Proliant Microserver, to the Raspberry Pi system? This transfer would have to be done to maintain the integrity of the zpool newpool, and the filesystem systema. You would no longer need the facilities of NFSv4 to share the zpool or its filesystem. Detail exactly how you would accomplish this transfer.

Hint: The ZFS commands to achieve this are **export** and **import**.

1.14 If you completed the "unsharing" of the ZFS pool and file system on the server in sub-section IX above, how would you complete the deletion of everything done in this Example, on both server and client? Be sure to include the removal of the entry in the fstab file on the Raspberry Pi client, the "destruction" of the zpool and its filesystem on the server, and the restoration of an ext4 filesystem on /dev/sdb1 in your answer.

*ZFS RAID-Z is a type of data storage architecture used in the ZFS file system.

RAID-Z in ZFS is a form of software RAID (Redundant Array of Independent Disks) that provides data redundancy and protection against disk failures. It uses a flexible and scalable approach to distribute parity information across the disks in the array. This helps in protecting data and ensuring continued operation in case of disk failures.

There are several levels of RAID-Z in ZFS:

0. RAID-1
In ZFS, a two-disk mirror is referred to as "mirror" or "RAID-1" (which is a more common term used in traditional RAID configurations). In a ZFS mirror, data are duplicated between the two disks, providing redundancy. This means that if one disk fails, the data are still available on the other disk.

When you create a mirror in ZFS, you are essentially setting up a RAID-1 configuration. Each block of data is mirrored to both disks in the pair. This configuration provides fault tolerance, but it comes at the cost of using twice the amount of storage space compared to a single disk.

1. RAID-Z1 (Single Parity):
    a. Similar to RAID 5, it uses single parity for data protection.
    b. Can tolerate the failure of one disk without data loss.
    c. Requires a minimum of three disks.
2. RAID-Z2 (Double Parity):
    a. Similar to RAID 6, it uses double parity for data protection.
    b. Can tolerate the failure of up to two disks without data loss.
    c. Requires a minimum of four disks.
3. RAID-Z3 (Triple Parity):
    a. Provides triple parity for enhanced data protection.

b. Can tolerate the failure of up to three disks without data loss.

c. Requires a minimum of five disks.

RAID-Z offers some advantages over traditional hardware RAID solutions. It provides features like data integrity checking, automatic repair of silent data corruption (scrubbing), and the ability to dynamically expand storage pools. Additionally, ZFS has advanced features like snapshots, data deduplication, and compression.

It's important to note that while RAID-Z provides data protection, it is not a substitute for regular backups. Backups are essential to protect against other types of data loss, such as accidental deletions, data corruption, or catastrophic events affecting the entire storage system.

1.3 ZFS Commands and Operations

The following section is an abbreviated encyclopedia, or reference manual, that illustrates many uses of the two important ZFS commands, **zfs** and **zpool**. It shows the kinds of operations you can perform with those two commands, and with their options and sub-commands. In order to get a complete listing, with examples, of the commands, sub-commands, and options, consult the man pages for **zfs** or **zpool** on your Raspberry Pi system.

We first present a summary of the command categories and basic definitions for **zpool** and **zfs**. We then show several examples of **zpool** and **zfs** command, sub-command, option, and command argument usage.

This section also assumes that you have done at least one or more of the previous examples in Section 1.2.2 to get a feel for what ZFS can accomplish, and how it works on the Raspberry Pi OS.

All sample code you type on the command line is shown in **bold** text, and is always followed by pressing **<Enter>** on the keyboard. Comments specific to a command, operation, or term, usually appear after the item of interest.

1.3.1 Command Categories and Basic Definitions

1. *Directories and Files*

Where error messages appear: **/var/adm/messages**, **console**

2. *ZFS States*

DEGRADED One or more top-level devices is in the degraded state because they have become offline. Sufficient replicas exist to keep functioning.

FAULTED   One or more top-level devices is in the faulted state because they have become offline. Insufficient replicas exist to keep functioning.

OFFLINE   The device was explicitly taken offline by the **zpool off-line** command.

ONLINE   The device is online and functioning.

REMOVED   The device was physically removed while the system was running.

UNAVAIL   The device could not be opened.

3. *Scrubbing and Resilvering*

Scrubbing: Examines all data to discover hardware faults or disk failures. Only one scrub may be running at one time, and you can manually scrub.

Resilvering: The same concept as rebuilding or resyncing data on to new disks into an array. The smart thing resilvering does is it does not rebuild the whole disk, only the data that are required (the data blocks not the free blocks), thus reducing the time to *resync* a disk. Resilvering is automatic when you replace disks and so on. If a scrub is already running, it is suspended until the resilvering has finished, then the scrubbing will continue.

4. *ZFS Devices and Device Terminology*

Disk:	A physical disk drive.
File:	The absolute path of preallocated files/images.
Mirror:	Standard RAID1 mirror.
RAID-Z1/2/3:	Nonstandard distributed parity-based software RAID levels. Basically, if a power failure occurs in the middle of a write then you have the data plus the parity, or you don't. Also, ZFS supports *self-healing*, which means that if it cannot read a bad block it will reconstruct it using the parity, and repair or indicate that this block should not be used.

RAID-Z1:	3, 5, 9 disks
RAID-Z2:	4, 6, 8, 10, 18 disks
RAID-Z3:	5, 7, 11, 19 disks

The more parity bits, the longer it takes to resilver an array. Standard mirroring does not have the problem of creating the parity, so it is quicker in resilvering. RAID-Z is more like RAID3 than RAID5 on another file system, but does use parity to protect from disk failures.

RAID-Z/RAID-Z1:   A minimum of three devices (one parity disk); you can suffer a one-disk loss.

RAID-Z2:   A minimum of four devices (two parity disks); you can suffer a two-disk loss.

RAID-Z3:   A minimum of five devices (three parity disks); you can suffer a three-disk loss.

Spare: Hard drives marked as *hot spare* for ZFS RAID. By default, hot spares are not used in a disk failure; you must turn on the *autoreplace* feature.

5. *Cache*

A zfs cache caches both the least recently used (LRU) and least frequently used (LFU) block requests; the cache device uses level-2 adaptive read cache (L2ARC).

6. *Log*

There are two log types used:

ZFS intent log (ZIL): A logging mechanism where all the data to be written are stored, then later flushed, as a transactional write; this is similar to a journal file system (**ext3** or **ext4**).

Separate intent log (SLOG): A separate logging device that caches the synchronous parts of the ZIL before flushing them to the slower disk; it does not cache asynchronous data (asynchronous data are flushed directly to the disk). If the SLOG exists, the ZIL will be moved to it rather than residing on the platter disk; everything in the SLOG will always be in the system memory. Basically, the SLOG is the device and the ZIL is data on the device.

1.3.2 ZFS Storage Pools and the zpool Command

The sub-commands and options shown in this section are presented in this general way:
   x. What the command, sub-command, and options accomplish.
The command, sub-command, options, and command arguments

Commentary or explanation.
Further examples:

More variations of the command, sub-command, options and command arguments
Additional commentary or explanation.

1. How to display zpools:

   zpool list

   Further examples:
   zpool list -o poolname, size, altroot

   There are a number of properties that you can select, the default is:
   name, size, used, available, capacity, health, altroot.

2. How to display zpool status:

   zpool status

   Further examples:
   zpool status -xv

   Shows only errored pools with more verbosity.

3. How to show zpool statistics:

   zpool iostat -v 5 5

   Use this command like you would **iostat**

4. How to show zpool history:

   zpool history -il

   Once a pool has been removed, the history is gone!

5. a) How to create a zpool:

   zpool create -n data2 /dev/sdb1

   The **-n** option performs a dry run but doesn't actually perform the
   creation.
   Further examples:

   b) **zpool create data2 /dev/sdb1 /dev/sdc1**
   You cannot shrink a pool, only grow it! Assumes there are two disks
   called **/dev/sdb1** and **/dev/sdc1** .

   c) **zpool create data2a /dev/sdb1**
   Using a standard disk slice on **/dev/sdb**, the first partition, numbered 1.

d) **zpool create -m /zfspool data2a /dev/sdb1**
Using a different mount point than the default /<pool name>.

e) **zpool create data3 mirror /dev/sdb1 /dev/sdc1 mirror /dev/sdd1\
/dev/sde1**
zpool create data4 mirror /dev/sdb1 /dev/sdc1 spare /dev/sdd1

Mirror and hot spare disk examples. "Hot spares" are not used by default, so you need to turn on the auto-replace feature with **zpool setautoreplace=on** for each pool!
f) **zpool create data5 mirror /dev/sdb1 /dev/sdc1 log mirror /dev/\
sdd1 /dev/sde1**

Setting up a log device and mirroring it.
g) **zpool create data6 mirror /dev/sdb1 /dev/sdc1 cache /dev/sdd1 /\
dev/sde1**

Setting up a cache device.
h) **zpool create data7 raidz2 /dev/sdb1 /dev/sdc1 /dev/sdd1 /dev/\
sde1 /dev/sdf1**

You can also create RAID pools (RAID-Z/RAID-Z1: mirror; RAID-Z2: single parity; RAID-Z3: double parity).

In-Chapter Exercise

1.15 How many discrete disks would you need to be able to actually implement the three levels of RAID-Z that you can create?

6. How to destroy a zpool:

zpool destroy data2
Further examples:

zpool import -f -D -d /mypool/data2
You can re-import a destroyed pool.

***Note ***
Another very powerful use of zpool importing is to enable you to completely replace your bootable system disk with the Raspberry Pi OS built on it (which cannot at the current time be a ZFS vdev!) by keeping your user data on a second hard disk with a ZFS zpool on it (possibly mirrored onto other disks in RAID arrays). This is our recommended storage model. Then, when you are ready to replace the system disk, you export the user data disk(s) with the **zpool export** command, and then once you've

replaced the system disk and installed ZFS on it, you can simply **import** the user data disk.

7. How to add a device to a zpool:

    zpool add data01 /dev/sdc1

    The zpool command only supports the removal of hot spares and cache disks! Therefore, be sure you want to add the device to the pool, because you cannot ordinarily remove it with the zpool remove command. For adding to mirrors, see the attach and detach sub-commands that follow.

8. How to resize a zpool:

    zpool set autoreplace=on pool_name
    zpool set autoexpand=on pool_name

    This is not about resizing partitions on an existing vdev that is contained in a zpool. It is about replacing an entire existing vdev, of smaller capacity, with another piece of hardware that has a larger capacity. When replacing a smaller disk with a larger one you must enable the autoreplace and autoexpand features to allow you to use the larger space. You must do this before replacing the first smaller capacity disk with the larger capacity second disk.

9. How to remove a zpool:

    zpool remove data01 /dev/sdb1

    zpool only supports the removal of hot spares and cache disks! Therefore, be sure you want to add the device to the pool, because you cannot ordinarily remove it with the **zpool remove** command. For adding to mirrors, see the **attach** and **detach** sub-commands that follow.

10. How to clear faults:

    zpool clear data01

    Further examples:
    zpool clear data01 /dev/sdb1

    Clears a specific disk fault.

11. Attaching additional drives as a mirror:

    zpool attach data01 /dev/sdb1 /dev/sdc1

/dev/sdb1 is an existing disk that is not mirrored, so by attaching **/dev/sdc1** to the pool **data01**, both disks will become a mirrored pair.

In-Chapter Exercise

   1.16   What level of RAID is this?

   12. How to detach a mirror disk:

       zpool detach data01 /dev/sdb1

       See the previous note on attaching additional drives as a mirror.

   13. How to *online* a zpool (put the pool online):

       zpool online data01 /dev/sdb1

   14. How to *offline* a zpool (take the pool offline):

       zpool offline data01 /dev/sdb1

       Further examples:
       zpool offline data01 -t /dev/sdb1

       This achieves temporary offlining using **-t** (will revert back to online after a reboot).

   15. How to replace pools:

       zpool replace data03 /dev/sdb1

       Replaces one disk that uses the same designation in **/dev** as another disk.

       Further examples:
       zpool replace data03 /dev/sdb1 /dev/sdc1

       Replaces one disk with another disk in **/dev** that has a different designation. As mentioned above, make sure to set the autoreplace and autoexpand features on before doing this operation.

   16. How to do scrubbing:

       zpool scrub data01

       Further examples:
       zpool scrub -s data01

Stop a scrubbing in progress; check the scrub line using zpool status data01 to see any errors.

17. How to do exporting.

As mentioned above, and detailed in our recommended storage model, this command, in combination with the **zpool import** command, enables you to completely replace your bootable system disk with the Raspberry Pi OS built on it (which cannot at the current time be a ZFS vdev!) by keeping your user data on a second hard disk with a ZFS zpool on it (possibly mirrored onto other disks in RAID arrays). Then, when you are ready to replace the system disk, you export the user data disk(s) with the **zpool export** command. Once you've replaced the system disk and installed ZFS on it, you can simply **import** the user data disk. This is a very powerful commercial system administration technique.

zpool export data01

You can list exported pools using the import command **zpool import** to find what the names of exported zpools are, if any.

18. How to do importing:

zpool import data01

When using standard disk devices—that is, **/dev/sdb1**. Further examples:

zpool import -d /zfs

If using files in the **/zfs** file system

zpool import -f -D -d /zfs1 data2

Imports a destroyed pool.

19. Getting zpool parameters:

zpool get all data01

The source column denotes if the value has been changed from its default value; a dash in this column means it is a read-only value.

20. Setting zpool parameters:

zpool set autoreplace=on data01

Use the command **zpool get all <pool>** to obtain a list of current settings.

21. How to upgrade pools:

zpool upgrade -v

Lists upgrade paths.
Further examples:

zpool upgrade -a

Upgrades all pools.

zpool upgrade data01

Upgrades a specific pool; use **zpool get all poolname** to obtain the version number of a pool.

zpool upgrade -V 10 data01

Upgrades to a specific version.

22. Replace a failed disk:

zpool list

Lists the zpools and identifies the failed disk.
Further examples:

zpool replace data01 /dev/sdb1
zpool replace data01 /dev/sdb1 /dev/sdc1

Replaces the disk. You can use the same capacity disk or a new disk of equal or larger capacity. As mentioned above, make sure to set the autoreplace and autoexpand features on before doing this operation.
zpool clear data01

Clears any existing errors.
zpool scrub data01

Scrub the pool to check for any more errors (this depends on the size of the zpool, as it can take a long time to complete). You can now remove the failed disk in the normal way, depending on your hardware.

23. How to expand a pool's capacity:

zpool set autoexpand=on data01
zpool set autoreplace=on data01
zpool replace data01 /dev/sdb1 /dev/sdc1

You cannot remove a disk from a pool and you cannot shrink the pool, but you can enlarge it by replacing existing disks with larger disks!

1.3.3 ZFS File System Commands and the zfs Command

The sub-commands and options shown in this section are presented in the following general way:

What the command, sub-command, and options accomplish.
The command, sub-command, options, and command arguments

Commentary or explanation.
Further examples:

More variations of the command, sub-command, options and command arguments
Commentary or explanation.

1. Displaying ZFS file systems:

   zfs list

   Lists all ZFS file systems

   Further examples:

   zfs list -t filesystem
   zfs list -t snapshot

   zfs list -t volume
   zfs list -t all -r poolname

   Lists different types (file system, snapshot, volume) by **poolname**.
   zfs list -r data01/bob

   Recursive display.
   zfs list -o poolname,mounted,sharenfs,mountpoint

   Complex listing: there are a number of attributes that you can use in a complex listing; see the man page for **zfs**.

2. How to create a file system:

   zfs create data01/bob

   Assumes a pool exists named **data01**, and creates a **/data01/bob** ZFS file system on that pool.

   Further examples:

   zfs create -o mountpoint=/users/data01/users

   Creates the ZFS filesystem at a different mount point.

3. How to destroy a file system:

   zfs destroy data01/bob

   Further examples:

   zfs destroy -r data01/bob
   zfs destroy -R data01/bob

   Uses the recursive options **-r** (all children), **-R** (all dependents).

4. How to mount a file system:

   zfs mount data01

   Further examples:

   zfs mount -o mountpoint=/tmpmnt data01/bob

   You can create temporary mount that expires after unmounting. You can apply all the normal mount options, i.e., **ro/rw, setuid,** etc..

5. How to unmount a file system:

   zfs umount data01

6. How to share a file system:

   zfs share data01

   Further examples:

   zfs set sharenfs=on data01

This file system persists after reboots!

zfs set sharenfs="rw=@192.168.0.13/24" data01/bob

Shares with specific hosts.

7. How to unshare a file system:

zfs unshare data01

Further examples:

zfs set sharenfs=off data01

This file system persists after reboot!

8. How to take snapshots of file systems:

Taking a "snapshot" of a file system is like taking a picture: changes are recorded to the snapshot when the original file system changes; to remove a dataset all previous snapshots have to be removed. You can also rename snapshots. You cannot destroy a snapshot if it has a clone.

zfs snapshot data01@10022010

Creates a snapshot.

Further examples:

zfs snapshot rename data01@10022010 data01@mybackup

Renames a snapshot.

zfs destroy data01@10022010

Destroys a snapshot.

9. How to roll back a file system:

By default, you can only roll back to the latest snapshot. To roll back to older ones, you must delete all newer snapshots.

zfs rollback data01@10022010

10. Cloning/promoting file systems:

Clones are writable file systems that have been upgraded from a snapshot. A dependency will remain on the snapshot as long as the clone exists. A clone uses the data from the snapshot to exist. As you use the clone, it uses space separate from the snapshot. Clones cannot be created across zpools, you need to use the **zfs send/receive** commands to do this, as shown in Example 1.2.

zfs clone data7@10022010 data8/clone
zfs clone -o mountpoint=/clone data7@10022010 data8/clone

Clones, changes the mount point of the clone.
Further examples:

zfs promote data8/clone

Promotes a clone. This allows you to destroy the original file system that the clone is attached to. The clone must reside in the same pool!

11. Renaming a file system:

zfs rename data03/koretsky_disk01 data03/koretsky_d01

The dataset must be kept within the same pool. There are two options on this command: **-p** creates all the nonexistent parent datasets; **-r** recursively renames the snapshots of all descendent datasets (used with snapshots only).

12. Compression of file systems:

zfs set compression=lzjb data03/bob

You enable compression by setting a feature. Compressions are on, off, lzjb, gzip, gzip[1–9], and zle. Compression only starts when you turn it on; other existing data will not be compressed.
Further examples:

zfs get compressratio data03/bob

You can get the compression ratio.

13. Deduplication:

You can save disk space using *deduplication*.
zdb -b data01

Use this command to see the block the dataset consumes.
Further examples:

zfs set dedup=on data01/myfiles

To turn on deduplicate.

zfs get dedupratio data01/myfiles

To see the deduplication ratio.

zdb -DD poolname
To see a histogram of how many blocks are referenced how many times.

14. Getting file system parameters:

zfs get all data03/bob

Lists all the properties.
Further examples:

zfs get setuid data03/bob

Gets a specific property.

zfs get compression

Gets a list of specific properties for all datasets. The source column denotes if the value has been changed from its default value; a dash in this column means it is a read-only value.

15. Setting file system parameters:

zfs set copies=2 data03/bob

Sets the number of copies of dataset **bob** in the pool **data03** to 2; the default number of copies is 1. This is probably the most useful and important way to ensure redundancy on a nonredundant vdev, such as a single hard disk in a laptop computer. Although it doubles the storage space required to contain the dataset, error correction with **zpool scrub** can be achieved on the nonredundant vdev that contains the pool and its datasets that have copies set to 2.
Further examples:

zfs set quota=50M data03/bob
zfs set quota=none data03/bob

Sets and unsets the disk usage quota. Use the command **zfs get all**
<dataset> to obtain a list of current settings.

16. How to have a file system inherit attributes:

    zfs inherit compression data03/bob

    Sets back to the default value.

17. How to upgrade the ZFS version:

    zfs upgrade -v

    Lists the upgrade paths.
    Further examples:

    zfs upgrade

    Lists all the datasets that are not at the current level.

    upgrade -V <version> data03/linuxthetextbook2

    Upgrades a specific dataset.

18. How to use allow/unallow:

    zfs allow master

    Displays the permissions set and any user permissions.
    Further examples:

    zfs allow -s @permset1 create,mount,snapshot,clone,promote master

    Creates a permission set.

    zfs unallow -s @permset1 master

    Deletes a permission set.

    zfs allow vallep @permset1 master

    Grants a user permissions.

    zfs unallow vallep @permset1 master

Revokes a user's permissions. There are many permissions that you can set. Refer to the zfs man page, or just use the **zfs allow** command, to get help.

1.4 File System Backups Using zfs snapshot

Snapshots are the ZFS way of creating archives and backups automatically, or with very simple script file operations and embedded commands. As stated previously, taking a snapshot of a file system is like taking a picture; changes are recorded to the snapshot when the original file system changes.

Here are some important things to remember about snapshots:

a.   To remove a dataset, all previous snapshots have to be removed.

b.   You can rename snapshots.

c.   You cannot destroy a snapshot if it has a clone.

1.4.1 Examples of snapshot

An example of creating a snapshot:

zfs snapshot data01@10022010

An example of renaming a snapshot:

zfs snapshot data01@10022010 data01@mybackup

An example of destroying a snapshot:

zfs destroy data01@10022010

1.4.2 zfs rollback

It is possible to roll back a file system, or return it to a previous state. You must use the **zfs rollback** command. By default you can only roll back to the latest snapshot, to roll back to an older one you must delete all newer snapshots!

An example of rolling back to a snapshot is:

zfs rollback data01@10022010

1.4.3 Cloning/Promoting

As stated previously, clones are writable file systems that have been upgraded from a snapshot, and a dependency will remain on the snapshot as long as the clone exists. A clone uses the data from the snapshot to exist. As you use the clone it uses space separate from the snapshot. Clones cannot be created across zpools, you need to use the **zfs send/receive** commands to do this.

Two examples of cloning are:

zfs clone data7@10022010 data8/clone
zfs clone -o mountpoint=/clone data7@10022010 data8/clone

Promoting a clone allows you to destroy the original file system that the clone is attached to. An example of this is:

zfs promote data8/clone

The clone must reside in the same pool.

1.4.4 Renaming a Filesystem

The dataset must be kept within the same zpool! An example of this is:

zfs rename data03/koretsky_disk01 data03/koretsky_d01

There are two options on this command: **-p** creates all the nonexistent parent datasets; **-r** recursively renames the snapshots of all descendent datasets (used with snapshots only).

1.4.5 Compression of Filesystems

You enable compression by setting a feature. Compressions are on, off, lzjb, gzip, gzip[1–9], and zle. Compression starts when you turn it on; other existing data will not be compressed. A description of those forms of compression follows:

lzjb:
lzjb is a compression algorithm used in the ZFS file system, which is developed by Sun Microsystems (now part of Oracle). It is designed to provide good compression and decompression speed with relatively low resource usage.

gzip:
gzip is a widely used data compression and decompression tool. It uses the DEFLATE algorithm, which is a combination of LZ77 (a sliding window

compression algorithm) and Huffman coding (a variable-length prefix coding algorithm). Gzip is commonly used to compress files on Unix and Unix-like systems.

gzip[1–9]:
The numbers 1 through 9 after gzip indicate different compression levels. The higher the number, the better the compression, but at the cost of increased processing time. For example, gzip -9 will use the maximum compression level, while gzip -1 will use the fastest (but least efficient) compression.

zle:
zle is not a compression algorithm itself; rather, it is a feature of the Zsh (Z Shell) command-line interpreter. Zle stands for "Zsh Line Editor". It provides advanced line editing capabilities, including command history, completion, and other interactive features to enhance the command-line experience for users.

In summary, lzjb is a compression algorithm used in the ZFS file system, gzip is a general-purpose compression tool using the DEFLATE algorithm, gzip[1–9] refers to different compression levels in gzip, and zle is a feature of the Zsh shell for line editing.

An example of this is:

zfs set compression=lzjb data03/bob

You can get the compression ratio by using the following example:

zfs get compressratio data03/bob

1.5 Incremental ZFS Backups

In this section we give examples of how to utilize ZFS to accomplish an important system administration task for the ordinary user: backup of file systems and the files in them. The first example uses **zfs send/receive** to accomplish this backup. The second example uses a Bourne shell script to automate that process, in order to make it faster, more efficient, and auto-matic if desired.

Example 1.5: Sending and Receiving ZFS Snapshots Across a LAN

Objectives:
To create two zpools and their default datasets on two different flashdrives, mounted on two different systems on a LAN. To then take **zfs** *snapshots*

(backups) of the dataset on one system, and use **zfs send/receive** to transmit the contents of those snapshots to the other system.

Introduction:

ZFS snapshots are a feature of the ZFS file system that allows you to create read-only point-in-time copies of your file system. These snapshots are efficient, storage space-saving representations of the state of the file system at the time the snapshot is taken. Here are some key points about them, and what you might use them for on your Raspberry Pi systems:

1. Storage Space Efficiency: ZFS snapshots are storage space-efficient because they initially consume no additional media space. Instead, they reference the existing data blocks of the file system. As changes are made to the ZFS file system after the snapshot is taken, only the modified data blocks are allocated additional space. This makes it possible to have multiple snapshots, without consuming a lot of extra storage space.

2. Rapid Creation and Deletion: Creating a ZFS snapshot is a quick operation because it doesn't involve copying data. Deleting a snapshot is also fast, as it involves freeing up references, rather than deleting actual data.

3. Data Protection: ZFS snapshots are useful for data protection and recovery. If you accidentally delete or modify a file, you can roll back to a previous snapshot to restore the file system to its state at the time of the snapshot. This can help prevent data loss, and simplify backup and recovery processes.

4. Backup: While ZFS snapshots are not a full replacement for traditional backups, they can be part of an overall user data backup strategy. Snapshots provide a point-in-time copy of the file system that, can be used for backup purposes. You can use them in conjunction with tools like **zfs send** and **zfs receive**, to send snapshots to another system or storage device, creating a backup. And that should have become evident to you when you did Example 1.2, even though the snapshots were on files emulating vdevs, and were on the same Raspberry Pi system.

5. Cloning: ZFS snapshots can be used to create *clones*, which are writable copies of a file system at a specific point in time. Clones share data with the original snapshot until changes are made, at which point the data in them diverges.

6. Rollback: If you make changes to your file system that you later regret, you can use ZFS snapshots to roll back the file system to a previous state, effectively undoing the changes.

ZFS snapshots contribute to the overall flexibility, efficiency, and data integrity features of the ZFS file system. They are a powerful tool for managing and protecting data, and they can be particularly useful in environments where data consistency and reliability are critical.

To transmit ZFS snapshots between two computers on your LAN, you can use the **zfs send** and **zfs receive** commands. These commands are used to send and receive ZFS snapshots, respectively. Below is a sequentially organized basic description of how you can use these commands:

1. On the source machine (sending machine):
Identify the dataset and snapshot you want to send. For example, if you have a dataset named pool1/mydata and a snapshot named @backup1, you would use:

zfs send pool1/mydata@backup1 > /path/to/backup1.zfs

2. Transfer the snapshot to the destination machine:
You can use various methods like scp, rsync, or any other file transfer tool to move the backup1.zfs file to the destination machine.

3. On the destination machine (receiving machine):
Once the snapshot file is on the destination machine, you can use the **zfs receive** command to apply the snapshot:

zfs receive pool2/newdataset < /path/to/backup1.zfs

This will recreate the dataset pool2/newdataset on the destination machine using the data from the snapshot.

Here's an explanantion of the above commands:
zfs send: This command sends the ZFS dataset or snapshot to standard output, which can then be redirected to a file or transmitted over the network.

zfs receive: This command reads the stream from standard input and creates a new dataset, file system, or volume.

Remember to replace **pool1/mydata**, **@backup1**, **pool2/newdataset**, **/path/to/ backup1.zfs**, and other placeholders with your actual dataset, snapshot, and file paths. Additionally, you may want to consider using tools like ssh along with **zfs send** and **zfs receive** for secure communication over the network. For example, you can use ssh to execute the **zfs receive** command on the destination machine, like this:

**zfs send pool1/mydata@backup1 | ssh username@destination-machine 'zfs\
receive pool2/newdataset'**

There are a couple of important qualifiers on this general command:

1. If you've created the zpool on both machines as root, unless you change the access privileges on the destination machine, the username at that destination will have to be root. And you will need to modify the SSH configuration on the destination, so that root can login. We show this procedure in the two examples that follow.

2. Make sure to replace **username** and **destination-machine** with your actual SSH username and the address of the destination machine!

3. Ensure that the destination dataset (**pool2/newdataset** in the case of this example) does not already initially exist when you're transmitting the first snapshot.

Note
The two systems (sending and destination) could be Raspberry Pi systems, or a Raspberry Pi system as the sender, and another type or architecture machine as the receiver. As long as both of them have ZFS installed.

Prerequisites:

1. Completion of Examples 1.1 through 1.4.

2. Installation of ZFS on both Raspberry Pi systems, as shown in Section 1.1.

3. Having root access privileges on both systems, i.e. knowing root's password, particularly on the destination system.

4. You must be able to login as root via ssh on the destination host receiving the backup. This involves changing your sshd_config file to allow root login, and is a security risk if your machine has a public-facing IP address! This is achieved on a Raspberry Pi system by editing the */etc*/ssh/sshd_config file as root, and changing the line

   #PermitRootLogin prohibit-password to **PermitRootLogin yes**

5. Having two spare, and properly formatted flashdrives available for use. In our case, we used two flashdrives formatted to FAT32 to begin with.

Procedures:

Step 1. Prepare the two flashdrives as shown in Example 1.3.

Step 2. Insert the flashdrives on the two systems, and create one zpool on each named as follows:

   On the source system: **sender**

   On the destination system: **receiver**

Step 3. In the ZFS dataset named **sender** (by default mounted at /sender), which ZFS created by default in the source zpool created in Step 2, use a text editor to create a file named **newfile**.

Step 4. Take a zfs snapshot of the sender dataset with the following command:

bob@raspberrypi:~ $ **sudo zfs snapshot sender@2023-11-25**

The snapshot's name in this case includes the date, November 25, 2023.
To list the snapshots now taken, use the following command:

bob@raspberrypi:~ $ **sudo zfs list -t snapshot**

NAME	USED	AVAIL	REFER	MOUNTPOINT
sender@2023-11-25	0B	-	134K	-

bob@raspberrypi:~ $

Step 5. Send the snapshot stream to the second system, using ssh, as follows:

bob@raspberrypi:~ $ **sudo zfs send sender@2023-11-25 | ssh\
root@192.168.1.34 zfs \ receive -F receiver**
root@192.168.1.34's password: **Enter root's password here!**
Output truncated...
bob@raspberrypi:~ $

Step 6. On the second system, the file named newfile will be in the directory /receiver.

When you send a full stream, the destination dataset must not exist. The following commands on the second, destination system, shows the results of sending the snapshot:

$ **cd /receiver**
/receiver$ **ls**
newfile
/receiver$

Step 7. On the sender, add another file using your text editor to /sender, named **newfile2**. Take another snapshot of sender with the following command:

bob@raspberrypi:~ $ **sudo zfs snapshot sender@2023-11-26**
bob@raspberrypi:~ $

You can check the status of snapshots now with the following command:

```
bob@raspberrypi:~ $ sudo zfs list -t snapshot
NAME                    USED  AVAIL  REFER  MOUNTPOINT
sender@2023-11-25       13K   -      134K   -
sender@2023-11-26       0B    -      135K   -
bob@raspberrypi:~ $
```

Step 8. You can send incremental data by using the **zfs send -i** option. To send an incremental snapshot to the second machine, use the following command:

```
bob@raspberrypi:~ $ sudo zfs send -i sender@2023-11-25 sender@2023-\
11-26 | ssh \ root@192.168.1.34 zfs receive -F receiver
root@192.168.1.34's password: Enter root's password here!
Output truncated...
bob@raspberrypi:~ $
```

Note that the first argument, sender@2023 -11-25, is the earlier snapshot and the second argument, sender@2023-11-26, is the second snapshot. In this case, the dataset receiver must already exist for the incremental receive to be successful.

Step 9. On the second system, the files named newfile and newfile2 will be in the directory /receiver. The following command shows this:

```
/receiver$ ls
newfile newfile2
/receiver$
```

10. To clean up, use the **sudo zfs destroy** command to delete the snapshots on both systems. Then use the **sudo zpool destroy** command on both systems to destroy the datasets and pools created on the flashdrives. Finally, use the gparted program on your Raspberry Pi systems to reinitialize the flashdrives so that they can be used again, outside of ZFS, if that's what you desire.

Conclusion

You created two zpools, and their default datasets, on two different flashdrives, mounted on two different systems on a LAN. You then took zfs snapshots (backups) of the dataset on one system, and used **zfs send/receive** to transmit the contents of those snapshots to another system.

Example 1.6: Daily zfs snapshot Command Automation in a Bourne Shell Script

Objectives:

The following Bourne shell script, which should be run only once daily, achieves the incremental backing up of a file system on one Raspberry Pi system to a remote host system on a LAN, using **zfs snapshot send/receive**. It is very similar to, and a further extension of, the **zfs send/receive** examples shown in Examples 1.2 and 1.5.

Prerequisites:

1. Installation of ZFS on both Raspberry Pi systems, as shown in Section 1.1, and completion of Examples 1.1 through 1.5.

2. The host receiving the snapshot must be running the same or a higher version of ZFS than the sender, which, if you've installed them on two Raspberry Pi systems with the instructions from Section 1.1, will be the same.

3. You must be able to login as root via ssh on the destination host receiving the backup. This involves changing your sshd_config file to allow root login, and is a security risk if your machine has a public-facing IP address! This is achieved on a Raspberry Pi system by editing the /*etc*/ssh/sshd_config file as root, and changing the line

#PermitRootLogin prohibit-password to **PermitRootLogin yes**

4. You must be sending to an account that has ZFS create/receive properties.

5. The zfs dataset names for source and destination, and the LAN IP addresses shown, are specific to our system. You need to change these appropriately for your system.

Procedures:

Note
The script file that achieves the Objectives of this example should only be run once daily, perhaps automatically via a systemd timer. If you run it more than that in the same calendar day, you will get an error message, and over-write yesterday's snapshot! And then you'll have to redo all of the steps of this Procedure.

1. Insert USB-mounted media into source and destination Raspberry Pi systems, unmount them, and create zpools on them named **sender**

and **receiver**, exactly like was done in Example 1.5. **sender** would be the name of the source zpool, and **receiver** would be the name of the destination zpool. You can interrogate each system, in particular the /dev directory of each, to know the logical names of each of the USB-mounted medium you've added to them. Or, you can use the **df -hT** command to find out the same thing.

2. Create a snapshot of the **sender** filesystem with the following command:

   bob@raspberrypi:~ $ **sudo zfs snapshot sender@2023-11-24**

   where 2023-11-24 was yesterday's date (whatever that date is at the time you're doing this Example) on our system. You can check this on the source system with the following command:

   bob@raspberrypi:~ $ **sudo zfs list -t snapshot**
NAME	USED	AVAIL	REFER	MOUNTPOINT
sender@2023-11-24	0B	-	135K	-

3. In order for the Bourne shell script file that copies a snapshot between systems to work, the archived, or previous snapshot, must exist on both the source and destination filesystems. Copy the snapshot **sender@2023-11-24**, as shown in Example 1.5, Step 5. to the destination host.

4. Execute the script file listed below with the following command:

   bob@raspberrypi:~ $ **sudo ./Example_1_6.sh**
   taking todays snapshot, sender@2023-11-25
   yesterday snapshot, sender@2023-11-24, exists, send todays backup
   root@192.168.1.27's password: **Enter your root password on the destination machine!**

   backup complete destroying yesterdays snapshot
   bob@raspberrypi:~ $

5. On the destination Raspberry Pi, check that the snapshot has been received with the following command:

   $ **sudo zfs list -t snapshot**
NAME	USED	AVAIL	REFER	MOUNTPOINT
receiver@2023-11-24	0B	-	134K	-
receiver@2023-11-25	0B	-	134K	-
   $

Optional Step:

6. To clean up, use the **sudo zfs -r destroy** command to delete the snapshots on both systems. Then use the **sudo zpool destroy** command on both systems to destroy the datasets and pools created on the USB-mounted media. Finally, use the Gparted program on your Raspberry Pi systems to reinitialize that media, so that they can be used again, with perhaps a FAT32, or ext4 filesystem on them.

Code for Example_1_6.sh:

```
# !/bin/sh
# This assigns a local filesystem as the source to be transmitted
pool="sender"
# This assigns a remote destination
destination="receiver"
# This names the IP address of the remote target host
host="192.168.1.27"
# Sets the date format for today
today=$(date +"%Y-%m-%d")
# This sets the date format for yesterday
yesterday=$(date +"%Y-%m-%d" -d"-1 day")
# Create today's snapshot
snapshot_today="$pool@$today"
# look for a snapshot with this name, and if none exists, take the snapshot
if zfs list -H -o name -t snapshot | sort | grep "$snapshot_today$" > /dev/null\
    then
        echo " snapshot, $snapshot_today, already exists"
        exit 1
    else
        echo " taking todays snapshot, $snapshot_today"
        zfs snapshot -r $snapshot_today
fi
# look for yesterdays snapshot
snapshot_yesterday="$pool@$yesterday"
# If it exists, zfs send todays snapshot
if zfs list -H -o name -t snapshot | sort | grep "$snapshot_yesterday$" > /dev/\
null
    then
        echo " yesterday snapshot, $snapshot_yesterday, exists, send todays\
        backup"
        zfs send -R -i $snapshot_yesterday $snapshot_today | ssh root@$host \
            zfs receive -F $destination
```

```
        echo " backup complete destroying yesterdays snapshot"
        zfs destroy -r $snapshot_yesterday
        exit 0
    else
        echo " missing yesterday snapshot aborting, $snapshot_yesterday"
        exit 1
fi
```

In-Chapter Exercise

1.17   If you run this Bourne shell script once every day for three days in
       a row, how many snapshots will exist on the destination Raspberry
       Pi, in the filesystem **receiver**?

Summary
This chapter provided someone just beginning to use the Raspberry Pi OS
with the basic techniques of working with the Zettabyte File System (ZFS). It
covered the following topics:

1.   Definition of essential terms used in ZFS and a description of what
     ZFS is from the user perspective.

2.   What differentiates ZFS from other file systems. ZFS file systems are
     mapped onto pool storage facilities, known as zpools, rather than onto
     physical storage media, like disk drives. The zpools are then mapped
     onto the physical media. That means that the file system's storage
     requirements can grow, or can be made redundant using mirroring, as
     more physical media devices are added to the zpools.

3.   Six fundamental and useful worked examples of deploying various
     ZFS commands, primarily **zpool** and **zfs**. These worked examples illus-
     trate for the beginner some of the basic operations that can be used to
     create zpools, and file systems on them.

4.   A command reference section that gives many ZFS command usage
     examples.

5.   File system backup procedures, with a Bourne shell script example,
     that uses the **zfs snapshot**, **zfs send**, and **zfs receive** commands.

2

The X Windows System, Wayland, Xwayland, Wayfire, GTK, Qt, and Gnuplot

2.0 Objectives

* To give a basic overview of how a GUI desktop system on the Raspberry Pi OS works

* To give the basic concepts behind the X Window System, the Wayland protocol, XWayland, Wayfire, XCB, Qt5, and GTK4 graphics

* To present the following model of developing practical GUI client applications:

* Data Generation → Window Generation/Construction → Data Mapping to the Constructed Window

* To provide simple examples of using the Qt5 and GTK4 toolkits to create widget graphics that comprise the Window Generation/Construction phase of the above model

* To detail the use of a Data Generation application, gnuplot, and how gnuplot can be used to map its data to windows created by Qt5

* To cover the commands and primitives

gcc, gnuplot, make, raspi-config, Wayfire, Wayland, qmake, XCB

2.1 Introductory Remarks

You've done the default installation of the Raspberry Pi OS, but are not happy with Wayland and Wayfire as your backend graphics system and window manager, which are the default GUI systems used on a Debian Bookworm-based Raspberry Pi OS. And the system is unstable, and is giving you a lot of problems while you're in the middle of doing important work on applications-related material.

DOI: 10.1201/9781003473268-3

So what do you do, if you want to use an X11 backend on your Raspberry Pi 3, 4b, 400 or 5, and have installed and are running the Debian Bookworm-based Raspberry Pi OS? You haven't completely swallowed the Wayland fanboy hype coming out of the Raspberry Pi Forums, or on the Internet, your system is always crashing in bizarre ways, and most importantly, you have attributed that behavior to the Wayland and Wayfire system and window manager. I've determined that I can eliminate those problems, simply by switching from Wayland to X11.

The following instructions allow you to simply and easily achieve that switch to an X11 window manager and backend on your Debian Bookworm-based Raspberry Pi OS.

1. Use the raspi-config tool. To launch it, type this command:

   $ **sudo raspi-config**

   A text-based configuration tool appears on screen.

2. Use the arrow keys on your keyboard to scroll down to choice **6 Advanced Options Configure advanced settings**, and press **<Enter>**.

3. Your screen looks something like Figure 2.1. Highlight menu choice **A6 Wayland Switch between X and Wayland backends**, and press **<Enter>**.

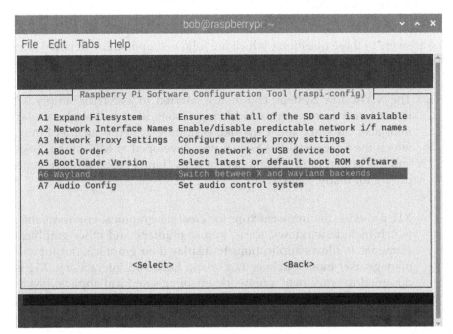

FIGURE 2.1
raspi-config A6 Selection.

4. The final choices are presented on the menu that appears. They are:

W1 X11 Openbox window manager with X11 backend

W2 Wayfire Wayfire window manager with Wayland backend

Choose by highlighting W1 with keyboard arrow keys, then press **<Enter>**. You can then have your system reboot into whichever menu choice you've made, W1 for X11.

2.1.1 What Constitutes a Raspberry Pi OS GUI?

In the spirit of many of the previous chapters and sections found in the volumes of this series, and as far as the Debian Bookworm-based Raspberry Pi OS released for the Raspberry Pi 5 is concerned, you also have to ask yourself these questions before you begin this chapter on the contemporary Raspberry Pi GUI:

1. What is the X Window System?
2. What is Wayland?
3. What is Xwayland
4. What is Wayfire?
5. What is GTK?
6. What is Qt?

The answers to these questions, which are followed up in more detail by this chapter's sections, examples, and problems, are as follows:

1. The X Window System, commonly referred to as X11(or simply X,) is a network-transparent windowing system used for graphical user interfaces on Unix and Unix-like operating systems such as Linux, which the Raspberyy Pi OS is. It was developed at MIT in the 1980s and has been a fundamental part of Unix/Linux-based desktop computing for many years.

    X11 provides the infrastructure for creating graphical environments, which include windows, icons, mouse pointers, and other graphical elements. It allows applications to display their graphical output and manage user input, such as mouse and keyboard interactions. X11 is designed to work over a network, enabling graphical applications to run on one machine and display output on another.

Note

As repeated below in Section 2.3.4, a key concept of the X Window System that sometimes causes confusion is the difference between *server* and *client*. One possible cause for confusion here is that traditionally, on a computer network, a server is thought of as a machine that serves files to many other machines (clients), which is certainly a different function from an X Window System server, and its client(s). In the X Window System, a server is the hardware and/or software that actually takes input from and displays output to the user. For example, the keyboard, mouse, and OLED display screen in front of the user are part of the server; they graphically *serve* information to the user. The client is an application program that connects to, receives input events from, and makes output requests to the server to show, or display something.

Some additional key features and concepts of the X Window System include:

a. Network Transparency: X11 is known for its network transparency, which means that applications can be run on one computer and displayed on another. This is useful for remote desktop applications and for distributing computational tasks to remote servers while displaying the results locally.

b. Window Management: X11 provides basic window management features, allowing users to move, resize, and manipulate windows.

c. Extension Support: X11 supports extensions that can add extra functionality to the core X protocol, such as the X Render extension for improved graphics rendering.

d. Multiple Window Managers: X11 is window manager-agnostic, meaning users can choose from a variety of window managers, each with its own look, feel, and features. Popular window managers include GNOME, KDE, Xfce, and many others.

It's worth noting that while X11 has been the standard for graphical environments on Unix and Linux systems for many years, Wayland is a newer alternative that aims to provide a more modern and efficient way of handling graphical rendering with a focus on security and performance. Many Linux distributions and desktop environments are gradually transitioning from X11 to Wayland as the default display protocol, and the Raspberry Pi OS has done that.

2. Wayland is a protocol for communication between a display server and its clients, designed as a replacement for the older X Window System. In simpler terms, it's a technology that manages graphical displays on Linux-based systems. Wayland aims to provide a more modern and efficient way of handling graphical rendering, improving performance and security compared to X. It's an integral part of many Linux desktop environments, like GNOME and KDE, and helps manage windows, input devices, and other graphical elements on your computer.

3. Xwayland is a compatibility layer that allows application specifically built for the X Window System, to run on a Wayland display server. It bridges the gap between the older X11 protocol and the newer

Wayland protocol, providing a way for legacy X11 applications to work seamlessly in a Wayland-based graphical environment.

The need for Xwayland arises because many existing Linux applications and window managers were developed for X11, and transitioning everything to Wayland natively would be a massive undertaking. Xwayland essentially acts as a translator, enabling X11 applications to draw their graphical elements and interact with a Wayland compositor, making it possible to run X11 applications alongside native Wayland applications in a Wayland session.

This compatibility layer is an important component of Wayland desktop environments, ensuring that users can continue to use their favorite X11 applications while benefiting from the improved performance and security features offered by Wayland.

4.   Wayfire is a 3-D Wayland compositor for Linux.

Note

Wayfire is essentially a window manager that works with the Wayland display protocol, and gives a desktop experience on the Debian Bookworm-based Raspberry Pi OS exactly like the Debian Bullseye-based Raspberry Pi OS Openbox LXDE desktop .

Wayfire aims to provide a visually appealing and feature-rich environment for Linux users who run Wayland-based desktops. Wayfire allows users to create visually stunning and highly customizable desktop environments on Wayland-based systems.

5.   GTK4 (the version we show here, and which was formerly known as the GIMP Toolkit) is an open-source graphical user interface (GUI) toolkit for creating graphical user interfaces in applications. It is primarily associated with the GNOME desktop environment, a popular Linux and Unix-based desktop environment, but it can also be used on other platforms, including Windows and macOS.

GTK4 provides a set of libraries and tools for building graphical user interfaces. It includes a wide range of graphical widgets (such as buttons, text fields, menus, and more) and facilities for handling events, drawing graphics, and managing windows. GTK4 is written in the C programming language, but it has bindings for various other programming languages, making it accessible to developers with different language preferences.

GTK4 has been widely used in the Linux and Unix software ecosystem and serves as the foundation for many applications, including text editors, file managers, and desktop environments like GNOME. It is known for its flexibility, extensibility, and the ability to create attractive and functional user interfaces.

6.   Qt5 is a cross-platform application framework and toolkit that is widely used for developing software with graphical user interfaces (GUIs). It is

known for its C++ libraries and tools that simplify the process of creating interactive and visually appealing applications that can run on multiple operating systems, including Windows, macOS, Linux, Android, and more. Qt5 is developed and maintained by The Qt Company.

Key features and components of Qt5 include:

a.   **Qt Widgets**: Qt5 provides a set of GUI widgets that can be used to create windows, dialogs, buttons, text input fields, and various other interface elements.
b.   **Qt Quick**: This is a framework for creating modern, fluid, and touch-enabled user interfaces. It uses the QML (Qt Meta-Object Language) scripting language and is particularly well-suited for applications with dynamic, animated user interfaces.
c.   **Qt Creator**: Qt Creator is an integrated development environment (IDE) designed for developing applications with Qt. It provides a code editor, visual GUI design tools, a debugger, and other features to streamline the development process.

Note
We really don't show Qt Creator, it's a rather complex framework.

d.   **Cross-Platform Support**: Qt5 enables developers to write code once and deploy it on multiple platforms without major modifications. This is achieved through the use of Qt5's abstraction of platform-specific features.
e.   **Open Source**: Qt5 is available under both open source and commercial licenses, making it accessible to a wide range of developers.

Qt5 and Qt Creator provide a robust and flexible environment for developing cross-platform applications with rich and responsive graphical user interfaces. It is used in a wide range of applications, from desktop software to mobile apps and embedded systems.

In the following sections, we describe all of the above topics in more detail, to allow the beginner to appreciate how sophisticated, complex, and useful, constructing a Raspberry Pi GUI is.

2.2 A Bit of Wayland History

Kristian Høgsberg, a Linux graphics and X.Org developer, started working on Wayland as a spare-time project in 2008. His goal at that time was to develop a system in which "every frame is perfect, which means that applications are able to control the rendering enough that you will never see tearing, lag, redrawing or flicker". The origin story of the title "Wayland" is as follows: he was driving through the town of Wayland, Massachusetts when the under-lying concepts for the project "crystallized", hence the name.

In October 2010, Wayland became a freedesktop.org project. As part of that move, the prior Google Group was replaced by the *Wayland-devel* mailing list as the project's central point of discussion and development. Mailing lists are kind of like forums where developers discuss important project issues, argue for their points of view, vent, and generally brainstorm for ideas.

The Wayland client and server libraries were initially released under the MIT License, while the reference compositor Weston and some example clients used the GNU General Public License version 2. Later all the GPL code was relicensed under the MIT license "to make it easier to move code between the reference implementation and the actual libraries". In 2015 it was discovered that the license text used by Wayland was a slightly different and older version of the MIT license, and the license text was updated to the current version used by the X.Org project (known as MIT Expat License).

Wayland works with all Mesa-compatible drivers with DRI2 support as well as Android drivers via the Hybris project.

2.2.1 How Do You Know You're Running Wayland, Xwayland, and the Wayfire Compositor, or for That Matter, How Do You Know If You're Running an X11 Backend?

Use the following two commands on your Raspberry Pi system, on a default install of the Debian Bookworm-based Raspberry Pi OS. If **inxi** is already installed, skip the first command:

> $ **sudo apt install inxi**
> Output truncated…

> $ **sudo inxi -GSCMm -t c -P -x**
> Output truncated...

Display: Wayland server: X.org v: 1.21.1.7 with: Xwayland v: 22.1.9 com-positor: wayfire
v: 0.7.5 driver: N/A tty: 104x46
API: EGL/GBM Message: No known Wayland EGL/GBM data sources.
Output truncated...

On our Raspberry Pi 4b running the Raspberry Pi OS, Debian-based Bookworm version, we got the above output.

Using the same **inxi** command on our Raspberry Pi 400 system, where we've switched to the X11 backend (via Xwayland), we got the following output:
Output truncated...

Display: x11 server: X.Org v: 1.21.1.7 with: Xwayland v: 22.1.9 driver: X: loaded: modesetting unloaded: fbdev dri: vc4
gpu: vc4-drm,vc4_crtc,vc4_dpi,vc4_dsi,vc4_firmware_kms,vc4_hdmi,vc4_hvs,vc4_txp,vc4_v3d,vc4_vec
resolution: 1920x1080~60Hz
API: OpenGL v: 3.1 Mesa 23.2.1-1~bpo12+rpt2 renderer: V3D 4.2
direct-render: Yes
Output truncated...

2.2.2 The Wayland Protocol

Wayland isn't like a new version of X or even an X server. Instead, it's more like a message system that helps your computer's visual elements work together. It's supposed to make your computer screen look better and run smoother.

In the past, older systems had to display disparate elements in an organized and efficient way, because each app had to handle its own display, which could lead to operating system crashes. These older systems were called "stacking window managers". Wayland is different in that it gives each app its own protected segment of memory to work with. It then combines these segments to create what you see on OLED display. This makes things stable and less prone to operating system crashing, and it also makes visual presentations like streaming video smoother, eliminating flicker.

The critical aspect of Wayland is that it can work with different parts of your computer, like your display server, X apps, or even special Wayland-compatible programs. It also provides modern visual effects like blur in animations, realistic coloring, shading, and shadows, and a lot more.

Some popular graphics programs that use Wayland are Xfwm, Cairo, KWin, Mutter, and Compiz. Some of them are working to fully support, or become native Wayland programs in the future. Wayland is becoming more popular in the Linux world, and even big names like the Raspberry Pi OS are moving towards fully supporting it.

Wayland takes care of many tasks that X did, such as drawing on your screen, handling multiple monitors, and rendering fonts.

Note
Instead of relying on the X server, Wayland connects the Linux kernel directly to your graphics card, which is faster and more efficient. This is very critical, especially in streaming video, because graphics cards can handle video processing much better than your computer's CPU, no matter how many cores it has.

Wayland is simpler, has cleaner code, and is more flexible than the X Window System. It's impossible to completely get rid of X due to all the legacy code and apps that are built with it. But Wayland can work alongside X, for example with the Xwayland system, for compatibility, while providing a better platform for modern apps.

The way Wayland handles graphics in Linux has shifted from being centered around the X server to a different type of system. Wayland's creator, Kristian Høgsberg, decided to move away from X because a lot of the functions that used to be handled by the X server are now handled by the Linux kernel or libraries. Wayland allows the X server to become an optional part of the system.

Wayland includes a protocol and a reference system called Weston. It also provides versions of popular libraries like GTK4 and Qt5 that work with Wayland instead of X. Most apps will eventually support Wayland without needing major changes.

Initially, Wayland lacked network transparency, which is the ability to run apps remotely. Developers are working on solutions for this, such as VNC-like pixel-scraping and sending rendering commands across networks.

In the Wayland protocol, a client (an app) and a compositor (a service that controls what you see on your screen) communicate through the Wayland protocol. This protocol follows the client-server model, where clients request the display of visual elements, and the compositor handles how they appear on the screen.

The Wayland protocol is split into two parts: a low-level layer for communication, and a high-level layer for basic window system features. The low-level layer does data exchange between the client and compositor, while the high-level layer handles the information both need to create the display. This high-level layer is flexible and easy to update, because it uses automatic code generation via an XML file.

The Wayland protocol includes two libraries: one library for Wayland clients, and one for Wayland compositors. These libraries expedite development of apps and services that work directly with Wayland.

2.2.3 Wayland Protocol Overview

The Wayland protocol is a language that communicates between different components of your hardware and software. There are two main types of items in the language: global items and non-global items. When your hardware or software wants to provide a service, it's pretty much immediate.

Your system can send messages back and forth to offer or request services. The Wayland protocol has its own special "language" for these messages. It has different "words" to describe what services are available and what's needed to use them. These "words" can have extra details, like what they're called, what they do, and how they work. This makes your system more versatile and flexible. So, think of the Wayland protocol as a message-passing machine that your computer uses to communicate internally and externally.

2.2.4 Wayland Core Interfaces

The interfaces of the current version of the Wayland protocol are in a file, which is the Wayland source code. It's an XML file that lists the existing interfaces in the current version of Wayland, along with their requests, events, and attributes. These interfaces are the minimum required to be implemented by any Wayland compositor, such as Wayfire.

2.2.5 Window System Comparison

A good way to understand the Wayland architecture, and how it is different from X, is to follow an event from the input device to the point where the change it affects appears on screen.

2.2.5.1 Wayland Architecture

Here are the steps through the Event/Request loop with the X Window System:

1. The kernel gets an event from an input device and sends it to X through the evdev input driver. The kernel does all the hard work here by driving the device and translating the different device-specific event protocols to the Linux evdev input event standard.

2. The X server determines which window the event affects, and sends it to the clients that have selected for the event in question on that window. The X server doesn't actually know how to do this right, since the window location on screen is controlled by the compositor and may be transformed in a number of ways that the X server doesn't understand (scaled down, rotated, wobbling, etc.).

3. The client looks at the event and decides what to do. Often the UI will have to change in response to the event—perhaps a check box was clicked or the pointer entered a button that must be highlighted. Thus the client sends a rendering request back to the X server.

4. When the X server receives the rendering request, it sends it to the driver to let it program the hardware to do the rendering. The X server also calculates the bounding region of the rendering, and sends that to the compositor as a *damage event*.

5. The damage event tells the compositor that something changed in the window and that it has to recomposite the part of the screen where that window is visible. The compositor is responsible for rendering the entire screen contents based on its scenegraph and the contents of the X windows. Yet, it has to go through the X server to render this.

6. The X server receives the rendering requests from the compositor and either copies the compositor back buffer to the front buffer or does a

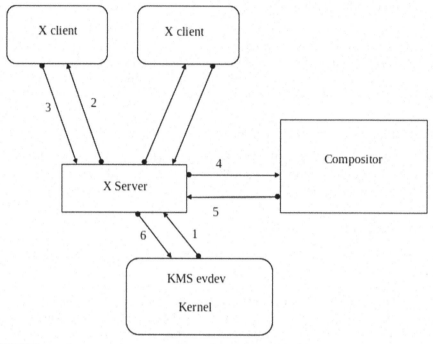

FIGURE 2.2
Event/Request loop in X.

pageflip. In the general case, the X server has to do this step so it can account for overlapping windows, which may require clipping and determine whether or not it can page flip. However, for a compositor, which is always fullscreen, this is another unnecessary context switch.

As seen in Figure 2.2, there are a few performance concerns with this approach. The X server doesn't have the information to decide which window should receive the event, nor can it transform the screen coordinates to window-local coordinates. And even though X has handed responsibility for the final painting of the screen to the compositing manager, X still controls the front buffer and modesetting. Most of the complexity that the X server used to handle is now available in the kernel or self-contained libraries (KMS, evdev, mesa, fontconfig, freetype, cairo, Qt, etc.). In general, the X server is now just a middle man that introduces an extra step between applications and the compositor and an extra step between the compositor and the hardware.

In Wayland, the compositor *is* the display server. We transfer the control of KMS and evdev to the compositor. The Wayland protocol lets the compositor send the input events directly to the clients and lets the client send the damage event directly to the compositor. This is seen in Figure 2.3.

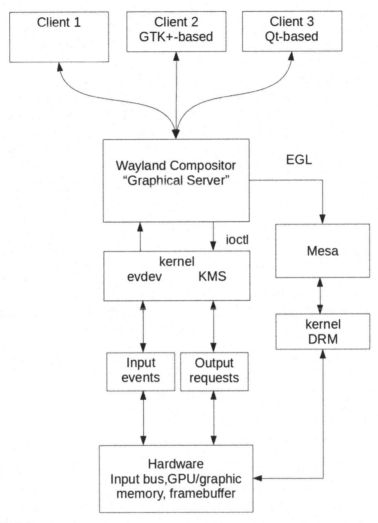

FIGURE 2.3
Wayland Event/Request map.

1. The kernel gets an event via the evdev facility, and sends it to the compositor. This is similar to the X case, because of the continual reuse of all the input drivers in the kernel.

2. The Wayfire compositor looks through its scenegraph to determine which window should receive the event. The scenegraph corresponds to what's on screen and Wayfire understands the transformations that it may have applied to all the elements. So Wayfire can pick the right window and transform the screen coordinates to window-local

coordinates, by applying the inverse transformations. The types of transformation that can be applied to a window are only restricted to what Wayfire can do, as long as it can compute the inverse transformation for the input events.

3. As in the X case, when the client receives the event, it updates the user interface in response. But in the Wayland case, the rendering happens in the client, and the client just sends a request to Wayfire to indicate the region, or surface that was updated.

4. Wayfire also collects damage requests from its clients and then "recomposites" the screen. Wayfire can then directly issue an ioctl to schedule a pageflip with KMS in the kernel.

2.2.6 Wayland Rendering

One of the details omitted from the above overview is how clients actually render under Wayland. By removing the X server from the picture we also removed the mechanism by which X clients typically render. But there's another mechanism that we're already using with DRI2 under X: *direct rendering*. With direct rendering, the client and the server share a video memory buffer. The client links to a rendering library such as OpenGL that knows how to program the hardware and renders directly into the buffer. The compositor in turn can take the buffer and use it as a texture when it composites the desktop. After the initial setup, the client only needs to tell the compositor which buffer to use and when and where it has rendered new content into it.

This leaves an application with two ways to update its window contents:

1. Render the new content into a new buffer and tell the compositor to use that instead of the old buffer. The application can allocate a new buffer every time it needs to update the window contents or it can keep two (or more) buffers around and cycle between them. The buffer management is entirely under application control.

2. Render the new content into the buffer that it previously told the compositor to use. While it's possible to just render directly into the buffer shared with the compositor, this might race with the compositor. What can happen is that repainting the window contents could be interrupted by the compositor repainting the desktop. If the application gets interrupted just after clearing the window but before rendering the contents, the compositor will texture from a blank buffer. The result is that the application window will flicker between a blank window or half-rendered content. The traditional way to avoid this is to render the new content into a back buffer and then copy from there

into the compositor surface. The back buffer can be allocated on the fly and just big enough to hold the new content, or the application can keep a buffer around. Again, this is under application control.

In either case, the application must tell the compositor which area of the surface holds new contents. When the application renders directly to the shared buffer, the compositor needs to be notified that there is new content. But also when exchanging buffers, the compositor doesn't assume anything changed, and needs a request from the application before it will repaint the desktop. The idea is that even if an application passes a new buffer to the compositor, only a small part of the buffer may be different, like a blinking cursor or a spinner.

2.2.7 Differences between Wayland and X

There are several differences between Wayland and X in regards to performance, code maintainability, and security:

Architecture:
The composition manager is a separate component in X, while Wayland merges display server and compositor as a single function. Also, it incorporates some of the tasks of the window manager, which in X is a separate client process.

Compositing:
Compositing is optional in X, but mandatory in Wayland. Compositing in X is "active"; that is, the compositor gets all pixel data, which introduces display latency, or delay. In Wayland, compositing is "passive", which means the compositor receives pixel data directly from client programs.

Rendering:
The X server itself is able to perform rendering, and it can be instructed to display a rendered window sent by a client program. In contrast, Wayland does not expose any API for rendering, but delegates to clients those things (including the rendering of fonts, widgets, etc.).

Note
Window decorations can be rendered by the client (via a graphics toolkit), or by the server (via the compositor).

Security:
Perhaps more important in server installs of other distros, Wayland isolates the input and output of every window, so that less code needs to run with *root* privileges, improving security. But in modern, and popular Linux distros, a system without a GUI can be run without root privileges nowadays.

FIGURE 2.4
Xwayland Wayfire-based desktop on the Debian Bookworm-based Raspberry Pi OS.

Inter-Process Communication (IPC):
Important for the Raspberry Pi OS, the Wayland core protocol does not support communication between Wayland clients at all, and that functionality (if needed) should be implemented by other distro desktop environments, or by a third party (for example, by using native IPC of the underlying kernel).

Networking:
The X Window System architecture was designed to run over a network. Wayland does not offer network transparency, however, a compositor like Wayfire can implement any remote desktop protocol to achieve remote displaying. Virtual Network Computing (VNC) is not yet mature in Wayland (Figure 2.4).

2.2.8 Xwayland

Xwayland is an X Server running as a Wayland client, and is capable of displaying native X11 client applications in a Wayland compositor environment. That's currently the way that Wayland, using the Wayfire compositor, works as of the Debian Bookworm-based release of the Raspberry Pi OS. The goal of Xwayland is to facilitate the transition from X Window System to Wayland environments, providing a way to run X applications in the meantime. When and how that transition will be completed is a matter that has severely affected many other releases and distros of Linux. Ubuntu being the prime example of this.

Widget toolkits such as Qt 5 and GTK4 can switch their graphical back-end at run time, allowing users to choose at run time whether they want to execute the application purely over X, or over Wayland. In fact, both Qt5 and GTK4 support Wayland directly.

2.2.8.1 Wayland Compositors—A Historical Perspective

Neither Wayland, nor X11, strictly specifies what software is responsible for rendering the window decoration. For example, with Wayfire, the client has the choice to either draw the window decorations, or designates that the compositor draws them.

Display servers that implement the Wayland display server protocol are also called *Wayland compositors*, because they additionally perform the task of a "compositing" window manager.

A compositing window manager is a type of window manager for graphical user interfaces that provides compositing functionality for windowing systems. In simple terms, it's a component of a graphical desktop environment that manages the placement and appearance of individual application windows on the screen.

The term "compositing" refers to the ability to combine multiple graphical elements or layers to create a final image. In the context of window managers, compositing involves blending and rendering windows with various visual effects, such as transparency, shadows, and animations. This results in a more visually appealing and dynamic user interface.

Compositing window managers use hardware acceleration and graphics processing capabilities to efficiently handle the graphical effects. Some popular compositing window managers include Wayfire, Compiz, KWin (used in the KDE Plasma desktop environment), and Mutter (used in the GNOME desktop environment). These window managers provide a range of visual effects and customization options to enhance the overall user experience.

Compositing window managers are commonly associated with modern desktop environments that aim to provide a visually rich and interactive user interface. They contribute to the overall aesthetics and usability of the desktop environment by adding graphical enhancements to window management.

Examples of compositing window managers are Weston, the reference implementation of a Wayland compositor, and Wayfire, the compositor used in the Raspberry Pi OS Debian Bookworm-based operating system version.

2.2.8.2 Xwayland and the Wayfire Compositor

As noted in Section 2.1, Xwayland is a compatibility layer that allows application specifically built for the X Window System, to run on a Wayland display server. It bridges the gap between the older X11 protocol and the newer

Wayland protocol, providing a way for legacy X11 applications to work seamlessly in a Wayland-based graphical environment.

The need for Xwayland arises because many existing Debian Linux, and Raspberry Pi applications, were developed for X11, and transitioning everything to Wayland natively would be a massive undertaking. And that transition is nowhere near to being achieved, even as of the time this book was written. Xwayland essentially acts as a translator, enabling X11 applications to draw their graphical elements and interact with a Wayland compositor, making it possible to run X11 applications alongside native Wayland applications in a Wayland session.

This compatibility layer is an important component of Wayland desktop environments, ensuring that users can continue to use their favorite X11 applications while benefiting from the improved performance and security features offered by Wayland.

And also as noted in Section 2.1, Wayfire, the 3-D Wayland compositor for the Raspberry Pi OS, is essentially a window manager that works with the Wayland display protocol, and gives a desktop experience on the Debian

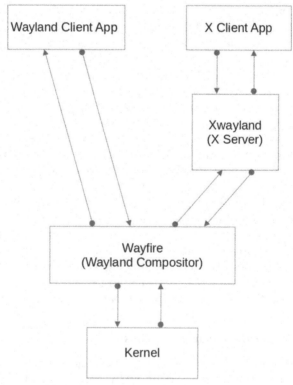

FIGURE 2.5
Wayland compositor general architecture.

Bookworm-based Raspberry Pi OS exactly like the Debian Bullseye-based Raspberry Pi OS Openbox LXDE desktop.

Wayfire aims to provide a visually appealing and feature-rich environment for Linux users who run Wayland-based desktops. Wayfire allows users to create visually stunning and highly customizable desktop environments on Wayland-based systems.

Figure 2.5 depicts how a Wayland compositor is situated between server and client components, and the kernel, and shows the interactivity between those components.

2.3 X Window System GUI Basics

The objectives of this section, and those that follow, are:

- To explain the relationship of the components of an X Window System-based graphical user interface to the Raspberry Pi OS.
- To describe the basic concepts and implementation of the X Window System.
- To give examples of client application program coding for the X Window System.

2.3.1 Introduction

This section presents these major topics. To get the most out of it, the beginner should go through each topic listed in the order shown.

X Window System model: We first define the X Window System, a *network protocol* for graphical interaction between a user and one or more computer systems running the Raspberry Pi OS. This means that it is a software system specifically designed to work over a network, to pass user-generated events to an application program, and then channel graphical responses as graphical output back to the user. The forms of interactivity, via event-driven input and multi-window display output, are detailed from the user's perspective. We illustrate and explain the basic X Window System at a high level—that is, closer to the user rather than the nearest the hardware, and its operability and functionality.

X Window System client application program coding: We then go on to describe how to work with the X Window System at a lower level of operability. We give a basic description of how to write a client application program for the X Window System, and then show the use of some programming toolkits that facilitate this process. We give basic examples of various methodologies: programming using Xlib, XCB, Qt5, GTK4, and gnuplot.

2.3.2 User–Application Software Interaction Model

When you sit at a computer monitor, with the keyboard and mouse in front of you, and work with an application program to accomplish specific tasks, you are primarily concerned with achieving some results, either textual or graphical, that the computer provides. You are shielded from the details of exactly how the computer turns the motions of your hands and fingers into those results. One way of seeing the process that the computer goes through is shown in Figure 2.6, where you, the *user*, harness the intermediary facilities of software components, either locally on the same workstation, or globally over a network or the Internet, to work with an application program. The fundamental assumption of this chapter is that a graphical user interface (GUI) can be used to most efficiently control the dialog between a single user and an application program running on a stand-alone or networked computer, using the intermediaries of the X Window System and the Raspberry Pi OS. The components of a user's dialog with an application program can be simplified to the software component blocks shown in Figure 2.6, applied to the traditional UNIX operating system.

For example, a user presses a mouse button to signify a graphical "pick" in an application window shown on screen. That choice, or event, is recognized by and acted upon by the window manager controlling that window. This event is passed along to the desktop manager, which uses the protocols of the X Window System to pass the request to the operating system. The operating system then passes the request to the application software program for further

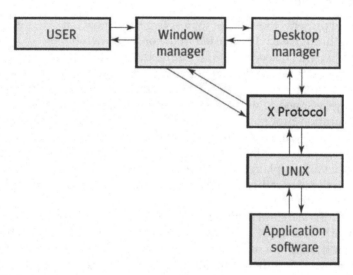

FIGURE 2.6
General components of a GUI.

disposition. Another example is the reverse of the previous one. An application software program generates a request for graphical service, passes this request to the operating system, which in turn passes the request via the X Window System protocols to the desktop manager and window manager to display the graphical request on the screen of the user's computer.

In-Chapter Exercise

2.1 Would you ever want to switch between a GUI and a text-based interface during the course of one session when working with the Raspberry Pi OS? Why would you want to do this? And most importantly, how would you do this, given the facilities of control of systemd?

2.3.3 Basics of the X Window System

To illustrate the functionality of the X Window System, we detail the following aspects of it in this section:

* What it is similar to, and what advantages it has.
* The Event/Request Model.

2.3.3.1 What Is the X Window System Similar to and What Advantage(s) Does It Have?

Contemporary user–computer interactivity falls into two basic categories. In one category, where a *character user interface* (CUI) is implemented, the user types commands on a command line presented in a terminal window using a keyboard, and components of the operating system handle this input and take appropriate action. In the other category, the user gives input via a *graphical user interface* (GUI), and components of the operating system take appropriate action. Of course there are also hybrid styles of interactivity which are a mixture of these two categories. Up to this point, you have relied almost entirely on a CUI to activate the functionality of the Raspberry Pi OS. Here, you will be introduced to a GUI system, known as the X Window System. The two foremost questions for the beginner concerning the X Window System are:

What is it similar to, and what advantage does it give me over, the traditional Linux CUI?

The answer to the first question is twofold. The X Window System is a network protocol developed to provide a GUI to the Linux operating system; on the surface it appears to the user like other popular operating system window managers, such as those found on an Apple or in Microsoft Windows. (The current version of the X Window System [Release 7.7] is what we used for our base Raspberry Pi system.) There is an important differentiation to make here between *window system, window manager,* and *desktop manager.* Briefly stated, a window system provides the generic functionality of the GUI, a window manager simply has particular implementations of the functionality provided by the window system, and a desktop manager provides a graphical method of interacting with the operating system. For example, interactive resizing of a window by the user is a generic function of a window system, whereas using icons or slider buttons is how it is accomplished in a particular window manager. The desktop manager provides the user with the graphic means to work with operating system functions such as file maintenance. A desktop manager might present a picture of folders connected in a tree-like structure and allow the user to manipulate files in those folders by dragging and dropping icons. Certainly, a modern window manager can include some or all of the functional features of a desktop manager.

In-Chapter Exercises

2.2 What is the name of the desktop management system on the Raspberry Pi OS Debian Bookworm-based release?

2.3 What is the name of the desktop management system on the Raspberry Pi OS Debian Bullseye-based release?

The first question above can also be answered by giving an analogy: what the X Window System does for a user of networked computers is exactly like what an operating system, and by extension, systemd, does for the user of a stand-alone computer. On a stand-alone computer, the complex details of managing the resources of the hardware of the computer to accomplish tasks is left to the operating system, with a large proportion of that management done by systemd. The user is shielded by the operating system from the complex hardware details of actually accomplishing a task, such as copying a file from one place to another on a USB-mounted medium, such as an SSD. On a system of networked computers, the X Window System manages the resources of the hardware of possibly many computers across the network to accomplish tasks for an individual user. Also, in a networked, distributed-system environment, where many machines are hooked up via a communications link, the X Window System serves *transparently* as a manager of the components of your interaction with application programs and system resources; in other words, you can run an application program on a machine that you are not sitting in front of, and the mechanics of interaction with the application work exactly as if the application were executing on a stand-alone machine that was right on the desk in front of you.

The most obvious answer to the second question is that you are able to quickly and easily accomplish predefined tasks by using a GUI on the Raspberry Pi OS. For example, dragging icons to delete files is faster than typing commands to do the same thing, particularly if the file names are long and complex! Another not so obvious answer is that your style of interaction with the operating system will be very similar to your style of interaction with applications. For example, modern computer programming and engineering applications are graphics based, and have a common look and feel; pull-down menus almost always include functions such as cut, copy, paste, and so on. Having a GUI for your Raspberry Pi desktop makes for uniformity of interaction between operating system and application.

2.3.4 The Key Components of Interactivity: Events and Requests

When you work with a computer, you provide input in a variety of ways, and the computer, after doing some processing, gives you feedback in return. Limiting this feedback to text and graphics, usually the computer responds by displaying information on the screen, or executing processes in the background, behind what you can actually see on the display.

On a modern computer workstation, you are able to use several devices, such as keyboard, mouse buttons, etc., to provide input to an application program in a style of interaction known as *interrupt-driven interaction*. The application is processing data, or in a wait state until signaled by a particular input device. Interrupts are known as input *events* from one or more devices, which can be ordered in time by forming a list or *queue*. With applications written for the X Window System, the client application can then process this queue of input events, do the work necessary to form responses to the events, and then output the responses as *requests* for graphical output to the server.

A schematic illustration of this is shown in Figure 2.7.

A key concept of the X Window System that sometimes causes confusion is the difference between *server* and *client*. One possible cause of confusion

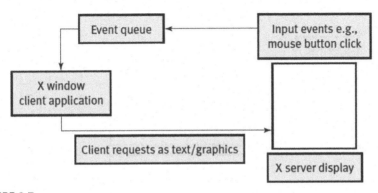

FIGURE 2.7
Event–request model.

here is that traditionally, on a computer network, a server is thought of as a machine that serves files to many other machines, which is certainly a different function than an X Window System server. In the X Window System, a server is the hardware and/or software that actually takes input from and displays output to the user. For example, the keyboard, mouse, and display screen in front of the user are part of the server; they graphically *serve* information to the user. The client is an application program that connects to, receives input events from, and makes output requests to the server. Be aware that sometimes (confusingly!) in X Window System jargon, the client is spoken of as a hardware device, like a workstation or computer. We will always use the term *client* to refer to application program code, rather than to a piece of hardware. In the X Window System, a server and client can exist on the same workstation or computer, and use InterProcess Communication (IPC) mechanisms, such as Linux sockets, to transfer information between them. A *local client* can be simply thought of as an application that is running on the same machine that you are either sitting in front of, or have a one-to-one relationship with. A *remote client* is an application that is running on a machine connected to your server via a TCP/IP, or other network connection. Whether a client application is local or remote, it still looks and feels exactly the same to the user of the X Window System.

Looking at Figure 2.8, you will see three client applications, X, Y, and Z, displaying their output on an X Window System server. Each of these applications is running on a different machine. Client X is running on a machine linked to the X Window System server via a LAN hookup,

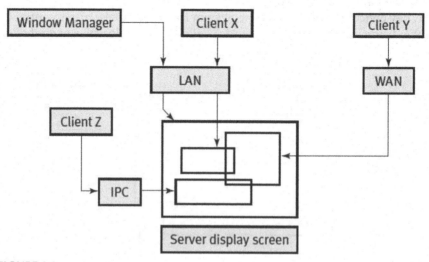

FIGURE 2.8
Client and server topologies.

an Ethernet. Client Y is running on a machine linked to the X Window System server via a wide area network, the Internet. Client Z is running directly on the workstation that is the server, and uses Linux sockets to display output requests on the server screen. Something not illustrated in Figure 2.8 is that each of the clients X, Y, and Z gets input events via this server as well.

Another critical aspect of the X Window System is that the GUI for each client is independent of the GUI of the window manager itself. In other words, each client application can open a window on the server screen, use its own style of GUI buttons, icons, pull-down menus, and so on, and the window manager, which is simply just another client application, handles the display of all other client windows. Figure 2.8 illustrates this point.

In-Chapter Exercises

2.4 If the client can queue events, do you think it would be advantageous for the server to queue requests? Why?

2.5 From what you know of network programming in Linux, is the meaning of client–server the same in network programming as it is in the X Window System? If it is not the same, what is the salient difference?

The important aspect of the window manager being just another client of the X Window System server is that you can use any of the available X Window System window managers to suit your particular needs. You can even use your own window manager, if you have the time and resources to write the program code for one! Have a look at the mechanics of writing a Wayland compositor, for example. It is worth noting that only one window manager can be active on a given server at one time.

2.3.5 Functions and Appearance of the Window Manager Interface

Similar to the look and feel and functionality of Microsoft Windows or OS X, you will recognize many of the general functions that an X Window System window manager provides, shown in Table 2.1. These functions are particular implementations of possibly more than one generic window system service, those provided by the X Window System protocol.

In-Chapter Exercise

2.6 With the Wayfire window manager active, test the functions in Table 2.1. Then, when you are using Wayfire, compare the window manager functions in terms of style of interaction, ease of use and availability, and most importantly customization capability.

TABLE 2.1

Window Manager General Functions

Item	Function	Description
A	(De)iconify window	Reduce window to a small, representative picture, or enlarge to a full size window
B	Create new window	Launch or run a new client application
C	CUI to operating system	Allows user to open one or more windows and type commands into those windows
D	Desktop management	Graphical file maintenance, speed buttons, special clients like time-of-day clock
E	Destroy window	Close connection between server and client
F	Event focus	Specifies which client is receiving events from devices like mouse, keyboard, etc.
G	Modify window	Resize, move, stack, tile one or more windows
H	Virtual screens	More than one screen area mapped onto the physical screen of the server
I	Pop-up/pull-down menus	Utility menus activated by holding down mouse buttons to run client application

2.3.6 Creating X Window System Client Application Programs

The two guiding principles explained in this section are:

1. A client application program is made up of two separate parts: a data generation part, and a User Interface (UI) part, which must work together.

2. The basic structure of a client application program is: initialization, start an event–request loop, cleanup.

In order to adhere to these principles, you can approach creating an X Windows client application program like this:

Use a GUI-based *Integrated Development Environment* (IDE), such as Geany, to generate the UI and program data generation code. This means coding the graphical interface by programming directly in Qt5, GTK4, XCB, or the older Xlib. Then, create the program data generation code in C, C++, or Python, and finally combine the graphical interface and program data generation code together.

The first component of this process is ostensibly easier. But to create the UI component of a client application, and in order to "hook" the data-generating or processing component of your program to that UI, you have to be very familiar with two things:

a. How to do advanced data structure programming in C++, or another available language library interface like Python3.

b. Knowing the data structure and operability of programming in Qt5 or GTK4.

The second way requires that you know the structure of an X Window System client application program, and if you use Xlib, are familiar with C.

The structure of a client application program is: initialize a connection with the X server, create an *event loop*, cleanup, and leave. Most of what follows details this structure more fully, and gives some simple examples.

The short way through the sections below are as follows:

Carefully examine the following examples, and find in them the two important points to remember in those examples. Then you will have a top-down view of how to create client application programs.

2.3.7 Client Application Program Structure and Development Model

In this section, we show where and how a user-written client application program fits into the overall scheme of the components of the X Window System. We then show the simplified structure of such a program. Following from these two illustrations, we detail in a simple and direct fashion how to develop C code for an X Window System client application program.

2.3.7.1 Model Overview

Here are two descriptions of the model:

1. First, a picture (Figure 2.9) showing how the components, such as a client application, Xlib, XCB, Qt5, or GTK4, the X.org server, and the actual display, are connected via the X Protocol over a network (or locally).
2. Then a verbal description of the coding process that shapes that model.

The X Window System, as seen from a software development model point of view, is a combination of these components:

1. Toolkit IDEs such as Qt Creator, or frameworks such as Qt5 or GTK4
2. X libraries such as XCB and Xlib
3. The X protocol or display server protocol
4. X display server, X.org server
5. Window manager

This model is arranged, from top to bottom, in a suitable order for a user writing an application program. The user generates the code either in

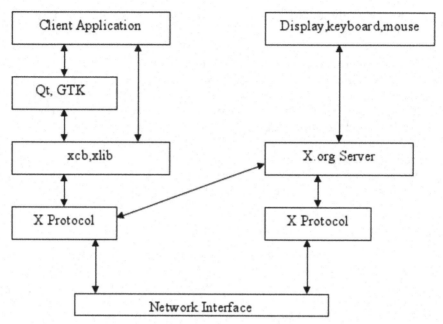

FIGURE 2.9
X Window System client/libraries/protocol components.

component 1 or 2; components 3 through 5 are processes that the application program code interprets and executes.

A more detailed textual description of the components is as follows:

Toolkit IDEs such as Qt Creator are used to arrange/write and put together the code itself, and integrate it, either internally in the programming language framework of the IDE, or externally by linking the code of the IDE with data generation code, for a particular application.

X client libraries are graphical routines or C language bindings that the toolkits generate. The two most important ones are XCB and Xlib. For example, Xlib is a legacy library of more than 300 utility routines that programmers can use to activate the X protocol. The Xlib utilities are used to accomplish the major tasks in an X Window System user-written application. XCB is the contemporary replacement for Xlib.

X clients communicate with X servers (and not necessarily over a network!) using the X protocol. In the X protocol, data are exchanged in an synchronous or asynchronous manner over a two-way communication channel.

The X display server (or X server) is the process executing on a computer and managing the graphics output and input from the computer display (its monitor[s], keyboard, and mouse). The window manager, like any of those that can be used on a Raspberry Pi system, is a program that handles the graphic activities sent to the X display server.

X clients are application programs that use the computer display to illustrate, or present, their information. The X clients, whether running locally or on a remote computer, send requests to the X server using a communication channel. The X client application program and the X server program can run on the same machine, using Linux sockets as the communication channel. As long as there is a common networking protocol (e.g., TCP/IP) to provide the communication channel, the X server can display output from any X client regardless of where it is actually running, and the operating system under which the client runs. With the X protocol running on a particular computer, the X server is listening to the network connections at a specific port and acting on the X protocol requests sent by X clients. The X server manages regions of the screen known as *windows*, where the output from an X client is displayed. When X application programs are running, everything on the screen appears in windows and each window is associated with a specific X client.

Creating a window is one of the basic X protocol requests that an X server handles. The X server considers anything you do with the keyboard and mouse as an event, to be reported to the X clients. When you press and release a mouse button, the X server sends these input events to the X client that created the window containing the mouse pointer. The X server also sends other kinds of events to X clients. These events inform an X client if anything happens to its window.

X client application programs, to a very large extent, have toolkit function calls, or routines, in them. The client application may be composed purely in the Qt5 programming language (C++), which in turn calls Xlib and/or XCB library functions. An X client application can also make some direct calls to Xlib and/or XCB routines for generating text and graphics output in a window. The client application can be a mixture of data generation code, toolkit functions, and Xlib and/or XCB function calls. The complicating factors here are the complexity of the data structures holding all three possible sources of information, the means of integrating these data structures, and the complexity of the modular system of code that the client application becomes.

In-Chapter Exercise

2.7   On your Raspberry Pi system, are there any X Windows applications running? Where are the X Window System clients running? Where are the X Window System servers running?

2.3.7.2 The Structure of a Typical X Client Application Program

A simple description of an X application program would divide it into three major sections:

I.   Initialization: Open a display that the application can use
II. Event loop: Start an event-driven loop that allows the application to communicate with the display
III. Cleanup: Clean up and gracefully exit

This description can be further expanded as follows:

I.   Initialization
   1. Perform initialization routines
   2. Connect to the X server
   3. Perform X-related initialization
II. Event loop (while not finished)
   1. Receive the next event from the X server
   2. Handle the event, possibly sending various drawing requests to the X server
   3. If the event was a quit message, exit the loop
III. Cleanup
   1. Close down the connection to the X server
   2. Perform cleanup operations

The initialization section sets up the window system for user interaction. After initialization, the program enters a loop in which it repeatedly tries to get events from the window system and process them. Finally, before exiting, the program performs any necessary cleanups. Usually the exit code is in a program that is called when the user clicks on the **Exit** button provided by the application (or on the **Close** button on the window frame typically on the top right of the window).

2.3.7.3 Specifying Resources

All X Window client application programs have resource files where options for colors, fonts, and other displayed attributes and components can be specified. To take advantage of this capability, programs should be written such that hard coding of resources doesn't happen in the client application per se, so that resources specified in the configuration files are used instead.

Those resources can reside in a file, named .XResources, in your home directory, or can be located in the directory where the application is launched.

2.3.7.4 Writing the Code for an X Windows Client Application

Why show four different libraries and methods of writing client application programs? There are a few good reasons.

Xlib and XCB are basically procedural programming paradigm libraries, where XCB has a more complex, but smaller module data structuring and API than Xlib. Qt5 uses an *Object-Oriented client Programming* (OOP) paradigm, with attendant data structures and classes, and is coded in C++. GTK4 is coded in C, with some special extensions. So whichever of the four libraries and methods appeals most to you, and whichever one is most intuitive and fits best with what you, or your programming team, already know about programming, is the best one for you to use. We try here to expose you to all four to so that you can get a feel for the varieties available.

Application code for Xlib or XCB can be written in C, C++, or Python, and compiled using any of the available compilers on the system, with the compiler directives we indicate.

When programming in C++ for Qt5, that library has its own facilities to compile, link, and assemble a client application and place it in the context of a Qt5 project. We also show that in detail.

In-Chapter Exercise

2.8   Before beginning into Xlib, XCB, QT5, or GTK4, you might want to take stock of your own experiences and familiarity with C, C++, the OOP methodolgy, and your knowledge of data structures in these areas.

2.3.8 Xlib versus XCB

The reason we include examples of Xlib and XCB client programs is that they are the two official C libraries for the X Window protocol. Xlib, the predecessor of XCB, was the original X client library, and was the only official X client library, until the introduction of XCB. The two libraries are based upon different approaches to client-side programs: Xlib is a layer further from the X protocol that uses a traditional, and programmer-friendly C API, whereas XCB is a lower-level software framework closer to the X protocol, and does not have as transparent and friendly an API. As you can see from our presentation on both Xlib and XCB, the documentation that exists currently for XCB, from a top-down perspective, is far less transparent, complete, and descriptive. These two aspects of XCB, documentation and user-friendliness, are a function of its closer relationship with its complex data structure implementation of the X protocol itself.

In practice, the difference in organizing schemes is most evident in how the two libraries handle the fundamental asynchronous event–request model between server and client of the X protocol itself. Xlib attempts to implement the asynchronous X protocol behind a mixed synchronous and asynchronous API, whereas the XCB API is asynchronous.

For example, to look up the attributes (e.g., size and position) of a window, you would write the following code using Xlib:

```
XWindowAttributes attrs;
XGetWindowAttributes(display, window, &attrs);
/*Execute some code*/
```

The Xlib call to XGetWindowAttributes() in the client-side program sends a request to the X server and blocks until it receives a reply from the X server. This is a synchronous request–event sequence.

The following is the code for the same thing in XCB:

```
xcb_get_window_attributes_cookie_t cookie =
        xcb_get_window_attributes(
            connection, window);
/*Execute other code while waiting for the reply from the server*/
xcb_get_window_attributes_reply_t* reply =
        xcb_get_window_attributes_reply(
            connection, cookie, nullptr);
/*Execute some code based on the reply*/
free(reply);
```

The function xcb_get_window_attributes sends the request to the X server, and returns immediately without waiting for the reply. This is an asynchronous request–event sequence. The client program must call xcb_get_window_attributes_reply to block on the reply.

The advantage of the asynchronous approach is gained when we need to retrieve the attributes of multiple windows at the same time. Using XCB, we can make multiple requests to the X server at once and then wait for multiple replies. With Xlib, we have to wait for the response to each request before we can send the next one. XCB only blocks for one round-trip network latency period, compared to multiple latency period waits with Xlib.

To be fully asynchronous, the XCB approach leads to a more complex data structure approach, and a less programmer-friendly API. The preceding Xlib code looks like your average C library call; the XCB code has a more complex data structure implementation.

XCB is fully asynchronous, whereas Xlib is not fully synchronous. Xlib has a mixture of synchronous and asynchronous APIs. Functions that do not return values (e.g., XResizeWindow, which changes the size of a window) are asynchronous, while functions that return values (e.g.,XGetGeometry, which returns the size and position of a window) are synchronous. Here is a quote from Volume 1 of the *Xlib Programming Manual* dealing with Xlib's synchronicity:

"Buffering Xlib saves up requests instead of sending them to the server immediately, so that the client program can continue running instead of waiting to gain access to the network after every Xlib call. This is possible because most

Xlib calls do not require immediate action by the server. Caching of requests by the client before sending them over the network increases the performance speed over most networks, because it makes the network transactions longer and less numerous, reducing the total time involved in creating an asynchronous set of transactions".

2.3.9 Xlib

In this section, we describe some important considerations when doing Xlib programming, show how to compile an Xlib client application program on a Raspberry Pi system, and then give C programming examples for an X Windows client application program that uses Xlib. It would be useful for you to compare the complexity of the code given here, with the code given for XCB programming in the following section. Also at this point, it would be very helpful to compare the extant documentation for Xlib to the documentation available for XCB. We provide an exercise that details what you should be looking for in the documentation sets for each of these official libraries. Xlib operates on the client–server model, which can be directly contrasted to the traditional networking model of those components. Essentially, the client–server model used for Xlib reverses the role of client and server assumed in the networking model.

In-Chapter Exercise

2.9   Create your own documentation set for Xlib, and for XCB from the next section, using online sources and printed documents and books.

Note
The most important component of a documentation comparison is cataloging and organizing that catalog to effectively serve you personally in showing how the documents for each system proceed from a top-down overview to the lowest level details of using the libraries. This method, which we can only partly illustrate and prescribe here, would then allow you to take our examples and expand upon them to enable you to write more complex X Windows client applications given the use cases you might encounter.

2.3.9.1 Basic Xlib Top-Down Considerations

Every Xlib client application program conforms to the basic structure shown in Section 2.3.9.2. In this section, we give that basic structure more articulation, and show how that basic structure could be implemented using some fundamental Xlib function calls.

This is basically how an X Windows Xlib client application operates:

1. Initialization: Establishes a connection to an X server with **XOpenDisplay()**, and if the connection can't be made, gracefully terminates the program.

   a) Requests server information such as the physical screen, with **XGetGeometry()** or **XGetWindowAttributes()** and uses the information obtained to calculate window parameters, like size, position, etc.,

   b) Creates a window on the physical screen with **XCreateSimpleWindow()**.

   c) Sets standard properties for the window manager with **XSetWMProperties()**.

   d) Selects and specifies the types of events it needs to receive, and respond to, in order to work, with **XSelectInput()**.

   e) If text will be output in the window, loads the font to be used for that text.

   f) Creates a GC to control the action of drawing request events.

   g) Displays the window with **XMapWindow()**.

2. Begins and continues to indeterminately (or *logically*) iterate (or "loop"), to handle events from the server and send callbacks to the client, using **XNextEvent()**.

   a) Possibly does the actual drawing operations in the window. Achieves this by responding to an *expose event* resulting from mapping the window, and other subsequent expose events, by calling routines to draw text and bit mapped graphics.

   b) Keeps handling events until a KeyPress or ButtonPress event arrives, which ends the indeterminate iteration.

3. Closes the display connection, cleans up, and exits, possibly with **XUnloadFont()**, **XFreeGC()**, and **XcloseDisplay()** .

One of the key features of a structured computer program, that is not detailed completely in the above operation presentation, is error handling at key junctures, other than at step 1. Of course, judicious additions of this would add to what is commonly referred to as the program's *robustness*.

Following we provide a helpful documentation table of the major Xlib function categories, descriptions of inclusive functions, and representative examples of these function categories (Table 2.2).

2.3.9.2 X Window and Xlib Description of Hostname, Display, Screen, and Window

Even though a multi-monitor ensemble for a computer workstation is usually used in only special cases, it is worth knowing the difference between

TABLE 2.2

Xlib Function Categories, Descriptions, and Examples

Function Category	Description of Functions as Programmed
	Representative Examples
Display Connection	Functions to connect and disconnect an application with a display, possibly across the network.
	XOpenDisplay(), XCloseDisplay()
Window Attributes	Functions for setting and getting the current characteristics of a window.
	XChangeWindowAttributes(), XSetWindowBackground(), XSetWindowBorder()
Window Life	Functions to create or destroy a window.
	XCreateWindow(), XCreateSimpleWindow()
Window Management	Functions to allow the manipulation of windows around the screen, changing their size, their visibility on the screen, and their apparent position above or below other windows.
	XConfigureWindow(), XLowerWindow(), XMoveResizeWindow(), XMoveWindow(), XRaiseWindow(), XResizeWindow(), XSetWindowBorderWidth(), XMapWindow(), XMapSubwindows(), XSetWMProperties()
Graphics Context (GC)	Functions to set the way drawing requests are interpreted.
	XCreateGC(), XChangeGC(), XCopyGC(), XSetLineAttributes(), XSetForeground()
Cursors	Functions to change the shape and colors of the image that tracks the pointer around the screen.
	XCreateFontCursor(), XcreateGlyphCursor(), XcreatePixmapCursor()
Drawing	Functions to draw dots, lines, rectangles, polygons, and arcs, and an analogous set to fill the last three.
	XDrawArcs(), XDrawLines(), XDrawPoints(), XDrawRectangles(), XDrawSegments(), XDrawText(), XFillArcs(), and XFillRectangles()
Fonts	Functions to list available fonts, load fonts, and find out font characteristics.
	XlistFonts(), XloadFont(), XQueryFont()
Images	Functions to get, display, or manipulate screen images.
	XGetImage(), XPutImage()
Regions	Functions to perform mathematical operations on polygonal regions.
	XCreateRegion(), XpolygonRegion(), XDestroyRegion()
Text	Functions for drawing text and for determining the size of a string to be drawn.
	XDrawString(), XdrawImageString(), XDrawText()
Color	Functions to change the way colors drawn by a client application are interpreted on the screen.
	XAllocColor(), XAllocNamedColor(), XParseColor(), BlackPixel(), WhitePixel()

(Continued)

TABLE 2.2 (Continued)

Xlib Function Categories, Descriptions, and Examples

Function Category	Description of Functions as Programmed
Events	Functions to get input from the user, from other applications, and from the server. XSelectInput(), XNextEvent(), XMaskEvent(), XWindowEvent()
Geometry	Functions to manipulate and translate geometry specifications. XWMGeometry(), XParseGeometry(), XSetWMProperties()
Resource Management	Functions to make managing user preferences and command line arguments easier. XGetDefault(), XrmGetDatabase(), XrmGetDatabase()
Keyboard	Functions to get and change keyboard input, and keyboard mapping. XLookupString(), XChangeKeyboardMapping(), XRefreshKeyboardMapping(), XGrabKeyboard()
Pointer	Functions to change the pointer and its input. XQueryPointer(), XGetMotionEvents(), XGetPointerMapping(), XSetPointerMapping(),XGrabPointer()
Keyboard and Pointer Preferences	Functions for setting and getting the keyboard and pointer parameters. XChangeKeyboardControl(), XChangePointerControl()
Interclient Communication	Functions enabling any client to make available information for any other client to read. XConvertSelection()
Internationalization	Functions to handle user input and draw text independent of language. setlocale, XSupportsLocale(), XSetLocaleModifiers(), XCreateFontSet()
Extensions	Functions to find out what extensions are available on a particular server and get information about how to use one. XListExtensions(), XQueryExtension(), XFreeExtensionList()
Data Management	Several mechanisms to associate data with windows or numbers. XUniqueContext(), XSaveContext(), XFindContext(), XDeleteContext()
Host Access	Functions to control access to a server from other machines connected on a network. XAddHost(), XAddHosts(), XListHosts(), XRemoveHost(), XRemoveHosts()
Screen Saver	Functions to set the screensaver program and invoke it. XGetScreenSaver(), XSetScreenSaver(), XActivateScreenSaver(), XResetScreenSaver()
Errors	Functions to set the user-written functions called when errors occur. XErrorHandler, XSetIOErrorHandler(), XSetErrorHandler(), XGetErrorText()

what the X Window System, and Xlib in particular, considers to be a display, a screen, and a window. A display can possibly consist of one or more monitors that have a single shared keyboard and mouse. A screen is a single physical monitor. A window is a rectangular portion of any screen, sort of like a mini-monitor. A vast majority of ordinary users are looking at a single-monitor display, with only one screen, and that screen usually has multiple windows shown on it.

In the context of, and to contrast and compare, graphics systems and display protocols, a *Wayland surface* refers to a drawable region within the Wayland display server protocol. In the Wayland protocol, a surface represents a drawable area that a client can use to display its content.

In simpler terms, a Wayland surface is an abstraction for a window or a graphical element that applications can create and use to render their user interfaces. The Wayfire compositor manages these surfaces, handling their placement, stacking order, and other aspects of their display on the screen.

Compared to the traditional X Window System, Wayland is designed to be more lightweight and modern. It aims to provide better performance, improved security, and a more direct interaction between applications and the display hardware. Wayland surfaces play a key role in this architecture by serving as the fundamental building blocks for graphical content within the Wayland display server environment.

Furthermore, and from the programmers' perspective, an X Window System server's display is designated as hostname:displaynumber.screennumber.

This designation, as an argument in the coding of a client application program, determines what graphical server to connect to, and which screen to portray information on. Since the X Windows Protocol is equally applied via networked connections between various host computers, the *hostname* designates the name of the machine to which any display is physically connected to. The term *displaynumber* (starting at 0) refers to the particular collection of monitors, on a possibly multi-monitor workstation. The term *screennumber* (starting at 0) refers to any single particular monitor in the displays collection.

2.3.9.3 *The Xlib Graphics Context (GC)*

What exactly is the Graphics Context (GC), as a resource that Xlib uses to produce the simple types of graphics in X Windows displays? Basically, the GC defines how graphics primitives are drawn, and what characteristics and attributes the graphics, such as lines, rectangles, points, text, filled areas, etc., will have in any window display. GCs are kept in the server-side portion of the client–server software model, enhancing speed, performance, and storage requirements. There are basically two "targets" for the drawing of graphics primitives: windows and pixel maps, or *pixmaps*. These targets are referred to as *drawables* in X Window jargon.

Note

A given graphics primitive does not contain all the information needed to draw a particular instance of that primitive.

The appearance of everything that is drawn by a client-side program is controlled by the GC that is in effect for each graphics primitive. For example, when an application has reached a point where graphics primitives are to be drawn, a GC must be specified or be already in place, and then the GC is supplied as an argument in the argument list of the particular function that draws the graphics primitive. This arrangement, of having a single, or possibly multiple contexts available, retained at the server, for the drawing of many primitives speeds up the drawing of graphics primitives.

2.3.9.4 Compiling an Xlib Client Application Program

Be aware that, on a Raspberry Pi system, you may have to download and install the GNU C compiler for the following example programs to run, if that has not already been done by default at installation, or subsequently by your system administrator. This compiler was already available after installation of the Raspberry Pi OS on our systems, and therefore, by default, we did not have to do this on our Raspberry Pi system.

We used the following compiler command, with the options and option arguments shown.

gcc input_file.c –o output_file –lX11

Here, **input_file.c** is the name of your C source code file, **output_file** is the name of the executable program, and X11 is the library that already exists on the system that must be linked to.

In-Chapter Exercise

2.10   Is the X11 library you link to in the compiler command for an Xlib program a statically or dynamically linked library?

2.3.9.5 Sample Xlib Client Application Programs

In this section, we give you a practical introduction to programming using the Xlib model. The example programs presented in this section fulfill some or all of the requirements for a basic application shown in Section 2.3.9.2, and as detailed in Section 2.3.9.1. They illustrate some of the most important X11 concepts and programming issues.

Following are three elementary sample Xlib C programs. Each is preceded by a statement of what the program does, relevant background information, and a reference to Table 2.2, listing the X Window functions, along with a

TABLE 2.3

simple1_white.c Xlib Function Calls

Xlib Function Name	Description and Important Arguments
XOpenDisplay	Connects a client program to the server, via TCP or Linux IPC. Requires the display_name as a character argument.
WhitePixel	Returns the white pixel value of the screen default color map, as an unsigned long integer.
DefaultScreen	Returns the default integer screen number, in the last segment of the string referenced by the XOpenDisplay function.
XCreateSimpleWindow	Creates an unmapped **Input-Output** sub-window for a specified parent window. Arguments include Display, parent, x and y coordinate location, width, height. Also returns the window ID of the created window as a long unsigned integer.
DefaultRootWindow	Returns the ID of the root window on the default screen.
XMApWindow	Maps the window and all its sub-windows. Its actual display depends on its stacking order relative to siblings and ancestors. Arguments are Display and Window.
XFlush	Flushes or sends all requests to the server that have been buffered, but not yet sent. Takes Display as an argument.

description of what the functions do. To get more information about the function calls—for example, what their specific argument list data structure and contents are—consult your own documentation set for Xlib, or the online documentation.

Note

You can download these three programs from the book website repository (www.github.com/bobk48/RaspberryPiOS), and use the Geany IDE to build and run them on your version of the Raspberry Pi OS.

Xlib Example Program **simple1_white.c**

Objective: Draw an empty 500 × 400 pixel window, surrounded by the window manager decorations for whatever window manager you have running on your system.

Background: This simple Xlib program, in addition to conforming to the structure illustrated in Section 2.3.9.1 for an X Window System client application, conforms to (and includes requisite code for window creation) our X Window System model of Data Generation → Window Creation → Data Mapping into the Created Window. In this particular program, we include a C **printf** statement that prints the window ID of the created window to stdout, so that when mapping gnuplot graphics to the window for example, you can easily identify the window ID as a hex number.

Functions Called: See Table 2.3

Code:

```
#include <X11/Xlib.h>
#include <stdio.h>
int main()
{
    Display *d = XOpenDisplay(NULL);
    int white = WhitePixel(d, DefaultScreen(d));
    Window w = XCreateSimpleWindow(
            d, DefaultRootWindow(d), 0, 0, 500, 400, 0, white, white);
    printf("Window ID 0x%p\n", (void*)w);
    XMapWindow(d, w);
    XFlush(d);
    while (1);
}
```

In-Chapter Exercises

2.11 Identify, by listing them, the basic structural components of this X Window System client application program, as seen in the listing in Section 2.3.9.1. What basic structural components from the listing are included in this program? Which ones are missing?

2.12 What are the arguments supplied to the XCreateSimpleWindow function in the preceding program? Consult your Xlib documentation set to give a complete listing and description of all arguments that are shown.

TABLE 2.4

test1.c Xlib Function Calls

Xlib Function Name	Description and Important Arguments
RootWindow	Returns the window ID of the root window.
BlackPixel	Returns the black pixel value of the screen default color map, as an unsigned long integer.
XSelectInput	Arbitrates which events a window will respond to.
ExposureMask	Selects for any exposure event for a window except GraphicsExpose or NoExpose.
KeyPressMask	Selects for any KeyPress event for a window.
XNextEvent	Copies the first event from the event queue into the specified XEvent structure and then removes it from the queue
Expose	A type of event.
XFillRectangle	Fills the specified rectangle or rectangles as if a four-point FillPolygon protocol request were specified for each.
DefaultGC	Returns the default GC of the specified screen.
XCloseDisplay	Closes the connection to the X server for the display specified in the display structure, and destroys all windows and resource IDs
KeyPress	A type of event.

Xlib Example Program **test1.c**

Objective: Produce a simple window on the display that draws a small filled-in rectangle in black. It may be closed by pressing **<Ctrl>+C>**.

Background: This is an example of an Xlib client application that actually does some drawing in a window opened on the display.

New Function Called: See Table 2.4

Code:

```
/*
   * Simple Xlib application drawing a box in a window.
   */
#include <X11/Xlib.h>
#include <stdio.h>
#include <stdlib.h>
#include <string.h>
int main(void)
{
    Display *display;
    Window window;
    XEvent event;
    int s;

/*Initialization*/

    /* open connection with the server */
    display = XOpenDisplay(NULL);
    if (display == NULL)
    {
      fprintf(stderr, "Cannot open display\n");
      exit(1);
    }

    s = DefaultScreen(display);

    /* create window */
  window=XCreateSimpleWindow(display,RootWindow(display,s),10,10,\200,200,1,\
                    BlackPixel(display, s), WhitePixel(display, s));

    /* select kind of events we are interested in */
    XSelectInput(display, window, ExposureMask | KeyPressMask);
```

```
/* map (show) the window */
XMapWindow(display, window);

/* Start the Event-Request Loop*/

for (;;)
{
    XNextEvent(display, &event);

    /* draw or redraw the window */
    if (event.type == Expose)
    {
        XFillRectangle(display, window, DefaultGC(display, s), 20, 20, 10, 10);
    }
    /* exit on key press */
    if (event.type == KeyPress)
        break;
}

/* Cleanup */

XCloseDisplay(display);

return 0;
}
```

In-Chapter Exercise

2.13   What basic structural components from the listing in Section 2.3.9.1 of an X Window System client application program are included in this program? Which ones are missing?

Xlib Example Program **test4.c**

Objective: Open a window on the display with the title Report, and then place the text string Linux Rocks at any mouse click-indicated position in the window. In addition, you can press keyboard keys and they will be echoed on the console screen, telling you what key you pressed.

Background: This introduces in a straightforward and easy-to-understand manner the program model for X Window System client applications, and illustrates the concept of a Graphic Context (GC) that specifies many of the characteristics of windows and other objects.

TABLE 2.5

test4.c Xlib Function Calls

Xlib Function Name	Description and Important Arguments
XLookupString	Translates a key event to a KeySym and a string.
XSetForeground	Sets the foreground attributes of a given GC.
XDrawString	Draws text characters in a given drawable.
XSetStandardProperties	Provides a means by which simple applications set the most essential properties with a single call.
ButtonPressMask	Specifies that button presses are selected as events for the current window.
XSelectInput	Requests that the X server report the events associated with the specified event mask.
XCreateGC	Creates and returns a GC; can be used with any destination drawable with the same root and depth as the specified drawable.
XSetBackground	Sets the background attributes of a given GC.
XSetForeground	Sets the foreground pixel value components in a GC. Arguments are Display, GC, and foreground as an unsigned long integer
XClearWindow	Clears the entire area in the specified window.
XMapRaised	Maps the window and all of its sub-windows that have had map requests and raises the window to the top of the stack.
XFreeGC	Destroys the specified GC as well as all the associated storage.
XDestroyWindow	Destroys the specified window as well as all of its subwindows and causes the X server to generate a DestroyNotify event for each window.
XClearWindow	Clears a window, but does not signal an exposure event. Arguments are the Display and a designated window.

New Function Called: See Table 2.5

Code:

```c
/* Xlib and standard      C headers */
#include <X11/Xlib.h>
#include <X11/Xutil.h>
#include <X11/Xos.h>
#include <stdio.h>
#include <stdlib.h>
/* Declare the X variables and pointers*/
Display *dis;
int screen;
Window  win;
GC gc;
/* X routines */
void init_x();
```

```
void close_x();
void redraw();
main () {
/*Initialization*/
        XEvent event;           /* declare the XEvent */
        KeySym key;             /* KeyPress Events */
        char text[255];         /* char buffer for KeyPress Events */
        init_x();

/* Start the Event-Request Loop*/

        while(1) {
                /* get the next event.
                   We set the mask for events that we want detected
                */
                XNextEvent(dis, &event);
                if (event.type==Expose && event.xexpose.count==0) {
                /* the window was exposed redraw it! */
                    redraw();
                }
                if (event.type==KeyPress&&
                    XLookupString(&event.xkey,text,255,&key,0)==1) {
                /* use the XLookupString routine to convert the invent
                     KeyPress data into regular text.
                */
                        if (text[0]=='q') {
                            close_x();
                        }
                        printf("You pressed the %c key\n",text[0]);
                }
                if (event.type==ButtonPress) {
                /* report where the mouse Button was Pressed */
                        int x=event.xbutton.x,
                            y=event.xbutton.y;
                        strcpy(text,"Linux Rocks");
                        XSetForeground(dis,gc,rand()%event.xbutton.x%255);
                        XDrawString(dis,win,gc,x,y, text,\ strlen(text));
                }
        }
}
```

```
void init_x() {
/* Set the colors black and white */
    unsigned long black,white;

    dis=XOpenDisplay((char *)0);
    screen=DefaultScreen(dis);
    black=BlackPixel(dis,screen),
    white=WhitePixel(dis, screen);
    win=XCreateSimpleWindow(dis,DefaultRootWindow(dis),0,0,\
            300, 300, 5,black, white);
    XSetStandardProperties(dis,win,"Report","E",None,NULL,0,NULL);\
    XSelectInput(dis, win, ExposureMask | ButtonPressMask | KeyPressMask);\
            gc=XCreateGC(dis, win, 0,0);
    XSetBackground(dis,gc,white);
    XSetForeground(dis,gc,black);
    XClearWindow(dis, win);
    XMapRaised(dis, win);
};

void close_x() {

/* Cleanup */
    XFreeGC(dis, gc);
    XDestroyWindow(dis,win);
    XCloseDisplay(dis);
    exit(1);
};

void redraw() {
    XClearWindow(dis, win);
};
```

In-Chapter Exercises

    2.14   What basic structural components from the listing in Section 2.3.9.1 of an X Window System client application program are included in this program? Which ones are missing?

    2.15   Which function calls create and implement the GC in program test4.c?

Tables 2.6, 2.7, and 2.8 give additional information about Xlib display, drawing, and event functions.

TABLE 2.6

Xlib Display Functions

Xlib Function Name	Description and Important Arguments
XOpenDisplay	Connects a client program to the server, via TCP or Linux IPC. Requires the display_name as a character argument.
WhitePixel	Returns the white pixel value of the screen default color map, as an unsigned long integer.
DefaultScreen	Returns the default integer screen number, in the last segment of the string referenced by the XOpenDisplay function.
XCreateSimpleWindow	Creates an unmapped **Input-Output** sub-window for a specified parent window. Arguments include Display, parent, x and y coordinate location, width, height. Also returns the window ID of the created window as a long unsigned integer.
DefaultRootWindow	Returns the ID of the root window on the default screen.
XMApWindow	Maps the window and all its sub-windows. Its actual display depends on its stacking order relative to siblings and ancestors. Arguments are Display and Window.
XFlush	Flushes or sends all requests to the server that have been buffered, but not yet sent. Takes Display as an argument.

TABLE 2.7

Xlib Drawing Function

Xlib Function Name	Description and Important Arguments
RootWindow	Returns the window ID of the root window.
BlackPixel	Returns the black pixel value of the screen default color map, as an unsigned long integer.
XSelectInput	Arbitrates which events a window will respond to.
ExposureMask	Selects for any exposure event for a window except GraphicsExpose or NoExpose.
KeyPressMask	Selects for any KeyPress event for a window.
XNextEvent	Copies the first event from the event queue into the specified XEvent structure, and then removes it from the head of the event queue.
Expose	A type of event.
XFillRectangle	Fills a rectanglular area in the specified drawable entity using the supplied arguments of x and y location as integers, width and height as unsigned integers, and GC.
DefaultGC	Returns the default GC of the specified screen.
XCloseDisplay	Closes the connection to the X server for the display specified in the display structure, and destroys all windows and resource IDs
KeyPress	A type of event.

TABLE 2.8

Xlib Event Functions

Xlib Function Name	Description and Important Arguments
XLookupString	Translates a key event to an ASCII string, keysym, and ComposeStatus.
XSetForeground	Sets the foreground attributes of a given GC.
XDrawString	Draws text characters in a given drawable entity.
XSetStandardProperties	Provides a means by which simple applications set the most essential properties with a single call.
ButtonPressMask	Specifies that button presses are selected as events for the current window.
XSelectInput	Requests that the X server report the events associated with the specified event mask.
XCreateGC	Creates and returns a GC; can be used with any destination drawable entity with the same root window and depth as the specified drawable entity.
XSetBackground	Sets the background attributes of a given GC.
XSetForeground	Sets the foreground pixel value components in a GC. Arguments are Display, GC, and foreground as an unsigned long integer
XClearWindow	Clears the entire area in the specified window.
XMapRaised	Maps the window and all of its sub-windows that have had map requests and raises the window to the top of the stack.
XFreeGC	Destroys the specified GC as well as all the associated storage.
XDestroyWindow	Destroys the specified window as well as all of its subwindows and causes the X server to generate a DestroyNotify event for each window.
XClearWindow	Clears a window, but does not signal an exposure event. Arguments are the Display and a designated window.

2.4 Using XCB

In this section, we detail another official client-side library that can be used to produce interactive X Window System client applications. We show some of the basic top-down considerations you need to make before actually writing the code for an XCB client application. Then we show how to compile and link an XCB program. Finally, we give basic examples of programming in XCB.

As in Section 2.3.9.3 on Xlib, it would be helpful for you to assemble your own documentation set for XCB from on-line sources, and then make a comparison of these two libraries in terms of the documents available for each. We also encourage you to compare the basic structure and complexity of the examples in this section to the example programs we provided for Xlib.

In-Chapter Exercise

2.16   Create your own documentation set for XCB, and for Xlib from the previous section, using on-line sources and printed documents and books. The most important component of a documentation comparison is cataloging and organizing that catalog to effectively serve you personally in showing how the documents for each system proceed from a top-down overview to the lowest level details of using the libraries. This method, which we can only partly illustrate and prescribe here, would then allow you to take our examples and expand upon them to enable you to write more complex X Windows client applications given the use cases you might encounter.

2.4.1 XCB Top-Down Considerations

XCB is more efficient, in several dimensions which are highlighted in online documentation, than its older predecessor, Xlib. And for beginning programmers, XCB client application programs conform to the basic structure shown in Section 2.3.7.2. That basic structure, as implemented by calling XCB functions, and interacting with the XCB data structures, is very similar to the basic structure of an Xlib program as seen in Section 2.3.9.1. Of course, instead of Xlib function calls, you must substitute XCB function calls. We repeat that basic structure here, and make the appropriate substitutions of function calls where necessary:

A client application program written for XCB generally operates in this way:

1. Establishes a connection to an X server with **xcb_connect()**, and if the connection cannot be made, gracefully terminates the program.
2. Polls the server for information about the physical screen, and uses the information obtained to calculate window parameters, like size, position, etc.
3. Creates a window on the physical screen with **xcb_create_window()**.
4. Sets standard properties for the window manager.
5. Selects and specifies the types of events it needs to receive, and respond to, in order to work.
6. If text will be output in the window, loads the font to be used for that text.
7. Creates a GC to control the action of drawing requests.
8. Displays the window with **xcb_map_window()**.
9. Begins and continues to indeterminately (or logically) iterate (loop), to handle possible events from the server, and send callbacks to the client.
   a. Possibly does the actual drawing operations in the window. Achieves this by responding to an Expose event resulting from

mapping the window, and other subsequent expose events, by calling routines to draw text and bit mapped graphics.

b. Keeps handling events until a KeyPress or ButtonPress event arrives (which ends the indeterminate iteration), then closes the display connection, cleans up, and exits.

2.4.1.1 The XCB API

The Application Programming Interface (API) structure of XCB has two basic layers, a lower layer, *XCB Connection*, that supports the establishment of an X server connnection, and an intermediate XCB protocol layer. The XCB Protocol layer provides a direct C API for the core X Protocol. There are also many other APIs available that provide other types of interaction between client and server. The XCB API uses an Xlib-style "event loop" method of interaction. Unlike Xlib, which blocks and caches requests, XCB requests are converted into "reply cookies", which use a form of caching that makes the cache of event replies more efficient.

XCB has an efficient data structure form and interface. As can be seen in the examples in Section 2.4.1.3, the establishment of the server-side connection, using a closed data structure, is the first action a client-side application takes.

Contrary to the Xlib partitioning of hostname/display/screen, as we show in Section 2.3.9.1, XCB limits the connection data structure to a single display. The only idea of "screen" in XCB as defined in the X Window System Protocol, becomes the root window of that single display. Event and request queues are established and flushed in a manner that supports, most importantly, a purely asynchronous form of interaction between client and server.

The XCB data structure/function call API can be broken into a variety of categories, such as functions that create connections and XIDs, non-blocking requests such as drawing primitives, blocking requests, retrieval of data, and event and error handlers.

2.4.1.2 XCB Documentation

In order to supplement your own documentation set for XCB, we present an on-line alphabetized listing of a large collection of Core API and main XCB functions in the following repository of the book's Github site:

www.github.com/bobk48/unixthetextbook3

That listing is entitled xcb_functions.doc. Each entry in this listing takes the following form:

****

Function Prototype

Data Structure Function Name **(** **Type Def** *Argument 1*
                            Type Def *Argument 2*
                            ...   ...
)

Short description of what the function does.
Parameters

      Argument 1 Description.
      Argument 2 Description.
      ...   ...

Returns
    Description of what the function returns.

    Verbose description of what the function does.

    References What other functions this function refers to.

****

An example function taken from that listing of functions is as follows:

xcb_void_cookie_t xcb_create_window (xcb_connection_t * *c,*
                                       uint8_t   *depth,*
                                       xcb_window_t   *wid,*
                                       xcb_window_t   *parent,*
                                       int16_t   *x,*
                                       int16_t   *y,*
                                       uint16_t   *width,*
                                       uint16_t   *height,*
                                       uint16_t   *border_*
                                                          width,
                                       uint16_t   *_class,*
                                       xcb_visualid_t   *visual,*
                                       uint32_t   *value_mask,*
                                       const void *   *value_list*
)

Creates a window.

Parameters

c	The connection
depth	Specifies the new window's depth.
	The special value XCB_COPY_FROM_PARENT means
	the depth is taken from the *parent* window.
wid	The ID with which you will refer to the new window, created
	by xcb_generate_id.
parent	The parent window of the new window.
x	The X coordinate of the new window.
y	The Y coordinate of the new window.
width	The width of the new window.
height	The height of the new window.
border_width	Must be zero if the class is InputOnly or a xcb_match_
	error_t occurs.
_class	A bitmask of #xcb_window_class_t values.
_class	
visual	Specifies the id for the new window's visual.
	The special value XCB_COPY_FROM_PARENT means
	the visual is taken from the *parent* window.
value_mask	A bitmask of xcb_cw_t values.

Returns

A cookie

Creates an unmapped window as child of the specified parent window. A CreateNotify event will be generated. The new window is placed on top in the stacking order with respect to siblings.

The coordinate system has the X axis horizontal and the Y axis vertical with the origin [0, 0] at the upper-left corner. Coordinates are integral, in terms of pixels, and coincide with pixel centers. Each window and pixmap has its own coordinate system. For a window, the origin is inside the border at the inside, upper-left corner.

The created window is not yet displayed (mapped), call xcb_map_window to display it.

The created window will initially use the same cursor as its parent.

References XCB_CREATE_WINDOW.

****

In-Chapter Exercise

2.17   In the function listing for xcb_create_window, what is the argument xcb_connection_t*? What are the elements of xcb_connection_t*? From the documentation of what API did you get this information?

2.4.1.3 The XCB Graphics Context (GC)

Question:
What exactly is the graphics context, as a resource that XCB uses to produce the simple types of graphics in X Windows displays?

Answer:
In X Window System, the graphics context (often referred to as GC) is a resource that encapsulates various attributes used for drawing on the screen. XCB (X C Binding) is a low-level library for communicating with the X Window System protocol, and it provides a programming interface to interact with X servers.

The graphics context in XCB is a structure that holds information about how graphics operations should be performed. It includes attributes such as the foreground and background colors, line width, font, function (specifying how pixel values should be combined), and more. When you perform graphics operations in XCB, you use a graphics context to define the properties of the drawing.

Here's a brief overview of some key attributes commonly found in a graphics context:

1. Foreground and Background Colors: Specifies the colors used for drawing. The foreground color is typically used for drawing shapes, while the background color may be used for clearing areas.
2. Line Attributes: Includes properties like line width, line style (solid, dashed, etc.), and cap and join styles for line endings and intersections.
3. Font: Specifies the font used for text rendering.
4. Function: Defines how pixel values should be combined during drawing operations. Common functions include COPY (replace existing pixel values), XOR (bitwise exclusive OR), etc.
5. Clip Mask: Specifies a region that limits where drawing can occur. Anything outside this region is not affected by drawing operations.

When you perform a drawing operation using XCB, you pass the graphics context along with the drawable (such as a window or a pixmap) to specify how the drawing should be done.

Here's a simple example in pseudocode to illustrate the use of a graphics context:

```
// Assume we have a connection to the X server and a window (drawable)
xcb_connection_t* connection;
xcb_drawable_t window;

// Create a graphics context
xcb_gcontext_t gc = xcb_generate_id(connection);
xcb_create_gc(connection, gc, window, XCB_GC_FOREGROUND |
XCB_GC_GRAPHICS_EXPOSURES, values);
// Set the foreground color to black
uint32_t values[1] = { 0x000000 };

// Draw a line using the created graphics context
xcb_point_t points[] = { {10, 10}, {50, 50} };
xcb_poly_line(connection, XCB_COORD_MODE_ORIGIN, window, gc, 2, points);
```

In this example, we create a graphics context (gc) and set its foreground color to black. Then, we draw a line using the xcb_poly_line function, passing the graphics context and an array of points defining the line.

2.4.2 Installing and Compiling an XCB Program

Use the following commands to install XCB on your Raspberry Pi system:

```
$ sudo apt -y install xcb
$ sudo apt -y install libc6
$ sudo apt -y install libxcb-util-dev
```

Note
At the time we wrote this book, on our Raspberry Pi system, running the latest Raspberry Pi OS, based on Debian Bookworm, we didn't need to use the second command shown above, but you may need to use that command.

On our Raspberry Pi system, we used the following compiler command with the options and arguments shown, to compile XCB program code:

```
$ gcc –Wall input_file.c –o output_file –lxcb
```

In-Chapter Exercise

2.18   Instead of using the above compile command to produce an executable image, how would you use the Geany IDE, or Visual Studio Code, to compile and execute the XCB programs presented in Section 2.4.3?

2.4.3 Sample XCB Client Application Programs

Following are three elementary sample XCB programs, taken from the following source:

www.x.org/releases/X11R7.6/doc/libxcb/tutorial/index.html

Each is preceded by a statement of what the program does, and a short background description that illustrates important functions or concepts in the program listing. To gain a full explanation of how an XCB program works, it would be very helpful to review the documants found at the above web link. XCB Example Program **xcb_simple2.c**

Objective: Place a simple window on screen.

Background: This simple XCB program conforms to the structure illustrated in previous sections for an X Windows System client application. Most notably, it calls the xcb_create_window function that we give a complete documentation reference for in Section 2.4.1.2. It also conforms to (and includes requisite code for window creation) our X Window System model of Data Generation → Window Creation → Data Mapping into the Created Window. In this particular program, we generate the window ID with the xcb_generate function, and include a **printf** C language statement that prints the window ID of the created window to stdout. We do this so that when mapping gnuplot graphics to the window, as shown in Section 2.7.5, you can easily identify the window ID as a hex number.

Note
Use Geany to build and launch it.

Code:

```
#include <unistd.h>      /* pause() */
#include <stdio.h>
#include <xcb/xcb.h>
int
main ()
{
    xcb_connection_t    \*c;
    xcb_screen_t        *screen;
    xcb_window_t        win;

/* Initialization */
```

```
/* Open the connection to the X server */
c = xcb_connect (NULL, NULL);

/* Get the first screen */
screen = xcb_setup_roots_iterator (xcb_get_setup (c)).data;

/* Ask for our window's Id and print it in hex to stdout */
win = xcb_generate_id(c);
printf ("Window ID, 0x%x\n", win);

/* Create the window */
xcb_create_window (c,                             /* Connection         */
                XCB_COPY_FROM_PARENT,          /* depth (same as root) */
                win,                           /* window Id          */
                screen->root,                  /* parent window      */
                0, 0,                          /* x, y               */
                250, 250,                      /* width, height      */
                10,                            /* border_width       */
                XCB_WINDOW_CLASS_INPUT_OUTPUT, /* class              */
                screen->root_visual,           /* visual             */
                0, NULL);                      /* masks, not used yet */

/* Map the window on the screen */
xcb_map_window (c, win);
/* Make sure commands are sent before we pause, so window is shown */
xcb_flush (c);

pause ();        /* hold client */
/* Cleanup */

xcb_disconnect(c);
return 0;
}
```

In-Chapter Exercises

2.19   What basic component of an X Windows client application is missing
       from the preceding program, and particularly what aspect or part of
       that component? How do you close the window without using the
       window kill button?

2.20   What is contained in the background of the window drawn by xcb_
       simple.c? Why does this background appear as it does?

XCB Example Program **2ndxcbdraw.c**

Objective: Draw two rectangles in a window.

Background: The important new function and its associated XCB data structure introduced in this example, xcb_create_gc, creates a GC.
That GC is used to assign attributes to the rectangle drawing
primitives placed in the window, which is subsequently
mapped to a screen. Also notice that the member assignment
statement for elements of a C struct is used in several places in
this program to assign values to elements of a data structure. For
example, in the creation of the GC, the statements win = screen-
>root; and values[0] = screen→white_pixel;. As noted, this data
structure technique is used very frequently in XCB to supply
values to parameters of XCB functions. Additionally, the other
new function call in this example is to a drawing function, xcb_
poly_rectangle. This drawing function creates the two rectangles,
using the GC defined, within the programs event/request loop.

Note
Use Geany to build and launch the program.

Code:

```
#include <stdlib.h>
#include <stdio.h>
#include <xcb/xcb.h>
int
main ()
{
    xcb_connection_t          *c;
    xcb_screen_t              *screen;
    xcb_drawable_t            win;
    xcb_gcontext_t            foreground;
    xcb_generic_event_t       *e;
    uint32_t                  mask = 0;
    uint32_t                  values[2];

/* geometric objects */

    xcb_rectangle_t           rectangles[] = {
        { 10, 50, 40, 20},
        { 80, 50, 10, 40}};

/* Initialization */

    /* Open the connection to the X server */
    c = xcb_connect (NULL, NULL);
```

```
/* Get the first screen */
screen = xcb_setup_roots_iterator (xcb_get_setup (c)).data;

/* Create black (foreground) graphic context */
win = screen->root;

foreground = xcb_generate_id (c);
mask = XCB_GC_FOREGROUND | XCB_GC_GRAPHICS_EXPOSURES;
values[0] = screen->black_pixel;
values[1] = 0;
xcb_create_gc (c, foreground, win, mask, values);

/* Ask for our window's Id */
win = xcb_generate_id(c);

/* Create the window */
mask = XCB_CW_BACK_PIXEL | XCB_CW_EVENT_MASK;
values[0] = screen->white_pixel;
values[1] = XCB_EVENT_MASK_EXPOSURE;
xcb_create_window (c,                              /* Connection        */
        XCB_COPY_FROM_PARENT,                      /* depth             */
        win,                                       /* window Id         */
        screen->root,                              /* parent window     */
        0, 0,                                      /* x, y              */
        150, 150,                                  /* width, height     */
        10,                                        /* border_width      */
        XCB_WINDOW_CLASS_INPUT_OUTPUT,             /* class             */
        screen->root_visual,                       /* visual            */
        mask, values);

/* Map the window on the screen */
xcb_map_window (c, win);

/* Flush the request */
xcb_flush (c);

/* Start the Event-Request loop */

while ((e = xcb_wait_for_event (c))) {
    switch (e->response_type & ~0x80) {
    case XCB_EXPOSE: {

        /* Draw the rectangles */
        xcb_poly_rectangle (c, win, foreground, 2, rectangles);
```

```
       /* Flush the request */
       xcb_flush (c);

       break;
    }
    default: {
       /* Unknown event type, ignore it */
       break;
    }
    }
    /* Free the Generic Event */
    free (e);
  }
/* Cleanup */

  xcb_disconnect(c);
  return 0;
}
```

In-Chapter Exercises

2.21   Make a list of the lines in the code of 2ndxcbdraw.c that establish the GC for the graphics primitives that are drawn by that program.

2.22   Which segment of the program 2ndxcbdraw.c generates the data for the graphics primitives that are drawn by it?

XCB Example Program **xcb_events.c**

Objective: Report screen coordinates of three-button mouse presses, and movement of the current position in the window created. Both mouse press/release events and positional movement are reported on stdout.

Background: This program is a simple example of how to monitor XCB events of the types shown in the code.

Code:

```
#include <stdlib.h>
#include <stdio.h>

#include <xcb/xcb.h>

void
print_modifiers (uint32_t mask)
{
   const char **mod, *mods[] = {
      "Shift", "Lock", "Ctrl", "Alt",
```

```
        "Mod2", "Mod3", "Mod4", "Mod5",
        "Button1", "Button2", "Button3", "Button4", "Button5"
    };
    printf ("Modifier mask: ");
    for (mod = mods; mask; mask >>= 1, mod++)
        if (mask & 1)
            printf(*mod);
    putchar ('\n');
}

int
main ()
{
    xcb_connection_t        *c;
    xcb_screen_t            *screen;
    xcb_window_t            win;
    xcb_generic_event_t     *e;
    uint32_t                mask = 0;
    uint32_t                values[2];

    /* Open the connection to the X server */
    c = xcb_connect (NULL, NULL);

    /* Get the first screen */
    screen = xcb_setup_roots_iterator (xcb_get_setup (c)).data;

    /* Ask for our window's Id */
    win = xcb_generate_id (c);

    /* Create the window */
    mask = XCB_CW_BACK_PIXEL | XCB_CW_EVENT_MASK;
    values[0] = screen->white_pixel;
    values[1] = XCB_EVENT_MASK_EXPOSURE    |
XCB_EVENT_MASK_BUTTON_PRESS    |
                XCB_EVENT_MASK_BUTTON_RELEASE |
XCB_EVENT_MASK_POINTER_MOTION |
                XCB_EVENT_MASK_ENTER_WINDOW   |
XCB_EVENT_MASK_LEAVE_WINDOW   |
                XCB_EVENT_MASK_KEY_PRESS          |
XCB_EVENT_MASK_KEY_RELEASE;
    xcb_create_window (c,                   /* Connection        */
                    0,                      /* depth             */
                    win,                    /* window Id         */
                    screen->root,           /* parent window     */
                    0, 0,                   /* x, y              */
```

```
                    150, 150,              /* width, height          */
                    10,                    /* border_width           */
                    XCB_WINDOW_CLASS_INPUT_OUTPUT, /* class    */
                    screen->root_visual,/* visual                    */
                    mask, values);         /* masks                  */

   /* Map the window on the screen */
   xcb_map_window (c, win);

   xcb_flush (c);

   while ((e = xcb_wait_for_event (c))) {
      switch (e->response_type & ~0x80) {
      case XCB_EXPOSE: {
         xcb_expose_event_t *ev = (xcb_expose_event_t *)e;

         printf("Window %u exposed.Region to be redrawn at location(%d,%d), with\
dimension (%d,%d)\n",\
                   ev->window, ev->x, ev->y, ev->width, ev->height);
         break;
      }
      case XCB_BUTTON_PRESS: {
         xcb_button_press_event_t *ev = (xcb_button_press_event_t *)e;
         print_modifiers(ev->state);

         switch (ev->detail) {
         case 4:
            printf("Wheel Button up in window %u, at coordinates(%d,%d)\n",\
                      ev->event, ev->event_x, ev->event_y);
            break;
         case 5:
            printf ("Wheel Button down in window %u, at coordinates (%d,%d)\n",\
                      ev->event, ev->event_x, ev->event_y);
            break;
         default:
            printf("Button %d pressed in window %u, at coordinates(%d,%d)\n",\
                         ev->detail, ev->event, ev->event_x, ev->event_y);
         }
         break;
      }
       case XCB_BUTTON_RELEASE: {
          xcb_button_release_event_t *ev = (xcb_button_release_event_t *)e;
          print_modifiers(ev->state);
          printf("Button %d released in window %u, at coordinates(%d,%d)\n",
          ev->detail, ev->event, ev->event_x, ev->event_y);
```

```
        break;
    }

    default:
        /* Unknown event type, ignore it */
        printf("Unknown event: %d\n", e->response_type);
        break;
    }
    /* Free the Generic Event */
    free (e);
    }
    return 0;
}
```

2.5 Basics of the Qt5 and GTK4 Toolkits

The objective of the next two sections is to give a very concise overview of the Qt5 and GTK4 software frameworks. This will be based on a very simple model. The model can be summarized as:

Data Generation → Window Generation/Construction → Data Mapping to the Constructed Window.

The primary purpose of conforming to this model is that it portrays a very practical and useful method for using the X Window System programming to the beginner. As in the previous sections of this chapter, it does not require that you have any more than just a basic computer programming knowledge of the C (or in the case of this section, the C++) programming language.

Our aim is not to give you a reference tutorial on Qt5 or GTK4. There are numerous documentation sources online, and built into those frameworks that accomplish this. But that doesn't mean that we don't give the beginner at least a glimpse into the inner workings of these software frameworks. We encourage further exploration and experimentation, via the built-in help systems available for each system, and the extensive online documentation available. This is particularly true of the Qt5 framework.

It is important to realize that both Qt5 and GTK4, as we use them here, can create very basic GUI elements, such as a single window that is empty. And in advanced design and implementation, even entire window management systems.

There are basically two ways an X Window System client application program can use its program code to work in conjunction with the X protocol running on an X server. This can be done directly by using XCB or Xlib library calls in a C program, or by using a toolkit specifically designed to act as a simple-to-use intermediary that minimizes the coding complexity of dealing with X protocol structure and Xlib or XCB functions. Qt5 (pronounced "cute five") and GTK4 are this kind of intermediary toolkit. They are a "framework", or programming environment, that allows an ordinary user to modify the pre-built Qt5 or GTK4 system with user-written C++ (for Qt5) or C (for GTK4) code, to create a customized X Window System client application program. This framework as an abstraction frees the user from dealing with the lower level details of XCB and Xlib library calls, or the X protocol itself.

In the following sub-sections and exercises, we show the following:

* Installing the Qt5 Framework and Qt5.

* Creating an Executable Qt5 Program from the Command Line.

* GTK4 Basics and Creating a Simple Widget.

Note

It is not necessary to have complete and developed knowledge of C++ Object Oriented Programming (OOP) concepts and its syntax to complete the QT5 material in this section.

2.5.1 The Qt5 Framework

For our purposes in this chapter, Qt5 is used for developing X Window System client applications with a GUI. These applications range from the most basic GUI app, up to entire windowing systems. To work with Qt5, a user combines standard C++ with the built-in QT5 framework code. Among the most important C++ extensions of this framework are "signals" and "slots", the equivalent of event handling constructs in Xlib and XCB programming. Qt5 supports a variety of compilers, including the gcc C++ compiler we used in Volume 3 of this series. Qt5 can be also be interfaced, via other programming languages, using a highly developed system of language bindings. Most prominent among these bindings is the one for Python3.

2.5.2 Some Preliminary Qt5 Programming Considerations

It is essential that you have the GNU C++ Compiler (gcc), and a text editor such as nano installed on your system. Even though the Qt5 framework is based upon the OOP model of C++, and uses the syntax of that language, it also extends the syntax to include some Qt5-specific constructs and functionality. For example, the signals and slots features of Qt5 differ from and extend the C++ class model in significant ways.

2.5.3 Installing the Qt5 Framework with Qt Creator, and Obtaining Help

To begin to work with Qt5, you must first download and install it. This is done most effectively from the command line with the following commands:

```
$ sudo apt-get install qtbase5-dev qtchooser
$ sudo apt-get install qt5-qmake qtbase5-dev-tools
$ sudo apt-get install qtcreator
$ sudo apt-get install qtdeclarative5-dev
```

After the installation, Qt Creator is added as a menu choice on the Raspberry Pi Programming menu. If you launch Qt Creator, there is an extensive help system available when you make the Qt Creator Help menu choice. We do not offer any QT Creator examples in our presentation here.

2.5.4 Creating an Executable Qt5 Program from the Command Line

Qt5 has its own compiling, linking, and assembling procedure, as shown. The following steps illustrate how to use the Qt5 procedure to compile a Qt5 program, create a Qt5 project, and execute a client application program on your Raspberry Pi system.

Note
You do not use the GNU C++ compiler directly to do any of these operations!

2.5.4.1 *The Eight Steps to Creating a Qt5 Project and Program on the Command Line*

Qt5 Example 1 The Eight Steps

Step 0: Create an empty directory under your home directory, with a name like **qtprogs1**. Make that directory the present working directory. Use a text editor of your choice to enter and save the Qt5 code of any of the example exercises in this section into files with the file extension **.cpp**— for example, **hello.cpp**, as follows, which contains Qt5 client application program code.
   This is one of the simplest Qt5 client application programs you can enter, which we entered into the file **hello.cpp**.
   Notice how much shorter it is than the XCB or Xlib code shown in the preceding sections.!

```
#include <QtGui>
#include <QApplication>
#include <QLabel>

int main(int argc, char **argv) {
    QApplication app(argc, argv);
    QLabel label("Hello, world!");
    label.show();
    return app.exec();
}
```

Step 1: While the directory qtprogs1 is the current working directory, at the shell prompt, type:

qmake -project

This executed quickly on our Debian Bookworm-based Raspberry Pi OS.

Step 2: At the shell prompt, type **qmake**

Step 3. Now in the qtprogs1 directory, you will have three files: hello.cpp, Makefile, and hello.pro

Edit hello.pro with nano, and add these lines to it:

INCLUDEPATH += .

QT += gui
QT += widgets

Note
On our Raspberry Pi system, the line **INCLUDEPATH +=**. was already in our hello.pro file.

Step 4. At the shell prompt, type the following command:

$ **make**
/usr/lib/qt5/bin/qmake -o Makefile hello.pro
g++ -c -pipe -O2 -Wall -Wextra -D_REENTRANT -fPIC -DQT_NO_DEBUG -DQT_WIDGETS_LIB -DQT_GUI_LIB -DQT_CORE_ LIB -I. -I. -I/usr/include/aarch64-linux-gnu/qt5 -I/usr/include/aarch64-linux-gnu/qt5/QtWidgets -I/usr/include/aarch64-linux-gnu/qt5/QtGui -I/usr/include/aarch64-linux-gnu/qt5/QtCore -I. -I/usr/lib/aarch64-linux-gnu/qt5/mkspecs/linux-g++ -o hello.o hello.cpp

g++ -Wl,-O1 -o hello hello.o   /usr/lib/aarch64-linux-gnu/
libQt5Widgets.so /usr/lib/aarch64-linux-gnu/libQt5Gui.so /usr/lib/
aarch64-linux-gnu/libQt5Core.so -lGL -lpthread
$

Step 5. In the qtprogs1 directory, you will now have five files:
hello, hello.cpp, Makefile, hello.o, and hello.pro.

Step 6: At the shell prompt, type **./hello**

Step 7: The graphics contained in the Qt5 program you entered into hello.
cpp are now shown on the screen. These graphics should produce a
Qt5 "widget" (short for window gadget) that displays the text string
"Hello, World!", and you can enlarge the window by dragging the lower-
right corner of the widget down and to the right. Use the kill window
button (the X) in the window frame to close this Qt5 widget.

In-Chapter Exercise

2.23   Enter and save the above program using a text editor of your choice
into a file, with the file name exercise1.cpp. Then, following the
eight steps shown, execute the program on your system.

Qt5 Example 2 Text Edit

In this next example, we create and show a built-in Qt5 text edit capability,
created in a newly opened window. This represents another simple Qt
program entered and executed on the command line, rather than using a
GUI-based toolkit. We also give a line-by-line basic description of the functional parts of the program. The line numbers shown to the left of the code
should be omitted, they are only there for reference in the dialog of explanation that follows.
Here is the code:

```
1       #include <QApplication>
2       #include <QTextEdit>
3
4       int main(int argv, char **args)
5       {
6           QApplication app(argv, args);
7
8           QTextEdit textEdit;
9           textEdit.show();
10
```

```
11          return app.exec();
12      }
```

Dialog of explanation and description:

Lines 1 and 2 include the header files for QApplication and QTextEdit, which are the two classes that Qt5 uses. Qt5 is an object-oriented programming language that uses C++ class and object descriptions and functionality. All Qt5 classes have a header file named after them.

Lines 4 and 5 declare the variables and open the main program.

Line 6 creates a QApplication object. This object manages application-wide resources and is necessary to run any Qt5 program that has a GUI. It needs argv and args because Qt accepts a few command line arguments for this object.

Line 8 creates a QTextEdit object. A *text edit* is a visual element in the GUI. In Qt5, we call such elements *widgets*, short for *window gadgets*. Examples of other Qt5 widgets are scroll bars, labels, spin boxes, sliders, and radio buttons. A widget can also be a container for other widgets, a dialog area, or a main application window.

Line 9 invokes the text edit widget on the screen in its own window frame. Since widgets also function as containers. A container such as QMainWindow has toolbars, menus, a status bar, and a few other widgets. It is possible to show a single widget in its own window. Widgets are not visible by default; the method show() makes the widget visible.

Line 11 makes the QApplication object enter its event loop, similar to XCB and Xlib client application programs. When a Qt5 client application is running, events are generated and sent to the widgets of the application. Examples of events, as seen in XCB and Xlib, are mouse button presses, mouse cursor movements, and key strokes pressed on the keyboard. When you type text in the text edit widget, it receives key press events and responds by drawing the text that was typed.

In-Chapter Exercise

2.24   Enter and save the above example program using a text editor of your choice into a file, with the file name of your choice. Then, following the Eight Steps from Qt5 Example Qt5 1, execute the program on your system.

Qt5 Example 3 Adding a Quit Button

In a real application, you would usually create more than one widget to have a rich and varied dialog established between client application data-generating code and display system code. We will now show a simple example of a QPushButton beneath the text edit window created in Qt5 Example 2. The button will exit the QTextEdit application when pushed (i.e., clicked on with the mouse). Again, disregard the line numbers shown, since they are only used to reference the code in the dialog that follows the code.

Here's the code:

```
1 #include <QtGui>
2 #include <QApplication>
3 #include <QTextEdit>
4 #include <QPushButton>
5 #include <QObject>
6 #include <QVBoxLayout>
7 #include <QWidget>
8     int main(int argc, char **argv)
9     {
10        QApplication app(argc, argv);

11        QTextEdit *textEdit = new QTextEdit;
12        QPushButton *quitButton = new QPushButton("&Quit");

13        QObject::connect(quitButton, SIGNAL(clicked()), qApp, SLOT(quit()));

14        QVBoxLayout *layout = new QVBoxLayout;
15        layout->addWidget(textEdit);
16        layout->addWidget(quitButton);
17        QWidget window;
18        window.setLayout(layout);

19        window.show();

20        return app.exec();
21    }
```

We provide the following dialog of explanations and descriptions of the line numbers as follows:

Lines 1 through 7 The includes, which contains all of Qt5 GUI classes used in this program.

Lines 8 creates two pointer objects to be used to reference the classes of objects below.

The next line illustrates probably the most important Qt call.

Line 10 uses Qt's signals and slots mechanism to make the application exit when the Quit button is pushed. A slot is a function that can be invoked at run time using its name (as a literal string). A signal is a function that when called will invoke slots registered with it; we call that to connect the slot to the signal and to emit the signal. So, quit() is a slot of QApplication that exits the application; clicked() is a signal that QPushButton emits when it is pushed.

Note

As a programming reminder for C++, :: is called the (binary) scope resolution operator. By using the scope resolution operator, you can address member functions outside of a class. Also remember that the scope resolution operator specifies that the identifier which is on the right belongs to the data type or class on the left.

The static QObject::connect() function takes care of connecting the slot to the signal. SIGNAL() and SLOT() are two macros that take the function signatures of the signal and slot to connect. We also need to give pointers to the objects that should send and receive the signal.

Lines 14 through 17 create a QVBoxLayout. As mentioned, widgets can contain other widgets. It is possible to set the bounds (the location and size) of child widgets directly, but it is usually easier to use a layout. A layout manages the bounds of a widget's children. QVBoxLayout places the children in a vertical row.

Line 19 uncovers the window.

Line 20 starts the event loop.

Qt5 Example 4 Connecting Signals and Slots

Qt5, as a C++-based framework, essentially is OOP. In Qt5, *signals* and *slots* are a mechanism used for communication between objects. This is similar to C/C++ function pointers, but the signal/slot system makes sure that the callback arguments are type-correct.

Here's a simple C program that uses a *callback function* as an argument. In this example, the program defines a function called performOperation that takes two integers, and a callback function as arguments. The callback function is then invoked within performOperation to perform some operation on the two integers.

```
#include <stdio.h>

// Callback function type definition
typedef void (*OperationCallback)(int, int);

// Function that takes two integers and a callback function as arguments
void performOperation(int a, int b, OperationCallback callback) {
    printf("Performing operation on %d and %d:\n", a, b);
    callback(a, b);
}

// Callback function implementations
void addCallback(int a, int b) {
    printf("Sum: %d\n", a + b);
}
```

```
void multiplyCallback(int a, int b) {
    printf("Product: %d\n", a * b);
}
int main() {
    int num1 = 10, num2 = 5;

    // Using the performOperation function with addCallback
    performOperation(num1, num2, addCallback);

    // Using the performOperation function with multiplyCallback
    performOperation(num1, num2, multiplyCallback);

    return 0;
}
```

In this example, the performOperation function takes two integers (a and b) and a callback function (OperationCallback callback). It prints a message indicating that it is performing an operation on the two integers and then invokes the callback function with the provided integers.

The addCallback and multiplyCallback functions are examples of callback functions that can be passed to performOperation. They perform addition and multiplication operations, respectively. In the main function, performOperation is called twice with different callback functions to demonstrate the use of callback arguments.

When you compile and run this program, the results are as shown here:

$ ./whoscalling
Performing operation on 10 and 5:
Sum: 15
Performing operation on 10 and 5:
Product: 50
bob@raspberrypi:~ $

The signal/slot system can also be used in other non-GUI programming, for example in asynchronous I/O (Linux sockets, pipes, etc.) event notification, or to associate timeout events with appropriate object instances and methods or functions. It's also very similar to topics we cover in Volume 2 of this series, in Python3 Sections 2.4.4 Multi-threaded Concurrency, and Section 2.4.5 Talking Threads. In that latter section we show that there are a variety of approaches to the solution of concurrent, multicore computation in Python3, which is similar to, for example, using locks, semaphores, event synchronization, condition objects or variables, barriers, and the Python3 **queue** module.

Signals and slots are a fundamental part of the Qt5 framework, and are used extensively in Qt-based applications to handle events, and implement what's known as the *observer pattern*. The observer pattern is a behavioral program-ming design pattern where an entity, known as the *Subject*, maintains a list of its dependents, known as *Observers*, that are notified of any state changes, typically by calling one of their methods.

Here's the scheme of how you can implement the observer pattern in Qt5 using signals and slots:

Subject (Observable):
The Subject is the entity that contains the information of interest to possibly multiple Observers. That entity emits signals when its state changes.

Observer:
The Observer is an entity that needs to be notified of changes in the subject. It connects to the subject's signals using slots.

This scheme outlines a simple implementation of the observer pattern in Qt5 using signals and slots, allowing objects to communicate changes in their state to interested observers.

Here's a further, brief explanation of the processes of signals and slots:

Signal:
A signal is emitted when a particular event occurs in an object. It represents a specific change or action. For example, a button press, a value changing, or a timer timing out can be events that emit signals.

Slot:
A slot is a function that can be connected to a signal. It is called in response to a particular signal being emitted. Slots are the functions that handle the events or changes represented by signals.

Connection:
Connecting a signal to a slot establishes a communication link between them. When the signal is emitted, the connected slot is called. Connections are typ-ically established using the QObject::connect() function.

The following Qt5 code places three widgets in a window, and defines interconnections between the signal elements and slot elements of those widgets.

Here's the code:

```
#include <QtGui>
#include <QApplication>
#include <QVBoxLayout>
#include <QLabel>
#include <QSpinBox>
#include <QSlider>
#include <QWidget>
#include <QObject>

int main(int argc, char **argv)
```

```
{
        QApplication a(argc, argv);
        QWidget window;
        QVBoxLayout* mainLayout = new QVBoxLayout(&window);
        QLabel* label = new QLabel("0");
        QSpinBox* spinBox = new QSpinBox;
        QSlider* slider = new QSlider(Qt::Horizontal);
        mainLayout->addWidget(label);
        mainLayout->addWidget(spinBox);
        mainLayout->addWidget(slider);
        QObject::connect(spinBox, SIGNAL(valueChanged(int)),
        label, SLOT(setNum(int)));
        QObject::connect(spinBox, SIGNAL(valueChanged(int)),
        slider, SLOT(setValue(int)));
        QObject::connect(slider, SIGNAL(valueChanged(int)),
        label, SLOT(setNum(int)));
        QObject::connect(slider, SIGNAL(valueChanged(int)),
        spinBox, SLOT(setValue(int)));
        window.show();
        return a.exec();
}
```

When you execute this program using the eight-step method, can you tell which are the interconnected Subject and Observer? What are the widgets, and how are they interconnected?

2.6 The GTK Framework

For our purposes in this chapter, GTK4 (formerly the GIMP Toolkit) is used for developing X Window System client applications with a GUI. Very similar to the Qt5 framework shown in Section 2.5, these applications range from the most basic up to entire windowing systems. GTK4 is a "cross-platform" widget toolkit for creating graphical user interfaces. Cross-platform means that a GTK4 program can be transposed from the X Window System environment to another operating system's environment easily, so that the GUI developed for the X Window System can have the look and feel of some other operating system's graphical environment.

GDK (GIMP Drawing Kit) is a higher-level suite of tools that provides functionality to underlying windowing and graphics system. Each user interface created by GTK4 consists of widgets. These are implemented in C using the Glib Object System (GObject), that provides an object-oriented "framework" for the C language. A framework basically allows an ordinary user to customize the GUIs that are created using their own code on top of the code already provided by the GObject framework.

GTK4 is one of the most popular toolkits for the Wayland and X11 Window System, along with the Qt5 framework.

The GTK4 library contains a set of graphical control elements. GTK4 is an object-oriented widget toolkit written in the C programming language; it uses GObject, that is the GLib object system, for the object orientation. While GTK4 is primarily targeted at windowing systems based upon X11 and Wayland, it works on other platforms. There is also an HTML5 back-end called Broadway.

GTK4 can be configured to change the look of the widgets drawn; this is done using different display engines. Several display engines exist which try to emulate the look of the native widgets on the platform in use.

The following sections on GTK4 are taken from the tutorial for API Version 4.0, available online at:

https://docs.gtk.org/gtk4/getting_started.html

2.6.1 Installing GTK4

We installed the latest release of this framework, at the time this book was written, by using the the following command:

$ **sudo apt install libgtk-4-dev**

2.6.2 GTK4 Basics

Widgets are organized in a hierarchy. The window widget is the main container. The user interface is then built by adding buttons, drop-down menus, input fields, and other widgets to the window. If you are creating complex user interfaces it is recommended to use GtkBuilder and its GTK4-specific markup description language, instead of assembling the interface manually. You can also use a visual user interface editor, like Glade. GTK4 is very similar to the X11 protocol structure, in that it is event-driven. The toolkit listens for events on the X server, such as a mouse click, and passes the event notification to your client application. You can compile a GTK program on a Raspberry Pi system, using gcc, with the following command:

gcc $(pkg-config --cflags gtk4) -o example-0 example-0.c $(pkg-config --libs gtk4)

As noted in the GTK4 tutorial listed in Section 2.6, if that compilation doesn't work, there are some options that are spelled out in detail. This general form compilation command worked on our Raspberry Pi OS, Debian Bookworm-based installation.

But before we actually executed the code we needed to use the following **export** command:

$ **export GTK_A11Y=none**

This avoided the following error:

Gtk-WARNING **: 09:52:39.702: Unable to acquire the address of the accessibility bus: GDBus.Error:org.freedesktop.DBus.Error. ServiceUnknown: The name org.a11y.Bus was not provided by any .service files. If you are attempting to run GTK without a11y support, GTK_ A11Y should be set to "none".

However, please note that this will disable accessibility features for the application.

If you need accessibility support and it's not working due to a missing service, you can try to install or enable the accessibility service. In many Linux distributions, the accessibility service is provided by at-spi2-core. You can check if it's installed and enable it as follows:

$ **sudo apt-get install at-spi2-core** # For Debian/Ubuntu

You may have to restart your system for the command to take effect. Plus, there are other options, such as checking for other missing D-Bus services.

2.6.3 Example GTK4 Programs

GTK Example 0
In the context of the GTK4 framework, a *signal-based* application refers to an application that utilizes signals and callbacks to respond to events and user interactions. GTK4 is the latest version of the library that this framework relies upon.

Signals in GTK4 are a mechanism for handling events, such as button clicks, mouse movements, and widget changes. In a signal-based application, you define event handlers (callbacks) that are executed when specific signals are emitted by widgets or other components of your GUI.

Here's how it works in practice:

1. Widgets, like buttons, sliders, or text entry fields, emit signals when users interact with them. For example, a button widget may emit a "clicked" signal when it's clicked by the user.
2. You can connect callback functions to these signals. These callback functions are essentially event handlers that get executed when the associated signal is emitted. You define these functions to specify what should happen in response to the signal.

3.   When the associated signal is emitted, GTK4 calls the connected call-back function, which allows you to respond to the event. For example, you might use a callback to update the content of a label when a button is clicked.

To give a simple example of a GTK4 program, we'll illustrate with a simple, signal-based application. This program will create an empty 200 × 200 pixel window.

Create a new file with the content below, named **example-0.c**.

```
#include <gtk/gtk.h>

static void
activate (GtkApplication* app,
      gpointer     user_data)
{
GtkWidget *window;

 window = gtk_application_window_new (app);
 gtk_window_set_title (GTK_WINDOW (window), "Raspberry Pi OS");
 gtk_window_set_default_size (GTK_WINDOW (window), 200, 200);
 gtk_widget_show (window);
}

int
main (int argc,
   char **argv)
{
 GtkApplication *app;
 int status;

 app = gtk_application_new ("org.gtk.example", G_APPLICATION_DEFAULT_FLAGS);
 g_signal_connect (app, "activate", G_CALLBACK (activate), NULL);
 status = g_application_run (G_APPLICATION (app), argc, argv);
 g_object_unref (app);

 return status;
}
```

You can compile the program above with GCC using:

gcc $(pkg-config --cflags gtk4) -o example-0 example-0.c $(pkg-config --libs gtk4)

where:

example-0.c is the name of the C source code file containing valid GTK4 commands,

example-0 is the name of the output executable image.

To execute the program, type the following:

$ ./example-0

A few takeaways from this Example are as follows:

This is a C program, and as such, doesn't use the Object Oriented Programming (OOP) paradigm. While GTK4 is primarily OOP, you can still use it in a procedural or imperative manner if you prefer, which is what is done in the Examples presented here. You can write GTK4 applications in languages like C, which are procedural in nature. However, even in a procedural language, you can still be working with GTK4's OOP architecture. That's because GTK4 itself is designed around OOP principles.

Note

A C *cast*, or *C-style cast*, is a way to convert or reinterpret the type of a variable or pointer. It allows you to change the data type of an expression to another data type.

In a GTK4 C program, the main() function creates a GtkApplication object.

GtkApplication selects an application identifier (some name), and passes it to gtk_application_new() as an argument. org.gtk.example is the name here. Finally, gtk_application_new() takes GApplicationFlags as input for your application.

The "activate signal" is connected to the activate() function above the main() function. The activate signal is given when your application is run with g_application_run() on the line below.

Within g_application_run(), the activate signal is forwarded, and activate() function is invoked. This is where the GTK4 window is constructed, so that a window appears on screen when the program is run. The call to gtk_application_window_new() creates a new GtkApplicationWindow, and stores it inside the window pointer. The window will have a frame, a title bar, and window controls dependent upon the Window Manager backend.

A window title is established using gtk_window_set_title(). This function takes a GtkWindow pointer and a string as input. As our window pointer is a GtkWidget pointer, we need to cast it to GtkWindow; instead of casting window via a typical C cast, like (GtkWindow*), window can be cast using the macro GTK_WINDOW(). GTK_WINDOW() will check if the pointer is an instance of the GtkWindow class, before casting, and give a warning if the check fails.

The window size is set using gtk_window_set_default_size(,) and the window is then shown by GTK4 via gtk_widget_show().

When you close the window, by (for example) pressing the X button, the g_application_run() call returns with a number which is saved inside an integer variable named status. Then the GtkApplication object is released from memory with g_object_unref(). Then the status integer is returned, and the application exits.

While the program is running, GTK4 is getting and perhaps processing events. These are typically input events caused by the user interaction, via mouse and keyboard, with the program, but also things like messages from the Wayfire window manager, or even from other applications running on your Raspberry Pi. GTK4 processes these, and then signals are displayed in the widgets. Interconnecting handlers for these signals is how you make your program do something in response to user input.

GTK Example 1

Interactivity with windows is an essential feature of a GUI. This example extends what was presented in example-0.c, by adding a button to the window, with the label "Raspberry Pi Rocks" in it. Type in the following code, using nano, with the name **example-1.c**

```
#include <gtk/gtk.h>

static void
print_rocks (GtkWidget *widget,
        gpointer  data)
{
  g_print ("Raspberry Pi Rocks\n");
}

static void
activate (GtkApplication *app,
        gpointer    user_data)
{
  GtkWidget *window;
  GtkWidget *button;
  GtkWidget *box;

  window = gtk_application_window_new (app);
  gtk_window_set_title (GTK_WINDOW (window), "Window");
  gtk_window_set_default_size (GTK_WINDOW (window), 200, 200);

  box = gtk_box_new (GTK_ORIENTATION_VERTICAL, 0);
  gtk_widget_set_halign (box, GTK_ALIGN_CENTER);
  gtk_widget_set_valign (box, GTK_ALIGN_CENTER);
```

```
gtk_window_set_child (GTK_WINDOW (window), box);

button = gtk_button_new_with_label ("Raspberry Pi Rocks");
g_signal_connect (button, "clicked", G_CALLBACK (print_rocks), NULL);
g_signal_connect_swapped (button, "clicked", G_CALLBACK (gtk_window_destroy),\
window);

gtk_box_append (GTK_BOX (box), button);

gtk_widget_show (window);
}

int
main (int argc,
    char **argv)
{
  GtkApplication *app;
  int status;

  app = gtk_application_new ("org.gtk.example", G_APPLICATION_DEFAULT_FLAGS);
  g_signal_connect (app, "activate", G_CALLBACK (activate), NULL);
  status = g_application_run (G_APPLICATION (app), argc, argv);
  g_object_unref (app);

  return status;
}
```

A few takeaways from this Example are as follows:

Two new **GtkWidget** pointers are established to achieve this, **button** and **box** pointers. The **box** variable stores a **GtkBox**, which is GTK's method of controlling the size and layout of buttons.

The **GtkBox** widget is created with **gtk_box_new()**, which takes a **GtkOrientation** enum value as a placeholder, or parameter. The button orientation in this box will be either horizontal or vertical. It doesn't matter in this particular example, since we're only defining one button. After initializing **box** with the newly created **GtkBox**, our code adds the **box** widget to the window widget, using **gtk_window_set_child()**.

Next, the **button** variable is initialized, pretty much the same way. **gtk_button_new_with_label()** is called, which returns a **GtkButton** to be stored in button. Then **button** is added to our **box**.

Using **g_signal_connect()**, the button is connected to a function in our app called **print_rocks()**, so that when the button is clicked, GTK will call this function. As the **print_rocks()** function does not use any data as input, NULL is passed to it. **print_rocks()** calls **g_print()** with the string "Raspberry Pi

Rocks", which will print Raspberry Pi Rocks in a terminal, if the GTK application was started from one.

After connecting **print_rocks()**, another signal is connected to the "clicked" state of the button, using **g_signal_connect_swapped()**. This function is similar to a **g_signal_connect()**, with the big difference being how the callback function is treated. **g_signal_connect_swapped()** allows you to specify what the callback function should take as parameter by letting you pass it as data. In this case the function being called back is **gtk_window_destroy()**, and the window pointer is passed to it. This has the effect that when the button is clicked, the whole GTK window is destroyed. If a normal **g_signal_connect()** were used here to connect the "clicked" signal with **gtk_window_destroy()**, then the function would be called on the button (which wouldn't work, since the function expects a GtkWindow as argument).

The rest of the code in example-1.c is identical to example-0.c.

Compile the above program with the following command:

gcc $(pkg-config --cflags gtk4) -o example-1 example-1.c $(pkg-config --libs gtk4)

and execute it in the same manner that you executed example-0.

GTK Example 2

The next example will show how to add several GtkWidgets to your GTK4 application.

When creating an application, you'll want to put more than one widget inside a window. When you do so, it becomes important to control how each widget is positioned and sized. This is where packing comes in.

GTK4 comes with a large variety of layout containers whose purpose it is to control the layout of the child widgets that are added to them. Here are some descriptions of these containers, taken from the GTK4 documentation:

GtkBox

The GtkBox widget arranges child widgets into a single row or column. Whether it is a row or column depends on the value of its GtkOrientable:orientation property. Within the other dimension, all children are allocated the same size. Of course, the GtkWidget:valign and GtkWidget:valign properties can be used on the children to influence their allocation.

GtkGrid

GtkGrid is a container which arranges its child widgets in rows and columns. It supports arbitrary positions and horizontal/vertical spans. Children are added using gtk_grid_attach(). They can span multiple rows or columns. It is also possible to add a child next to an existing child, using gtk_grid_attach_next_to(). To remove a child from the grid, use gtk_grid_remove(). The behavior of GtkGrid when several children occupy the same grid cell is undefined.

GtkRevealer
A GtkRevealer animates the transition of its child from invisible to visible. The style of transition can be controlled with gtk_revealer_set_transition_type(). These animations respect the GtkSettings:gtk-enable-animations setting.

GtkStack
GtkStack is a container which only shows one of its children at a time. In contrast to GtkNotebook, GtkStack does not provide a means for users to change the visible child. Instead, a separate widget such as GtkStackSwitcher or GtkStackSidebar can be used with GtkStack to provide this functionality.

GtkOverlay
GtkOverlay is a container which contains a single main child, on top of which it can place "overlay" widgets. The position of each overlay widget is determined by its GtkWidget:halign and GtkWidget:valign properties. E.g. a widget with both alignments set to GTK_ALIGN_START will be placed at the top left corner of the GtkOverlay container, whereas an overlay with halign set to GTK_ALIGN_CENTER and valign set to GTK_ALIGN_END will be placed a the bottom edge of the GtkOverlay, horizontally centered. The position can be adjusted by setting the margin properties of the child to non-zero values.

GtkPaned
A widget with two panes, arranged either horizontally or vertically. The division between the two panes is adjustable by the user by dragging a handle. Child widgets are added to the panes of the widget with gtk_paned_set_start_child() and gtk_paned_set_end_child(). The division between the two children is set by default from the size requests of the children, but it can be adjusted by the user. A paned widget draws a separator between the two child widgets and a small handle that the user can drag to adjust the division. It does not draw any relief around the children or around the separator. (The space in which the separator is is called the gutter.) Often, it is useful to put each child inside a GtkFrame so that the gutter appears as a ridge. No separator is drawn if one of the children is missing.

GtkExpander
GtkExpander allows the user to reveal its child by clicking on an expander triangle. This is similar to the triangles used in a GtkTreeView. Normally you use an expander as you would use a frame; you create the child widget and use gtk_expander_set_child() to add it to the expander. When the expander is toggled, it will take care of showing and hiding the child automatically.

The following example shows how the GtkGrid container lets you arrange several buttons. Type it into a file named example-2.c using your favorite text editor:

```
#include <gtk/gtk.h>


static void
print_rocks (GtkWidget *widget,
        gpointer   data)
{
 g_print ("Raspberry Pi Rocks\n");
}

static void
activate (GtkApplication *app,
      gpointer       user_data)
{
 GtkWidget *window;
 GtkWidget *grid;
 GtkWidget *button;

 /* create a new window, and set its title */
 window = gtk_application_window_new (app);
 gtk_window_set_title (GTK_WINDOW (window), "Window Rocks");

 /* Here we construct the container that is going pack our buttons */
 grid = gtk_grid_new ();

 /* Pack the container in the window */
 gtk_window_set_child (GTK_WINDOW (window), grid);

 button = gtk_button_new_with_label ("Button A");
 g_signal_connect (button, "clicked", G_CALLBACK (print_rocks), NULL);
 /* Place the first button in the grid cell (0, 0), and make it fill
 * just 1 cell horizontally and vertically (ie no spanning)
 */
 gtk_grid_attach (GTK_GRID (grid), button, 0, 0, 1, 1);

 button = gtk_button_new_with_label ("Button B");
 g_signal_connect (button, "clicked", G_CALLBACK (print_rocks), NULL);

 /* Place the second button in the grid cell (1, 0), and make it fill
 * just 1 cell horizontally and vertically (ie no spanning)
 */
 gtk_grid_attach (GTK_GRID (grid), button, 1, 0, 1, 1);

 button = gtk_button_new_with_label ("Quit");
 g_signal_connect_swapped (button, "clicked", G_CALLBACK (gtk_window_destroy),\
window);
```

```
/* Place the Quit button in the grid cell (0, 1), and make it
 * span 2 columns.
 */
gtk_grid_attach (GTK_GRID (grid), button, 0, 1, 2, 1);

gtk_widget_show (window);

}

int
main (int argc,
    char **argv)
{
  GtkApplication *app;
  int status;

  app = gtk_application_new ("org.gtk.example",
G_APPLICATION_DEFAULT_FLAGS);
  g_signal_connect (app, "activate", G_CALLBACK (activate), NULL);
  status = g_application_run (G_APPLICATION (app), argc, argv);
  g_object_unref (app);

  return status;
}
```

Compile the program with the following command:

gcc $(pkg-config --cflags gtk4) -o example-2 example-2.c $(pkg-config --libs gtk4)

and execute it in the same manner as you did with example-0 and example-1.

2.6.4 Using Geany to Build and Execute a GTK4 Program

In the last section, you installed GTK4, used a text editor to create the source code for a GTK4 program, and then compiled it with the given command shown there. But what if you wanted to use an Integrated Development Environment (IDE) such as Geany, to do the same thing? Geany comes pre-installed on the latest Debian Bookworm-based Raspberry Pi OS. IDE creation and building is more efficient, and easier to do than the legacy text-editing methods of code creation. In Volume 3, we illustrated the use of Geany in a number of examples.

To use Geany for building and executing a GTK4 program, follow these general steps:

1. Install GTK4 Required Software:

Make sure you have Geany and the necessary development tools installed. Additionally, ensure that you have the GTK4 library and its development files installed. The command to install GTK4 is **sudo apt install libgtk-4-dev**

Also, **export GTK_A11Y=none** should be done on the command line before compilation is done.

2. Create a GTK4 Project:

Open Geany and create a new project for your GTK4 application. Set up your source code files and any other project-specific files.

3. Configure Build Settings:

In Geany, go to the "Build" menu and select "Set Build Commands". Configure the build commands for compiling and linking your GTK4 program. Use pkg-config to get the necessary compilation flags for GTK4. For example:

Compile: gcc -Wall -c "%f" 'pkg-config --cflags gtk4'
Build: gcc -o "%e" "%f" 'pkg-config --libs gtk4'

4. Write GTK4 Code:

Write your GTK4 application code in the source files. Ensure that you include the necessary GTK4 headers and follow the GTK4 programming conventions.

5. Save and Build:

Save your files and then build your project using Geany's build commands. Check the build output for any errors.

6. Execute the Program:

Once the build is successful, you can execute your GTK4 program directly from Geany. Use the "Execute" button or press F5.

7. Debugging:

If you encounter issues, use Geany's debugging features. Set breakpoints, inspect variables, and step through your code to identify and fix problems.

Remember that these are general steps, and the specifics may vary based on your project structure and specific development environment.

2.7 Gnuplot and the X Window System

To complete our study of Wayland, and the X Window System on a Raspberry Pi, we turn in this section to a plotting package named gnuplot. For our purposes, there is a very important reason for using gnuplot: it makes it possible to conform to a modularized idea of using the X Window System. You can have a discreet module create data, another discreet module create and orchestrate the window display you want to present the data in, and then finally have a discreet module map the data into the window display.

We encourage you to compare the particular use case we show in this section, and this modularized approach, to the specific design and programming details and methodologies that would accomplish the same end result in:

* a purely-Xlib or XCB C program,

* an "augmented" C program for the GTK framework, or

* a C++ Qt framework program.

This model's particular modularized use case does not replace using Xlib/ XCB, GTK, or Qt as we have shown them in the previous sections of this chapter. In addition, the window(s) you create are framed and constrained to a large extent by the particular window management system you are using. For example, by default we are using Wayfire, which has its own look and feel, window dressing, etc.

2.7.1 Installing gnuplot

There are two ways you can install gnuplot on your Raspberry Pi system.

The first way is the simplest: from the Raspberry Pi Menu, make the choice Preferences > Add/Remove Software. Then enter **gnuplot**, and press **<Enter>**. Put a check mark next to **Command-line driven interactive plotting program**, and click on the **Apply** button. The appropriate packages will be installed, along with the gnuplot-X11 package so you can get X Window System terminal output. At the time of the writing of this book, the latest gnuplot version and patches available was gnuplot5, which gave us gnuplot 5.4.1.

Or you can go the gnuplot homepage at www.gnuplot.info and follow the download and installation instructions found there.

Type the following to launch, and then exit from gnuplot:

$ **gnuplot**
>   G N U P L O T
>   Version 5.4 patchlevel 1   last modified 2020-12-01
>
>   Copyright (C) 1986-1993, 1998, 2004, 2007-2020
>   Thomas Williams, Colin Kelley and many others
>
>   gnuplot home: www.gnuplot.info
>   faq, bugs, etc: type "help FAQ"
>   immediate help: type "help"   (plot window: hit 'h')

Terminal type is now 'qt'
gnuplot> **exit**
$

2.7.2 What gnuplot Is and Basic Syntax for Interactive and Batch Modes

Gnuplot is an X Window System command-line data and scientific graphing package for Linux and UNIX. Gnuplot supports many types of plots in either 2D and 3D. It can draw using lines, points, boxes, contours, vector fields, surfaces, and various associated text. It also supports various specialized plot types. Gnuplot also supports many different types of output formats: interactive screen terminals (with mouse and keyboard input), printers, and to a variety file formats (eps, emf, fig, jpeg, LaTeX, pdf, png, postscript, etc.). Recent additions in Release 5 include wxWidgets terminals, and Qt-based graphics terminals.

The "interactive" command language is case sensitive. All command names have standardized abbreviations. Any number of interactive commands may appear on a line, separated by semicolons (;). String arguments to interactive commands may be delimited by either single or double quotes, although there are some differences in the interpretation of quoting.

Example:

gnuplot> **set title "My First Plot"; plot 'data'; print "all done!"**

Commands may extend over several input lines by ending each line (except the last one!) with a backslash (\). The backslash must be the last character on each line. In gnuplot documentation, curly braces ({}) denote optional arguments, and a vertical bar (|) separates mutually exclusive choices. Gnuplot keywords or help topics are indicated by backquotes, or are in **bold-face** type. Angle brackets (<>) are used to mark replaceable tokens. In many cases, a default value of the token will be taken for optional arguments if the token is omitted, but these cases are not always denoted with braces around the angle brackets. For built-in help on any topic, type **help**, followed by the name of the topic, or help? to get a menu of available topics.

When run from the Raspberry Pi command line in what is known as "Batch Mode", gnuplot is launched by using the syntax:

$ **gnuplot {OPTIONS} file1 file2 ...**

where:

file1, file2,... are validly formatted input files for the load command. The load command executes gnuplot commands contained in file1, file2... as if each line of the specified input file(s) had been typed in interactively. Files created by the save command can later be reloaded. Any text file containing valid gnuplot commands can be created, and then executed by the load command. Files being loaded may themselves contain load or call commands.

On X Window System-based systems, you can use:

$ **gnuplot {X11OPTIONS} {OPTIONS} file1 file2 ...**

2.7.3 Batch Mode Examples

Gnuplot may be executed in either Batch or Interactive modes, and the two may even be mixed together in valid ways. Any Batch mode arguments are assumed to be either program options (where the first character is -) or names of files containing gnuplot commands. The option **-e "command"** may be used to force execution of a gnuplot command. Each file or command string will be executed in the order specified. The special filename "-"indicates that commands are to be read from stdin. Gnuplot exits after the last file is processed. If no load files and no command strings are specified, gnuplot accepts interactive input from stdin.

Both the **exit** and **quit** commands terminate the current command file and load the next one, until all have been processed.

Examples:

To launch an interactive session:

$ **gnuplot**

To launch a Batch session using two gnuplot command files "input1" and "input2":

$ **gnuplot input1 input2**

To launch an interactive session after an initialization file "header" and followed by another command file "trailer":

$ **gnuplot header · trailer**

To give gnuplot commands directly on the Raspberry Pi command line, using the "-persist" option so that the plot remains on the screen afterwards:

$ **gnuplot -persist -e "set title 'Sine curve'; plot sin(x)"**

To set user-defined variables a and s prior to executing commands from a file:

$ **gnuplot -e "a=2; s='file.png'" input.gpl**

2.7.4 Batch Mode Plotting to a Terminal with Persistence of the Plot Window

Gnuplot terminals open separate display windows on the screen into which plots are drawn. One of the most important plot command options is the persist option. It tells gnuplot to leave these windows open when the main program exits. It has no effect on subsequent interactive terminal output. For example if you issue the following two batch mode commands:

$ **gnuplot -persist -e 'plot [-5:5] sinh(x)'**
$ **gnuplot -persist -e 'plot [-5:5] tanh(x)'**

After the first command, gnuplot will open a display window using the default terminal type, draw the sinh plot into it, and then exit, leaving the display window containing the sinh plot on the screen. After the second command, a new display window will open, using the default terminal type, and the tanh plot will be drawn into it.

2.7.5 Interactive Mode and Terminal Type

If you type **gnuplot** on the Bash command line, you enter what's known as gnuplot's "Interactive Mode". We gave a simple illustration of this mode in Section 2.7.1. Another simple example of this is as follows:

gnuplot> **plot [-5:5] tanh(x)**

Once this interactive command is given, a window opens on-screen that shows you a plot of tanh(x), with the x range varying from –5 to +5.

Without changing the default terminal type on our Raspberry Pi system when we installed gnuplot, as shown in Section 2.7.1, the terminal type was set to qt 0, or a Qt terminal. To find out what the current terminal is set to, type:

gnuplot> **show terminal**

In a Qt terminal, there are some menu choices seen at the top of the window, which we list here from left to right:

File Output—copy to clipboard, print, export to pdf, etc.

Replot (a green circular arrow)—replots the window

Grid—places a grid on the window

Previous Zoom (a minus signed magnifier)—goes to the previous zoom

Next Zoom (a plus sign magnifier)—goes to the next zoom

Settings—Allows changes of terminal configuration settings like background color, replot on resize, etc.

To zoom in a Qt terminal window, click the right-most mouse button once to designate a corner of the plot you want to zoom to, and then click the right-most button again to designate the opposite corner of the zoom.

In addition to persistence in both Batch and Interactive modes, there are various settings of a plot window that are interesting in this section. The following interactive commands lets you:

a) set the terminal type to x11,

b) designate a specific X Window System display ID (0x3200006) within which to plot,

c) have that window persist after the program exits,

d) set its size to 700 x 500,

e) plot sin(x) in that display, and

f) reset gnuplot to its defaults.

These settings and operations in gnuplot Interactive Mode are achieved as follows:

```
gnuplot> set term x11 window "0x3200006" persist size 700,500
Terminal type set to 'x11'
Options are "XID 0x3200006 persist enhanced size 700,500"
gnuplot> plot sin(x)
gnuplot> reset
gnuplot> exit
```

The important characteristic of using gnuplot that the first two commands illustrate is that if you have previously created an X Window System display using Xlib or XCB programming commands, and it has the display ID of 0x3200006, your plot of sin(x) will be drawn in that display. This now makes it possible to conform to our modularized idea of using the X Window System. You can have a discreet module create the data using your favorite programming language (C, Python, C++, bash, etc.), design the window display you want to present the data in with an Xlib or XCB module, and then map the data into the window with either a gnuplot batch or interactive module. We encourage you to compare, in this particular use case, this modularized approach to the specific details and methodologies of accomplishing the same end result in either a purely Xlib or XCB C program, in an "augmented" C program for the GTK framework, or in a C++ Qt framework program. Certainly this particular modularized use case does not replace using Xlib/XCB, GTK, or Qt in the situations where they excel, or are more germane to the task(s) at hand.

In-Chapter Exercise

   2.25   In gnuplot, type **set terminal**

You'll get a listing of the terminal types available for you to set for your installation of gnuplot.

The terminal types actually available to you are dependent upon what driver library packages you have installed previous to installing gnuplot!

Experiment with setting the terminal to some of the different types shown by the set terminal command in gnuplot.

2.7.6 Plotting in Interactive Mode

There are four basic gnuplot commands that create plots: **plot, splot, replot,** and **refresh. plot** generates 2D plots, **splot** generates 3D plots (2D projections onto a picture plane). **replot** appends its arguments to the previous **plot** or **splot** and executes the modified command. **refresh** re-executes the previous **plot** or **splot** command using previously stored data rather than rereading data from a file.

2.7.6.1 Plotting Data Contained in a File

Data contained in a file can be plotted with plot or splot by specifying the name of the properly formatted data file (enclosed in single or double quotes) on the `plot` command line.

Syntax:
```
plot '<file_name>' {binary <binary list>}
          {{nonuniform} matrix}
          {index <index list> | index "<name>"}
          {every <every list>}
          {skip <number-of-lines>}
          {using <using list>}
          {smooth <option>}
          {volatile} {noautoscale}
```

A short explanation of the arguments is: binary allows data entry from a binary file, index selects which data sets in a multi-data-set file are to be plotted, every specifies which points within a single data set are to be plotted, using determines how the columns within a single line are to be interpreted, and smooth allows for simple interpolation and approximation. splot has a similar syntax, but does not support the smooth option.

Data files should contain at least one data point per line (using can select one data point from the line). Lines beginning with # will be treated as comments and ignored.

Each data point represents an (x,y) pair. For plots with error bars or error bars with lines, each data point is (x,y,ydelta), (x,y,ylow,yhigh), (x,y,xdelta), (x,y,xlow,xhigh), or (x,y,xlow,xhigh,ylow,yhigh).

If line numbering is present at the beginning of each line of a data file, that numbering must be separated by white space (one or more blanks or tabs) from the remainder of the data on that line, unless a format specifier is provided by the using option. This white space divides each line into columns. However, white space inside a pair of double quotes is ignored when counting columns, so the following datafile line has three columns: **1.0 "second column" 3.0**

A data file can contain only one column (the y value). If x is omitted, gnuplot provides integer values for x, starting at 0.

In-Chapter Exercises

2.26 Create a data file of interest to you with your favorite text editor, containing at least 20 paired x-y data points. Then use gnuplot to read that data in from the file, and plot it in an XCB-created window.

2.27 Plot the following functions in a single, persistent Xlib-created window: 2tan(x), sin(x), cos (x), tanh(x).

2.7.6.2 Plotting Styles

There are many 2-D and 3-D plotting styles available in gnuplot, which have evolved over the long history of gnuplot use on both UNIX and Linux systems. We give a listing of them as they pertain to a particular kind of graphical presentation method (if applicable), and then give a few descriptions of the most important ones. For example, the commands **set style data** and **set style function** change the default plotting style for subsequent plot and splot commands. You can also specify the plot style explicitly as part of the plot or splot command. If you want to mix plot styles within a single plot, you must specify the plot style for each component.

An example of this would be as follows:

gnuplot> **plot 'statistics' with boxes, sin(x) with lines**

Each plot style has its own expected set of data entries in a data file. For example, by default the lines style expects either a single column of y values (with implicit x ordering) or a pair of columns with x in the first and y in the second.

Descriptive Statistics: Boxerrorbars, Boxes, Boxplot, Boxxyerrorbars, Candlesticks, Circles, Ellipses, Dots, Histograms, Newhistogram, Xerrorbars, Xyerrorbars, Yerrorbars, Xerrorlines, Xyerrorlines, Yerrorlines.

General Graphics: Filledcurves, Fillsteps, Histeps, Image, Impulses, Labels, Lines, Linespoints, Parallelaxes, Points, Polar, Steps, Vectors, 3D (surface) plots, 2D projection.

2.7.7 Obtaining Help on Important Commands

In Interactive mode, if you type help **topic**, where **topic** is any of the major or sub-topics listed in Table 2.9, you will get verbose help on that topic. We list all major topics in gnuplot help, and their major sub-topics for your convenience here.

TABLE 2.9

gnuplot Command Help Matrix

bind	call	cd	clear	do
evaluate	exit	fit	help	history
if	import	load	lower	pause
plot				
	acsplines	axes	bezier	binary
	cnormal	csplines	cumulative	data
	datafile	errorbars	errorlines	every
	example	for	frequency	functions
	index	kdensity	mcsplines	parametri
	ranges	sampling	sbezier	smooth
	special-filnames	style	thru	title
	uniques	unwrap	using	volatile
	with			
print	printerr	pwd	quit	raise
refresh	replot	reread	reset	save
set-show				
	angles	arrow	autoscale	bars
	bmargin	border	boxwidth	cbdata
	cbdtics	cblabel	cbmtics	cbrange
	cbtics	clabel	clip	cntrlabel
	cntrparam	color	colorbox	colorsequence
	contour	dashtype	decimalsign	dgrid3d

(continued)

TABLE 2.9 (Continued)

gnuplot Command Help Matrix

	dummy	encoding	fit	fontpath
	format	grid	hidden3d	history
	historysize	isosamples	key	
	linetype	link	lmargin	loadpath
	locale	logscale	macros	mapping
	margins	monochrome	mouse	multiplot
	mx2tics	mxtics	my2tics	mytics
	mztics	object	offsets	origin
	output	palette	parametric	paxis
	pm3d	pointintervalbox	pointsize	polar
	print	psdir	raxis	rmargin
	rrange	rtics	samples	size
	style	surface	table	terminal
	termoption	tics	ticscale	ticslevel
	timefmt	timestamp	title	tmargin
	trange	urange	view	vrange
	x2data	x2dtics	x2label	x2mtics
	x2range	x2tics	x2zeroaxis	xdata
	xdtics	xlabel	xmtics	xrange
	xtics	xyplane	xzeroaxis	y2data
	y2dtics	y2label	y2mtics	y2range
	y2tics	y2zeroaxis	ydata	ydtics
	ylabel	ymtics	yrange	ytics
	yzeroaxis	zdata	zdtics	zero
	zeroaxis	zlabel	zmtics	zrange
	ztics	zzeroaxis		
shell				
splot				
	binary	datafile	errorbars	errorlines
	example	for	grid_data	parametric
	ranges	style	surfaces	title
	with			
stats	system	test	undefine	unset
update	while			

2.7.8 Qt and X11 Terminals

In this sub-section, we describe the parameters of setting the two most important terminal types that are useful in gnuplot for the Raspberry Pi, and also for our modularized X Window System model. They are the Qt and X11 terminals.

2.7.8.1 Qt Terminal Type Parameters

The mainstay qt terminal device generates output in a separate window, using the Qt library.

a. **enhanced (or noenhanced)**: This parameter determines whether enhanced text mode is enabled or disabled. Enhanced text mode allows you to use special formatting and symbols in labels and titles. For example:

    set terminal qt enhanced (enables enhanced text mode)
    set terminal qt noenhanced (disables enhanced text mode)

b. **persist (or nopersist)**: This parameter specifies whether the Qt window should remain open after plotting. Enabling persist allows you to interact with the plot and keep it open, while nopersist closes the window when the script execution finishes. For example:

    set terminal qt persist (keeps the window open)
    set terminal qt nopersist (closes the window)

2.7.8.2 X11 Terminal Type Parameters

The terminal type useful for our modularized X Window System model is x11.

a. **enhanced (or noenhanced)**: Similar to the Qt terminal, this parameter controls enhanced text mode for the X11 terminal. It allows you to use special formatting and symbols in labels and titles. For example:

    set terminal x11 enhanced (enables enhanced text mode)
    set terminal x11 noenhanced (disables enhanced text mode)

b. **persist (or nopersist)**: This parameter specifies whether the X11 window should remain open after plotting. Enabling persist allows you to interact with the plot and keep it open, while nopersist closes the window when the script execution finishes. For example:

    set terminal x11 persist (keeps the window open)
    set terminal x11 nopersist (closes the window)

c. **title "Your Window Title"**: You can set a custom title for the X11 window. For example:

    set terminal x11 title "My Plot"

Here's an example of how you can use these parameters when setting the terminal type:

Set the terminal type to Qt with enhanced text and a persisting window
set terminal qt enhanced persist

\# Set the terminal type to X11 with a custom window title and enhanced text
set terminal x11 title "Custom Title" enhanced

\# Plot your data or functions
plot sin(x)

2.7.9 Plotting in Multiple Windows or Multiple Graphs in One Window

As seen in Section 2.7.5, you can plot graphs in multiple discreet windows by setting the current terminal to x11 window <n>, which outputs the graph to window number n.

Most importantly, as shown in that section, the gnuplot specification of an x11 terminal can connect to X windows previously created by an outside application via the window option.

The window option requires a string containing the X ID for the window in hexadecimal format as an option argument. Gnuplot uses that external X window as a container. In this way, gnuplot's mouse features work within the contained plot window. To repeat the example of setting the terminal type interactively:

gnuplot> **set term x11 window "0x360001"**

A plot window created in this way can be closed by pressing the letter **q** while that window is the active window (mouse cursor rolled into it), or by closing it from the desktop manager window border, and clicking the (X) in the upper right corner of the window.

Additionally, consider the following gnuplot Batch mode program:

```
set multiplot layout 2,2 rowsfirst
# --- GRAPH sin
set label 1 'x' at graph 0.92,0.9 font ',8'
plot sin(x) with lines ls 1 dt 2
# --- GRAPH cos
set label 1 'y' at graph 0.92,0.9 font ',8'
plot cos(x) with lines ls 1 dt 3
# --- GRAPH tan
set label 1 'z' at graph 0.92,0.9 font ',8'
plot tan(x) with lines ls 1 dt 4
# --- GRAPH hyperbolic tan
set label 1 't' at graph 0.92,0.9 font ',8'
plot tanh(x) with lines ls 1 dt 5
unset multiplot
```

It uses the **multiplot** option of the **set** command to "tile" the single current window into a 2 by 2 matrix, and then proceeds to plot graphs of sin, cos, tan, and tanh in each of the tiles of that single window. Also, it uses the

set command to place labels on each graph, and the **with** option of the **plot** command to customize the line type and color of each graphed function.

You can test these commands, one at a time, in gnuplot, to see the results they yield. To do this, on the gnuplot command line:

```
Terminal type is now 'qt'
gnuplot> set multiplot layout 2,2 rowsfirst
multiplot> set label 1 'x' at graph 0.92,0.9 font ',8'
multiplot> plot sin(x) with lines ls 1 dt 2
multiplot> set label 1 'y' at graph 0.92,0.9 font ',8'
multiplot> plot cos(x) with lines ls 1 dt 3
multiplot> set label 1 'z' at graph 0.92,0.9 font ',8'
multiplot> plot tan(x) with lines ls 1 dt 4
multiplot> set label 1 't' at graph 0.92,0.9 font ',8'
multiplot> plot tanh(x) with lines ls 1 dt 5
multiplot> unset multiplot
```

The resulting multiplot command is shown in Figure 2.10.

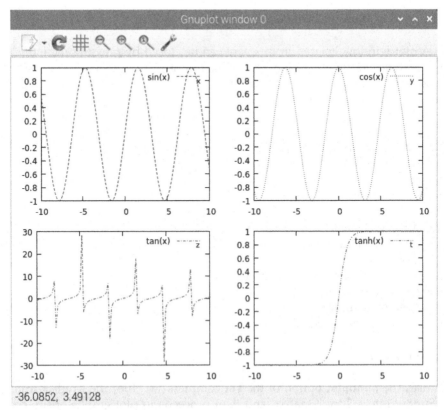

FIGURE 2.10
Gnuplot multiplot display.

The syntax, and other information concerning the multiplot option is as follows, as obtained from the gnuplot help command:

The command `set multiplot` places `gnuplot` in the multiplot mode, in which several plots are placed next to each other on the same page or screen window.

set multiplot
      { title \<page title> {font \<fontspec>} {enhanced|noenhanced} }
      { layout \<rows>,\<cols>
      {rowsfirst|columnsfirst} {downwards|upwards}
      {scale \<xscale>{,\<yscale>}} {offset \<xoff>{,\<yoff>}}
      {margins \<left>,\<right>,\<bottom>,\<top>}
      {spacing \<xspacing>{,\<yspacing>}}

set multiplot {next|previous}
      unset multiplot

For some terminals, no plot is displayed until the command `unset multiplot` is given, which causes the entire page to be drawn and then returns gnuplot

to its normal single-plot mode. For other terminals, each separate `plot` command produces an updated display.

The 'clear' command is used to erase the rectangular area of the page that will be used for the next plot. This is typically needed to inset a small plot inside a larger plot.

Any labels or arrows that have been defined will be drawn for each plot according to the current size and origin (unless their coordinates are defined in the 'screen' system). Just about everything else that can be 'set' is applied to each plot, too. If you want something to appear only once on the page, for instance a single time stamp, you'll need to put a 'set time'/'unset time' pair around one of the 'plot', 'splot', or 'replot' commands within the 'set multiplot'/'unset multiplot' block.

The multiplot title is separate from the individual plot titles, if any. Space is reserved for it at the top of the page, spanning the full width of the canvas.

The commands 'set origin' and 'set size' must be used to correctly position each plot if no layout is specified or if fine tuning is desired. See 'set origin' and 'set size' for details of their usage.

Example:
    set multiplot
    set size 0.4,0.4
    set origin 0.1,0.1
    plot cos(x)
    unset multiplot

This displays a plot of cos(x) stacked above a plot of sin(x).

'set size' and 'set origin' refer to the entire plotting area used for each plot. Please also see 'set term size'. If you want to have the axes themselves line up, you can guarantee that the margins are the same size with the 'set margin' commands. See 'set margin' for their use. Note that the margin settings are absolute, in character units, so the appearance of the graph in the remaining space will depend on the screen size of the display device, e.g., perhaps quite different on a video display and a printer.

   With the 'layout' option you can generate simple multiplots without having to give the 'set size' and 'set origin' commands before each plot: Those are generated automatically, but can be overridden at any time. With 'layout' the display will be divided by a grid with <rows> rows and <cols> columns. This grid is filled rows first or columns first depending on whether the corresponding option is given in the multiplot command.

In-Chapter Exercise

   2.28   Execute the Examples from gnuplot's multiplot help in windows created by the compiled Xlib program simple1_white.c, found above in Section 2.3.9.5.

2.8 Summary

The operation of the Raspberry Pi OS is greatly improved, from the ordinary user perspective, through the modern use of a *graphical user interface* (GUI). A traditional and common GUI for Linux is built upon a display and network protocol called the X Window System. The protocol used by the Debian Bookworm-based Raspberry Pi OS is Wayland. A GUI system can be classified as either *integrated* or *nonintegrated*. A nonintegrated system generally utilizes only the functionality of a window manager. An integrated system generally couples the window manager with other higher-level programs that achieve *desktop management* and *session management*. Examples of integrated systems are Gnome, KDE, Plasma, and Xfce.

   The X Window System, as a display and network protocol, contains device-specific drivers for Intel-based and ARM-based hardware. The X Window System is used for networked graphical interaction between a user and one or more computer systems. The chief arbiter of the interactive dialog between user and computer system is the *window manager*. The Wayfire compositor, and window manager, offers all of the amenities of other popular window systems, and additionally allows you to manage the graphical output from the entire contingent of application programs available. The user interface has two basic parts: the *application user interface* (AUI), which is how each client application presents itself in one or more windows on the server screen display, and the window manager or *management interface*, which controls the display of and organizes all client windows.

The basic model of interactivity in the X Window System is an *event–request* loop between the application *client* and the graphical *server*. With applications written for the X Window System, the client application can process input events, do the work necessary to form a response to the events, and then output the responses as requests for graphical output to the server.

The X Window System is highly customizable to suit the interactive needs of a wide range of users. In this chapter we covered two approaches to changing the appearance and functionality of a nonintegrated window system, and the window manager as well. Our approach involved changing the characteristics of applications that run under the X Window System by specifying command line options.

We covered the functionality of one of the predominant open-source integrated desktop management systems. We showed how this system can be used to expedite your work within the Raspberry Pi environment, particularly with regard to personal productivity and file management operations. We specifically showed the customization possible within this system to allow a user to work more efficiently.

We showed several elementary sample client application programs for the X Window System, coded to call upon four standard and very common toolkit libraries, Xlib, XCB, Qt, and GTK. We stressed the two most important aspects of client application program creation for the beginner:

- A client application program has two parts: a data generation part that uses code in C, C++, or another high-level programming language to produce the numbers, text, files, and data structures; and a user interface (UI) part which produces the actual graphics that display the data generation part.
- A client application program is made up of initialization, event–request loop, and cleanup sections.

We also showed many detailed examples of the toolkit code itself and what the code accomplished in the context of the sample programs.

Xlib and XCB programs, and a vast collection of legacy X Window System applications, are primarily designed to work with the X Window System, and they may not run natively on Wayland without a compatibility layer like XWayland. Wayland is a different display protocol and has a different architecture compared to X.

If you have Xlib and XCB programs that you want to run on a Wayland-based desktop environment without XWayland, you need to adapt or rewrite those programs to use Wayland's native protocol. Wayland offers a more modern and secure display and networking protocol, but it requires applications to be compatible with it. This typically involves using libraries like wlroots and implementing the Wayland protocol in your applications.

In summary, running Xlib and XCB programs directly on Wayland without XWayland may not be straightforward and could require significant changes to the applications. Most Linux distributions use Xwayland, including the latest version of the Raspberry Pi OS, to provide compatibility for running X applications on Wayland-based desktops.

3

The GNU Emacs Editor

3.0 Objectives

* To explain the general utility of editing text files on a Raspberry Pi system
* To show the basic capabilities of GNU Emacs
* To illustrate some of the important ways of customizing this editor
* To cover the commands and primitives:

cp, Emacs, ls, pwd, sh, who

3.1 Introduction

Question: Why use Emacs, rather than Geany, Thonny, or Visual Studio Code?

Answer: The basic process of typing text into Emacs is very similar to those Integral Development Environment (IDE) systems. But IDEs allow you to use that text in a more sophisticated, and necessarily complex way. Perhaps you just want to create the body of an email message as plain text, and then email a friend that message from within your text creation tool. The choice between using Emacs and an IDE like Geany, Thonny, or Visual Studio Code really comes down to personal preferences, and the specific needs of the developer in perhaps a team-oriented coding environment. Each tool has its own strengths and weaknesses, and the best choice depends on the individual's chosen workflow, programming languages, and requirements. Here are some reasons why a beginner might choose Emacs over other IDEs:

I.   Extensibility and Customization:

    1.   Emacs: Emacs is known for its powerful and extensible nature. It's highly customizable, and users can write custom scripts in

Emacs Lisp to extend the functionality of the editor itself. This makes it suitable for a wide range of tasks beyond coding, such as text editing that approaches the boundary of word processing, task management, and more.

2. IDEs: While modern IDEs offer customization to some extent, they may not be as flexible as Emacs in terms of deeper forms of personalized customization and extension.

II. Lightweight and Speed:

1. Emacs: Emacs is lightweight (consumes less system resources, such as main memory) compared to some IDEs, making it fast and efficient, especially on older hardware.

2. IDEs: Some IDEs, like Visual Studio Code, might be more resource-intensive due to their feature-rich nature.

III. Text Editing Features:

1. Emacs: Emacs is renowned for its powerful text editing capabilities. It has a wide range of keyboard shortcuts and commands for manipulating text efficiently.

2. IDEs: While IDEs also provide robust text editing features, Emacs enthusiasts often appreciate the depth and efficiency of Emacs for text-related tasks.

IV. Learning Curve:

1. Emacs: Emacs has a steeper learning curve, but users who invest time in learning it can become highly productive.

2. IDEs: Some IDEs are designed to be more user-friendly and may have a gentler learning curve, making them more approachable for beginners.

V. Coding Language Support:

1. Emacs: Emacs supports a wide variety of programming languages and file types.

2. IDEs: Depending on the IDE, language support might be optimized for specific ecosystems. For example, Visual Studio Code has a rich ecosystem and excellent support for languages like JavaScript and Python, and integration with GitHub for pull requests, and branch maintenance there.

VI. Community and Documentation:

1. Emacs: Emacs is the traditional UNIX/Linux text editor, and has a long history and a dedicated community. There are extensive documentation and a wealth of user-contributed packages.

2. IDEs: Popular IDEs also have active communities and documentation, but the depth and breadth might vary.

VII. Cross-Platform Compatibility:

1. Emacs: Emacs is highly portable and can run on various operating systems, Raspberry Pi OS being one of them.
2. IDEs: Most modern IDEs are also cross-platform, providing consistent experiences on different operating systems.

The choice between Emacs and an IDE really comes down to personal preference and workflow. Some developers prefer the lightweight and highly customizable nature of Emacs, while others may appreciate the integrated features and user-friendly interfaces of modern IDEs. It's worth trying out different tools to find the one that best fits your needs and preferences.

As noted in the answer to our primary question, the Emacs editor is the most complex and customizable of the Raspberry Pi keystroke-command text editors, and it gives you the most freedom, flexibility, and control over the way you edit text files. It can format text for very specific technical applications, such as program source code development, more effectively than a word processor. Its use in that application makes the process of program development more efficient. In addition, from within the Emacs program (deploying multiple windows) you can accomplish a wide variety of personal productivity and operating system tasks, such as sending e-mail and executing shell commands and scripts.

But along with more control, specificity, and capabilities comes a much steeper learning curve, which brings with it a more complex keystroke command structure. This complexity can be offset in part for some users, and totally for others, by using the graphical forms of input and command execution, that we will emphasize in some of the sections that follow.

As mentioned above, if you cannot run a "graphical" Emacs (as we do exclusively by running it in an interactive shell, GUI window in this section) because you are working in a login shell, text-only console or terminal.

No worries.

You can still gain access to the Menu Bar at the top of the Emacs screen by pressing <Esc> on the keyboard and then pressing the single back quote (`) key. You can then descend through the menu bar choices by pressing the letter key of the menu choice you want to make. For example, pressing the **f** key on your keyboard gives you access to the File pull-down menu choices, and then pressing the **s** key allows you to save the current buffer. The ways of descending and ascending these menus, and making menu choices, is rather intuitive, and we suggest you experiment as much as is reasonably possible with the non-graphical form of Emacs. We present a Problem at the end of this chapter that asks you to do this.

Unfortunately, you cannot access the speed button bar menu choices from within a text-only display of Emacs.

To stress how the keyboard keys are used in graphical GNU Emacs, we present the following notes:

1. Pressing the Escape key is signified as **<Esc>**.
2. Pressing the Enter key is signified as **<Enter>**.
3. Pressing the **<Ctrl>** key in combination with another single key is signified as **<Ctrl+X>**, where you hold down the **<Ctrl>** key and press the **X** key (or any valid key for that combination) at the same time.
4. Pressing the **<Alt>** key in combination with another single key is signified as **<Alt+X>**, where you hold down the **<Alt>** key and press the **X** key (or any valid key for that combination) at the same time.
5. A variant of 4 is shown as **<Ctrl+X>** a [b], where you first press and release **<Ctrl>** and **X** simultaneously, and then press the **a** key, and optionally press the **b** key (or any valid combination of single keys or strings of characters).
6. In GNU Emacs for our Raspberry Pi OS, which is based upon Debian Bookworm, the Meta key that is referred to in much of the literature on GNU Emacs is the **<Alt>** key.

It is important to realize before you begin that there are some common terms used in nano, vi, vim, and gvim (the editors covered in Volume 3 of this series) and Emacs, that describe the facilities of each editor. But the terms do not necessarily have the same meaning between the major families of editor.

As in vi, vim, and gvim, you can't immediately begin to enter text into any file you're editing. You have to be in **Insert mode** to do that, that's what typing **A** as the second step is doing. Vi, vim, and gvim have modes. In nano and GNU Emacs, you can start typing text into the file immediately.

Nano and Emacs are *modeless* editors.

Vi, vim, and gvim operate in three distinct modes: Command mode, Insert mode, and Last Line mode. Emacs is a *modeless* editor in the sense that, when you launch Emacs, you do not have to switch modes to immediately type characters on the keyboard and enter text into a buffer, or change modes to save the buffer to a file.

But Emacs does have major modes of operation, such as *Lisp mode*, *Python mode*, and *C mode*; they are for the special formatting of text, and for specialized operations when editing files for use in coding for those language applications. This is different from allowing you to switch between significant forms of action in the editor, as the vi, vim, and gvim Command, Insert, and Last Line modes do. The keystroke command syntax itself in Emacs is different and more complex than in vi, involving use of the **<Ctrl>** and **<Alt>** prefix characters, as previously noted. The Emacs concepts of *point* and the *cursor location* are also more refined and specific than in vi. In Emacs, the point is the location in the buffer where you are currently doing your editing; the point is assumed to be at the left edge of the cursor, or always between characters or white space (what you enter into a text file when you press the space bar). This difference becomes an important issue when you want to use the cut/copy/paste operations. In vi, yanking removes text from the main buffer, much like cutting/copying, whereas in Emacs yanking is more like pasting into the *main buffer*. The concept of a buffer is very important in Emacs, and is very much the same in Emacs as it is in vi.

Currently, there is one major "brand" of Emacs for the Raspberry Pi: GNU Emacs. We use the graphical form of GNU Emacs, version 28.2 on our Raspberry Pi OS, running in its own frame, and launched by typing **emacs** on a terminal command line. An example of how emacs appears when you launch it in this way is shown later in Figure 3.1. We also add options and command arguments to the basic Emacs command, while working with Emacs in the following illustrations, In-Chapter Exercises, Practice Sessions, and Problems.

A complete summary of Emacs commands is given later in Table 3.7, which we conveniently place at the end of this chapter, so that you can bookmark and use it as a handy reference when you are editing with Emacs.

3.2 Installing Emacs on the Raspberry Pi OS

The easiest and quickest way to install Emacs on a Raspberry Pi is to use the Raspberry Pi menu choice **Preferences> Add/Remove Software**. In the Add/ Remove Software window that opens on-screen, type emacs in the search bar, and press **<Enter>**. A number of packages are shown, none of which come pre-installed on our Raspberry Pi OS. Put a check mark next to GNU Emacs editor (metapackage), and then press the Apply button in the lower-right corner of the Add/Remove Software window. In a short time, you'll have the necessary packages installed on your system.

3.2.1 Launching Emacs, Emacs Screen Display, and General Emacs Concepts and Features

There are three graphical ways to launch Emacs on the Debian-bookworm version of the Raspberry Pi OS, all of which are presented to you after you've installed Emacs as we've shown in Section 3.2. These three ways are found on the Raspberry Pi menu > **Programming**. They are the Emacs GUI, Client, and Terminal icons. Basically they give you a more graphical presentation in the GUI version, less of a graphical front end in the Client version, and the least graphical presentation in the Terminal version. Again, it's a matter of personal preferences as to which one of these you want to use. You can also launch Emacs from a terminal window, simply by typing **emacs**, plus any options and command arguments on the command line.

The general syntax for launching the Emacs program from the command line in a terminal window is as follows (anything enclosed in square brackets [] is optional):

emacs [options][file(s)]
Purpose: Allows you to edit a new or existing file(s)
Output: With no options or file(s) specified, Emacs runs and begins or
               opens on the Welcome Screen buffer
Commonly used options/features:
+n   Begin to edit file(s) starting at line number **n**
-nw   Run Emacs without opening a window, useful in an elementary GUI
               environment
emacs file1 file2 file3   Open three buffers in Emacs on three different files
                               at the same time

For example, if you run the Emacs program the first time by typing **emacs
alien** in a terminal window on a Raspberry Pi, Emacs launches and shows
you a split-screen display, with a buffer open into the file alien, and the
Welcome Screen buffer down below. This is seen in Figure 3.1.

Note
At this point, you could click in the Welcome Screen buffer, and make the
choice to Dismiss this startup screen—Never show it again.

A brief description of the major components of the Emacs Graphical screen
display labeled in Figure 3.1 is as follows (note: items J, A, B, D, and C are
found on what is called the *mode line*):

A. Name of the current buffer: This is the name of the entity or "file"
    you are editing in this window. In Figure 3.1, the name of the buffer
    is **alien**.

B. Major and minor mode: Different major modes are used to edit
    different kinds of files, like C programs, Lisp, or HTML, and spe-
    cial configurations of the major modes define the minor modes. In
    Figure 3.1, only the major mode Fundamental is shown, with no minor
    mode set.

C. Percentage of the text shown on screen: This shows how much of the
    text in the buffer is seen on screen. In Figure 3.1, all of the text in the
    current buffer is shown on-screen.

D. Current line number: The line location of the cursor in the current
    buffer is displayed here.

E. Minibuffer: Information and questions/prompts from Emacs
    appear here.

F. Speed button bar: This allows you to do quick, common operations
    graphically.

G. Menu bar: This gives you pull-down menus that contain all of the
    important Emacs operations.

H. Text: The actual text you are editing appears here.

FIGURE 3.1

First GNU Emacs Graphical screen display.

I. Scroll bar: The scroll bar allows you to graphically scroll or move through the text.

J. Status indicator: Two-character codes are used to tell you about your file. In Figure 3.1, a **1:** and three hyphens (**---**) is shown.

In-Chapter Exercises

3.1 Launch Emacs on your Raspberry Pi system, and identify components A through J of the Emacs screen display.

3.2 If you launch Emacs on your Linux system by typing only the word **emacs** in a terminal or console window (without changing any of the defaults!), how does your screen display differ from what is shown in

Figure 3.1? What Emacs commands or menu choices can you make to close the Emacs Welcome Screen buffer, and begin to edit in a new, completely blank buffer?

To close the Welcome Screen buffer display that opens in the bottom window of the Emacs frame, while the cursor is flashing on the Emacs Tutorial choice, type **q** on your keyboard. Once you do this, you will only have one buffer shown in the screen display.

3.3 Emacs Help

Emacs provides a wide variety of help commands, all accessible through the key sequence **<Ctrl+H>** or graphically with the function key **<F1>**. You can also type **<Ctrl+H> <Ctrl+H>** to view a list of help commands. You can scroll the list with **<Space>** and **<Del>**, then type the help command you want. To cancel, type **<Ctrl+G>**. Many help commands display their information in a special help buffer. In this buffer, you can type **<Space>** and **<Del>** to scroll and press **<Enter>** to follow hyperlinks.

The following are the most general ways of obtaining help on a topic or command:

<Ctrl+H> a topic(s) <Enter>
This searches for commands whose names match the argument **topic(s)**. The argument can be a keyword, a list of keywords, or a regular expression.

<Ctrl+H> i d m Emacs <Enter> i topic <Enter>
This searches for **topic** in the indices of the Emacs Info manual, displaying the first match found. Press , (comma) to see subsequent matches. You can use a regular expression as a topic.

<Ctrl+H> i d m Emacs <Enter> s topic <Enter>
Similar to <Ctrl+H> ... I topic, but searches the text of the Emacs manual rather than the indices.

<Ctrl+H> <Ctrl+F>
This displays the Emacs FAQ, using Info.

<Ctrl+H> p
This displays the available Emacs packages based on keywords.
A summary of help command syntax is found in Table 3.1.

TABLE 3.1

Summary of Emacs Help Command Syntax

\<Ctrl+H> a topics \<Enter>	Display a list of commands whose names match topics (apropos-command).
\<Ctrl+H> b	Display all active key bindings—minor mode bindings first, then those of the major mode, then global bindings (describe-bindings).
\<Ctrl+H> c key	Show the name of the command that the key sequence key is bound to (describe-key-briefly). Here c stands for "character". For more extensive information on key, use \<Ctrl+H> k.
\<Ctrl+H> d topics \<Enter>	Display the commands and variables whose documentation matches topics (apropos-documentation).
\<Ctrl+H> e	Display the ***Messages*** buffer (view-echo-area-messages).
\<Ctrl+H> f function press \<Enter>	Display documentation on the Lisp function named function (describe-function). Since commands are Lisp functions, this works for commands too.
\<Ctrl+H> h	Display the **HELLO** file, which shows examples of various character sets.
\<Ctrl+H> i	Run Info, the GNU documentation browser (info). The Emacs manual is available in Info.
\<Ctrl+H> k key	Display the name and documentation of the command that key runs (describe-key).
\<Ctrl+H> l	Display a description of your last 300 keystrokes (view-lossage).
\<Ctrl+H> m	Display documentation of the current major mode (describe-mode).
\<Ctrl+H> n	Display news of recent Emacs changes (view-Emacs-news).
\<Ctrl+H> p	Find packages by topic keyword (finder-by-keyword). This lists packages using a package menu buffer.
\<Ctrl+H> P package \<Enter>	Display documentation about the package named package (describe-package).
\<Ctrl+H> r	Display the Emacs manual in Info (info-Emacs-manual).
\<Ctrl+H> s	Display the contents of the current syntax table (describe-syntax). The syntax table says which characters are opening delimiters, which are parts of words, and so on.
\<Ctrl+H> t	Enter the Emacs interactive tutorial (help-with-tutorial).
\<Ctrl+H> v var \<Enter>	Display the documentation of the Lisp variable var (describe-variable).
\<Ctrl+H> w command \<Enter>	Show which keys run the command named command (where-is).
\<Ctrl+H> C coding \<Enter>	Describe the coding system coding (describe-coding-system).
\<Ctrl+H> C \<Enter>	Describe the coding systems currently in use.
\<Ctrl+H> F command \<Enter>	Enter Info and go to the node that documents the Emacs command command (Info-goto-Emacs-command-node).

(Continued)

TABLE 3.1 (Continued)

Summary of Emacs Help Command Syntax

<Ctrl+H> I method <Enter>	Describe the input method method (describe-input-method).
<Ctrl+H> K key	Enter Info and go to the node that documents the key sequence key (Info-goto-Emacs-key-command-node).
<Ctrl+H> L language-env **<Enter>**	Display information on the character sets, coding systems, and input methods used in language environment language-env (describe-language-environment).
<Ctrl+H> S symbol <Enter>	Display the Info documentation on symbol symbol according to the programming language you are editing (info-lookup-symbol).
<Ctrl+H>	Display the help message for a special text area, if the point is in one (displaylocal-help). (These include, for example, links in ***Help*** buffers.)

In-Chapter Exercise

3.3 Use the Emacs command **<Ctrl+H> i d m Emacs <Enter> s topic <Enter>** to search for the following terms: point, minibuffer, modes, keys.

Then write a brief description, in your own words, of each of these terms, based upon what the help provided by Emacs yields.

3.4 Graphical Features

From a beginner's perspective, the most useful graphical features of Emacs are the menu bar and speed button bar, seen in Figure 3.1 as F and G. These features utilize all of Emacs's functionality with a graphical style of inter-action that is most agreeable to a novice, and also to the experienced user.

Note
When a menu choice is grayed out, that means it is not available at the current level you are operating at in Emacs. Depending on your display, this may be somewhat difficult to determine.

Following is a brief description of what tasks each menu bar item accomplishes:

File: Facilities for opening, saving, and closing buffers, files, windows, and frames

Edit: Means to modify text in buffers

Options:	Facilities to make configuration changes
Buffers:	A pull-down menu listing of the currently open buffers
Tools:	File and application functions
Help:	Extensive documentation and on-line manual for Emacs

The speed button bar contains single-button presses for (1) file and buffer operations; (2) common text-editing operations, such as cut and paste; and (3) printing, searching, and changing preferences.

3.5 Buffers, File, Windows, and Frames

The most important concept in Emacs is that of a buffer, or text object that is currently being edited by Emacs. This is different from a file, which is a text object stored on disk. The differentiation is made, in simple terms, because (1) the object currently being modified and viewed in Emacs is not the same object stored on disk, if you have not yet saved your edits; and (2) Emacs can work on text objects that are not files and never will be, such as the output from commands typed on the command line. When you first launch Emacs on the command line, and use the option to specify a file to edit, you are looking into the buffer created by Emacs for that file, in what is generally known as an Emacs frame. That frame may contain only a single window open, that allows you to see the buffer contents. A frame consists of one window, or possibly many windows, with the pull-down and speed button bar menus, the mode line, and a minibuffer.

In-Chapter Exercise

3.4   When you launch Emacs in a terminal, specifying a filename on the command line, and close the Welcome screen, how many buffers are open? What are their names? How did you find this out? How do you shift between working in different open buffers? How do you open a new frame on screen? How do you close a frame?

3.6 Point, Mark, and Region

The second most important concept in Emacs is that of the *point* and *mark*, and the *region* of text they demarcate. The point is located in the white space before the character the cursor is highlighting. The mark, set by placing the cursor over a character and then holding down **<Ctrl+Space>** or **<Ctrl+@>**, is also in the white space before the character the cursor is highlighting. The region or area of text you want to manipulate in operations, such as cutting and copying, is all text between the point and the mark. For example, in the line of text Now is the time for all good men, if the cursor is on or highlighting the N in the word Now (the point is in the white space before the N), and the mark has been set before the character i in the word time by placing the cursor on the letter i and holding down **<Ctrl+Space>**, then the region is defined as Now is the t.

To exit from Emacs without saving any of the buffers, make the pull-down menu choice **File > Quit** or type **<Ctrl+X>** then **<Ctrl+C>** on the keyboard.

In-Chapter Exercises

3.5   In a new Emacs file, type in the following text:

Now is the time for all good men

and then place the flashing cursor on the letter N. Define the region by holding down **<Ctrl+Space>** and then set the mark by using the arrow keys on the keyboard to place the cursor on the n in the word men. What is the region defined as? If you make the speed button bar choice "Copy", what is copied to the paste buffer? How did you find this out?

3.6   What signifies the region graphically on a Raspberry Pi system running with a GUI desktop?

3.7 How to Use Emacs to Do Shell Script File Creation, Editing, and Execution

The following practice session shows how to create a file to define aliases, or command name substitutes, that allow you to type DOS command names in a terminal at the command prompt, to execute some of the common file maintenance operations. DOS commands are similar to Linux commands, but are used in the Windows operating system environment. As you will see in the practice session, you can use an efficient combination of keyboard typing and graphical interaction to work with Emacs.

In this section, we assume that you are running the default shell on your Raspberry Pi system, the Bourne Again shell (Bash). Also, it is assumed in these practice sessions, exercises, and problems that you are creating and editing files in your home directory, where you have unaliased all of the aliases.

Practice Session 3.1

Step 1: At the shell prompt, type e**macs alien** and then press **<Enter>**.

> The Emacs screen appears in your display, similar to Figure 3.1. Close the Welcome Screen.

Step 2: Type # **DOS aliases** and then press **<Enter>**.

Step 3: Type **alias del=rm** and then press **<Enter>**.

Step 4: Type **alias dir='ls -la'** and then press **<Enter>**.

Step 5: Type **alias type=more** and then press **<Enter>**.

Step 6: Hold down the **<Ctrl+X>**, and then hold down **<Ctrl+S>** to save your file with the name **alien**. The display of your text should appear similar to Figure 3.2.

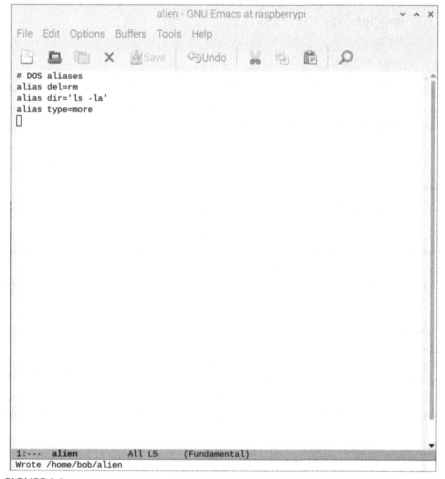

FIGURE 3.2

File alien after step 6.

Step 7:   Hold down **<Ctrl+X>**, and then hold down **<Ctrl+C>** to gracefully exit from Emacs and return to the Bash shell prompt.

In-Chapter Exercises

3.7   How did you get the Bash aliases created in the file alien in Practice Session 3.1 to work? List the specific steps you used to do this. The assumption here is that you are working in a GUI desktop system, and you are not in a login shell when you test the aliases.

3.8   As shown in Practice Session 3.1, use Emacs to create a text file that contains the following Bash aliases:

dir='ls -l'

rename='mv'

spr='lpr -Pspr'

lt='ls -ltr'

page='more'

Test the aliases on your system. Note that if your default printer has a designation other than spr, substitute the printer designation on your system. Then **unalias** all of the aliases created in this Exercise.

3.8 Visiting Files, Saving Files, and Exiting

Your Raspberry Pi OS stores data permanently in files, so a vast majority of the text a novice user, or even an advanced user, will edit with Emacs, comes from a file and is saved in a file. To edit a file while running Emacs, you need to read the file into a buffer and prepare that buffer containing a copy of the file's text. This is called *visiting* the file.

Note
The Emacs editing commands work on the text in the buffer inside Emacs. Your changes are written to the file itself, by default only when you save the buffer to the file!

In addition to visiting and saving files, Emacs can delete, copy, rename, and append to files, keep multiple versions of them, and operate on file directories.

The following are some of the basic operations you can do to visit files, save them, and then exit gracefully from Emacs:

* Visiting a New File

To visit a new file from within Emacs, make the pull-down menu choice **File>Visit New File**. In the Name bar that appears in the Find File window on screen, type in a new file name and then make the choice **OK**. If the only buffer open is the welcome window, it will close, and you will be editing a buffer named with the new file name. You can do the same thing by typing **<Ctrl+X> <Ctrl+F>**. Then in the minibuffer, type in the file name.

* Saving to a File without Quitting Emacs

After you have entered some text into the current buffer, make the pull-down menu choice **File> Save**.
    You can do the same thing by typing **<Ctrl+X> <Ctrl+S>**.

* Saving to a File with Unsaved Changes and Quitting Emacs

If you make unsaved changes to a buffer, and make the pull-down menu choice **File>Quit**, Emacs puts a Question dialog box on screen asking you the following:

Save file? Yes No
View This Buffer
View Changes in This Buffer
Save This but No More
Save All Buffers
No for All

If you make the last menu choice, you are presented with one additional Question Dialog box informing you that "Modified buffers exist; exit anyway?"
    You can do any of these things, depending on what you want to accomplish. You get the same choices, although they are less descriptive, when you type **<Ctrl+X> <Ctrl+C>** for the unsaved buffer.
    Experiment with all of the above editing and saving files and buffers methods, to establish a preferred personal operating procedure for yourself when using Emacs.

3.9 Cursor Movement and Editing Commands

In addition to general purpose commands, Emacs has some important cursor movement and editing commands that allow you to move quickly and easily around the text and make changes. Some of the most important of these commands are listed in Tables 3.2 and 3.3.

TABLE 3.2

Entities to Move Over

Entity to Move Over	Backward	Forward
Character		<Ctrl+B>	<Ctrl+F>
Word		<Alt+B>	<Alt+F>
Line		<Ctrl+P>	<Ctrl+N>
Go to line beginning (or end)		<Ctrl+A>	<Ctrl+E>
Sentence		<Alt+A>	<Alt+E>
Paragraph		<Alt+{>	<Alt+}>
Page		<Ctrl+X> [	<Ctrl+X>]
Sexp		<Ctrl+Alt+B>	<Ctrl+Alt+F>
Function		<Ctrl+Alt+A>	<Ctrl+Alt+E>
Go to buffer start (or end)		<Alt+<>	<Alt+>>
Scroll to next screen	<Ctrl+V>		
Scroll to previous screen	<Alt+V>		
Scroll left	<Ctrl+X> <		
Scroll right	<Ctrl+X> >		
Scroll current line to center, top, bottom	<Ctrl+L>		
Go to line	<Alt+G> g		
Back to indentation	<Alt+M>		

TABLE 3.3

Entities to Kill

Entity to Kill	Backward	Forward
Character (delete, not kill)		<Del>	<Ctrl+D>
Word		<Alt+Del>	<Alt+D>
Line (to end of)		<Alt+0><Ctrl+K>	<Ctrl+K>
Sentence		<Ctrl+X> DEL	<Alt+K>
Sexp		<Alt+-> <Ctrl+Alt+K>	<Ctrl+Alt+K>
Kill region	<Ctrl+W>		
Copy region to kill ring	<Alt+W>		
Kill through next occurrence of char	<Alt+Z> char		
Yank back last thing killed	<Ctrl+Y>		
Replace last yank with previous kill	<Alt+Y>		

Practice Session 3.2 illustrates the use of a mixture of keystroke commands and graphical methods in Emacs, and lets you edit the file **alien** that you created in Practice Session 3.1. In particular, Practice Session 3.2 instructs you to insert the file you created in Practice Session 3.1 into a special file you will create in your home directory, named .bash_aliases, so that, upon subsequent logins, these DOS-aliased commands will be permanently available. This insertion is achieved with an Emacs feature known as the *mini-buffer*. Before you begin Practice Session 3.2, do the following:

Preparatory Step 1. By default on a Raspberry Pi system, there is a .bashrc file in your home directory. In it, you will find the following lines of code that allow you to use a secondary aliases file to contain user-defined aliases. At the end of it, it has lines in it as follows:

```
#Alias definitions.
# You may want to put all your additions into a separate file like
# ~/.bash_aliases, instead of adding them here directly.
# See /usr/share/doc/bash-doc/examples in the bash-doc package.

if [ -f ~/.bash_aliases ]; then
  . ~/.bash_aliases
fi
```

Preparatory Step 2. In your home directory, create an empty file named .bash_ aliases using the touch command:

bob@raspberrypi:~ $ **touch .bash_aliases**

If you make a mistake anywhere in the following exercise, you can revert to using the graphical form of editing for expediency (using the mouse and pull-down menus, including undo, inside the Emacs window).

Practice Session 3.2

Step 1: At the shell prompt, type **emacs alien** and then press **<Enter>**. Close the Emacs Welcome Screen. The file you created in Practice Session 3.1 is loaded into the buffer, and your screen display should look similar to the one shown in Figure 3.1.

Step 2: Using the arrow keys, position the cursor to the right of the ' character at the end of the third line.

Step 3: Press **<Enter>**

Step 4: Type **alice dirw=ls**

Step 5: Hold down **<Ctrl+A>** The cursor moves to the beginning of the line.

Step 6: Hold down **<Alt+D>** The word alice has been cut from the buffer.

Step 7: Type **alias**.

Step 8: Hold down **<Alt+B>** The cursor moves to the beginning of the word alias.

Step 9: Position the cursor with the arrow keys on the keyboard at the beginning of the first blank line, below the line that reads **alias type=more**.

Step 10: Hold down **<Ctrl+Y>** The cut word alice has been put back into the buffer at the start of the line.

Step 11: Use the arrow keys to position the cursor in the space to the right of the word alice if it is not there already.

Step 12: Use the **<Delete>** or **<Backspace>** keys to delete the letters c and e from the word alice.

Step 13: Type **as copy=cp**.

Step 14: Hold down **<Ctrl+X>** **<Ctrl+W>**.

Step 15: At the Write file: prompt, type **alien2** and then press **<Enter>**. Your screen display should now look similar to the one shown in Figure 3.3.

FIGURE 3.3
Display after step 15.

Step 16: Hold down **<Ctrl+H>** and then press the **a** key. The minibuffer area shows a prompt for you to obtain help. Hold down **<Ctrl+G>**. Doing so cancels your help request.

Step 17: Hold down **<Ctrl+X>** **<Ctrl+C>** to quit Emacs and return to the shell prompt.

Step 18: From the shell prompt, type **emacs .bash_aliases** and then press **<Enter>**. Dismiss the startup screen. The blank contents of your **.bash_aliases** file now appear in the editing buffer.

Step 19: Position the cursor with the arrow keys on the keyboard on the first blank line in the file, if it isn't already there. Hold down **<Ctrl+X>** and then press the **i** key on the keyboard. This will allow you to insert the contents of a file into the current buffer at the position of the cursor.

Step 20: In the minibuffer, type **alien2**. The lines of text from **alien2**'s DOS aliases should now be inserted into the file **.bash_aliases** after and below where you positioned the cursor in Step 19.

Step 21: From the pull-down menu File, make the choice **File>Save (current buffer)**, or use **<Ctrl+X>** **<Ctrl+S>**.

Step 22: Hold down **<Ctrl+X>** **<Ctrl+C>** to quit Emacs and return to the shell prompt.

In-Chapter Exercises

3.9 Test the new **.bash_aliases** file created in Practice Session 3.2 . How did you do this?

The assumption here is that you arenot working in a login shell! In a terminal window, at the shell prompt, type one of the aliased commands, with its appropriate arguments if necessary, and note the results. Which aliases work, and which ones don't? Why?

3.10 Use Emacs to correct the Bash aliases that do not work in the **.bash_aliases** file. Then test them. Finally, unalias them.

3.10 Keystroke Macros

The Emacs text editor contains a simple-to-use facility that allows you to define *keystroke macros*, or collections of keystrokes that can be recorded and then played back at any time. This capability allows you to define repetitive multiple keystroke operations as a single command and then execute that command— as many times as you want. The keystrokes can include Emacs commands and

TABLE 3.4

Interactive Search and Replace

Search and Replace Action	Keystrokes
Search forward	<Ctrl+S>
Search backward	<Ctrl+R>
Regular expression search	<Ctrl+Alt+S>
Reverse regular expression search	<Ctrl+Alt+R>
Select previous search string	<Alt+P>
Select next later search string	<Alt+N>
Exit incremental search	<Enter>
Undo effect of last character	<Del>
Abort current search	<Ctrl+G>
Interactively replace a text string	<Alt+%>
Using regular expressions	<Alt+X> query-replace-regexp
Replace this one, go on to next	<Space> or y
Replace this one, don't move	,
Skip to next without replacing	<Del> or n
Replace all remaining matches	!
Back up to the previous match	^
Exit query-replace	<Enter>
Enter recursive edit (<Ctrl+Alt+C> to exit)	<Ctrl+R>

a series of keystrokes. A macro can also be saved with a name, or even be saved to a file, for use during subsequent Emacs editing sessions. Table 3.4 shows a list of some of the most important keyboard macro commands.

For a more complete description and detailed explanation of how to record, edit, list, and delete keystroke macros, see Section 3.16.9.

Practice Session 3.3 lets you create a new text file using some of the commands presented in Table 3.4.

Practice Session 3.3

Step 1: At the shell prompt, type **emacs datafile** and then press **<Enter>**.

The Emacs screen appears on your display. Dismiss the startup screen.

Step 2: Hold down **<Ctrl+X> <Shift+9>**. These actions begin your keyboard macro definition. If you make a mistake anywhere in subsequent steps, simply hold down **<Ctrl+G>** to cancel the current macro definition.

Step 3: Type **1 2 3 4 5 6 7 8 9 10** and then press **<Enter>**.

Step 4: Hold down **<Ctrl+X> <Shift+0>**. These actions end your macro definition.

Step 5: Hold down **<Ctrl+X> E**. Doing so replays the macro that you just defined, placing another line of the numbers 1 through 10 in the buffer.

Step 6: Press **E** eight more times so that your display looks similar to that shown in Figure 3.4.

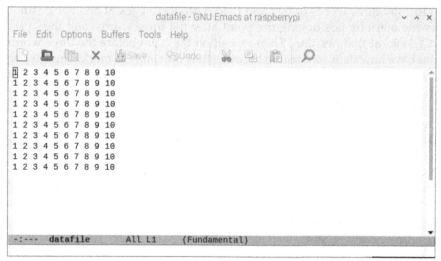

FIGURE 3.4
Display after step 6.

Step 7: Hold down **<Ctrl+X> <Ctrl+S>**. These actions save the buffer to the file datafile.

Step 8: Hold down **<Ctrl+X> <Ctrl+C>** to exit from Emacs.

3.11 Cut or Copy and Paste and Search and Replace

Every word processor has the capability to cut or copy text and then paste that text back into the document bring worked on, and to search for old text and replace it with new text. Because Emacs operations can be totally text activated, whereby you use sequences of keystrokes to execute commands, cutting or copying and pasting are fairly complex operations. They are accomplished with the *Kill Ring*, whereby text is held in a buffer by *killing* it and is then restored to the document at the desired position by *yanking* it. Global search and replace are somewhat less complex and are accomplished by either an unconditional replacement, or an interactive replacement.

The mark is simply a place holder in the buffer. For example, to cut three words from a document and then paste them back at another position, move the point before the first word you want to cut and press **<Esc+D>** three times. The three words are then cut to the Kill Ring. Because the Kill Ring is a First In First Out (FIFO) buffer, you can now move the point to where you want to restore the three words and press **<Ctrl+Y>**. The three words are yanked into the document in the same order, left to right, that they were cut from the document.

To copy three words of text and then paste them back at another position, set the mark by positioning the point after the three words, and then press **<Ctrl+@>** at that position. Then reposition the point before the three words; you have now defined a region between the point and the mark. There is only one mark in the document. Press **<Esc+W>** to send the text between the point and the mark to the Kill Ring; the text is sent, but it is not blanked from the screen display. To restore the three words at another position, move the point there and press **<Ctrl+Y>**. The three words are restored at the new position. Table 3.4 gives the important kill and yank commands for Emacs.

Global search and replace can be either unconditional, where every occurrence of old text you want to replace with new text is replaced without prompting, or it can be interactive, where you are prompted by Emacs before each occurrence of old text is replaced with new text. Also, the grammar of replacement can include regular expressions, which we do not cover here.

Note
On our Raspberry Pi system, the **<Alt>** key on the keyboard is the *Metacharacter*, signified in Emacs as **M**.

For example, to replace the word **men** unconditionally with the word **women** from the current position of the point to the end of the document, press **<Esc+%>**, type **replace-string**, and then press **<Enter>**. You are then prompted for the old string. Type **men** and then press **<Enter>**. You are then prompted for the new string. Type **women** and then press **<Enter>**. All occurrences are replaced with no further prompts.

To accomplish an interactive replacement, simply press **<Esc+X>**, type **query-replace**, and then press **<Enter>**. You can then input old and new strings, but you are given an opportunity at each occurrence of the old string to replace it or not to replace it with the new string. Table 3.4 shows the actions that you can take while doing an interactive search and replace.

Practice Session 3.4 contains further examples of copying and pasting and global search and replace, both unconditional and interactive. Your objective will be to type in one line of text, copy it into the Kill Ring, and then paste it into the document seven times. Then modify the contents of the original line and each pasted line by using both interactive search and replace and unconditional search and replace. Upon completion of Practice Session 3.4, your screen display should look similar to Figure 3.5.

Practice Session 3.4

Step 1: At the shell prompt, type **emacs osfile** and then press **<Enter>**. The Emacs screen appears on your display. Dismiss the startup screen.

Step 2: Type **Windows is the operating system of choice for everyone.**

Step 3: Position the cursor at the W in the word Windows. Press **<Ctrl+@>**. The mark is now set at the start of the line you typed in Step 2. Highlight

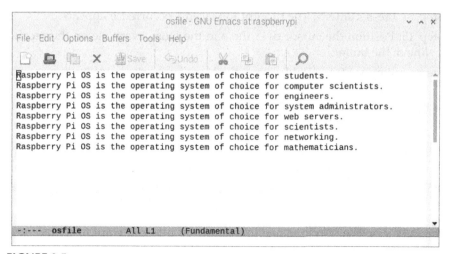

FIGURE 3.5
Display after step 21.

the whole first line with the graphics cursor and left mouse button, going from left to right, and including the period at the end of the line. This will define the region that will be put in the Kill Ring.

Step 4: Press **<Esc+W>**. This action copies the region to the Kill Ring.

Step 5: Press **<Enter>** to start a new line in the buffer, which should be blank. The cursor should be positioned at the start of this new line.

Step 6: Press **<Ctrl+Y>**. The first line of text is now pasted into the next blank line from the Kill Ring.

Step 7: Repeat Steps 5 and 6 six more times so that you now have eight lines of text in the buffer, all containing the text Windows is the operating system of choice for everyone.

Step 8: Position the cursor on the letter W in the word Windows on the first line of the buffer.

Step 9: Save the buffer at this point with **<Ctrl+X> <Ctrl+S>**.

Step 10: Press **<Alt+%>**. These actions begin an interactive search and replace. The prompt Query replace appears.

Step 11: Type **everyone** and then press **<Enter>**. All of the words everyone from the second line on down, are highlighted. The prompt Replace string everyone with: appears.

Step 12: Type **students** and then press **<Enter>**.

Step 13: Pressing **<Space>** on the keyboard replaces the word everyone on the first line with the word students, and the prompt Query replacing everyone with students: (? for help) appears again.

Step 14: Press **<Enter>**. The prompt Replaced 1 occurrence appears.

Step 15: Position the cursor over the e in the word everyone on the second line of the buffer.

Step 16: Repeat Steps 10–14, interactively replacing the word everyone each time it appears with the words computer scientists, engineers, system administrators, web servers, scientists, networking, and mathematicians on lines 2–8 of the buffer.

Note

On the second through last press of **<Alt+%>**, the previous replacement sequence will be presented. Override this by typing the word everyone at the prompt, pressing **<Enter>**, and the next replacement. And, be sure that the second through eighth times you do Step 16, you always position the cursor on the previous line to the current line you want to replace text on!

Step 17: Position the cursor on the **W** in Windows on the first line of the buffer.

Step 18: Press **<Alt+X>**. Then type **replace-string** and press **<Enter>**. These actions begin an unconditional search and replace. The prompt replace string: appears.

Step 19: Type **Windows** and then press **<Enter>**. The prompt Replace string Windows with: appears.

Step 20: Type **Raspberry Pi OS** and then press **<Enter>**. The prompt Replaced 8 occurrences appears. Correct?

Step 21: Save the buffer with **<Ctrl+X><Ctrl+S>**, print it using the facilities available on your computer system, and exit Emacs with **<Ctrl+X> <Ctrl+C>**. Your screen display should appear like Figure 3.5.

The following in-chapter exercises ask you to apply some of the operations you learned about in the previous practice sessions:

In-Chapter Exercises

3.11   Run Emacs and define keyboard macro commands that automatically delete

      a.   every other word in a line of unspecified length,

      b.   every other line in a file of unspecified length,

      c.   every other word and every other line in a file of unspecified length with lines of unspecified length.

3.12   Write a keyboard macro, as shown in Section 3.16.9, to do every-
        thing shown in Steps 10–14 of Practice Session 3.4.

3.12 How to Do Purely Graphical Editing with GNU Emacs

Up to this point in our work, it was possible to use Emacs in a single, text-
based terminal window, and obtain the results shown. As a beginner, you are
likely interfacing with the operating system via a GUI desktop system. This
would allow you to do all of your Emacs work in a graphical environment.
For the purposes of learning Emacs, you may exclusively want to run Emacs
in its own frame on your screen display, or even possibly in several frames on
your screen display simultaneously.

3.12.1 Editing Data Files

The following practice session demonstrates the use of graphical GNU
Emacs to do some further editing of the datafile created in Practice Session
3.4. The look and feel of GNU Emacs, running under a GUI desktop default
windowing environment on a Raspberry Pi system, is very similar to a word
processor or desktop publishing application running under any other operating system that has a GUI, such as Windows 11 or Mac OS X. In the practice
sessions that follow, we are using GNU Emacs 28.2.

Practice Session 3.5

Step 1: In a terminal or console window, at the shell prompt, type **emacs
    datafile** and then press **<Enter>**. Your screen display should look similar
    to the one shown in Figure 3.4.

Step 2: Use the mouse to position the cursor over the character 1 at the begin-
    ning of the tenth line in the buffer, and then click the left mouse button.
    The cursor is now positioned over the character 1.

Step 3: Click and hold down the left mouse button over the character 1, and
    then drag the mouse so that the entire tenth line is highlighted, including
    one character to the right of the 0 in the number 10 at the end of the line.
    Release the left mouse button.

    The whole first line should be highlighted.

Step 4: Position the cursor with the mouse so that the arrow points to the
    menu choice **Edit** at the top of the Emacs screen. Click the left mouse
    button. A set of pull-down menu choices appears, similar to that shown in
    Figure 3.6.

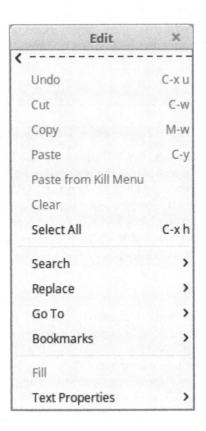

FIGURE 3.6
Edit pull-down menu.

Step 5: Make the **Copy** menu choice. The text that you highlighted (selected) in Step 3 is now held in a temporary buffer.

Step 6: Press **<Enter>**. This opens an eleventh line at the bottom of the buffer.

Step 7: Move the mouse so that the cursor is over the first character position on the eleventh line, and click the left mouse button. The cursor is now in that position in the buffer.

Step 8: Make the pull-down menu choice **Edit>Paste**. You have now pasted the 10 characters from the tenth line in the buffer into the eleventh line in the buffer. Your screen display should now look similar to Figure 3.7.

Step 9: Make the pull-down menu choice **File>Save (current buffer)**. In the Write file: dialog box that appears, save the file in your home directory as **datafile11**, and then make the pull-down menu choice **File>Exit Emacs**.

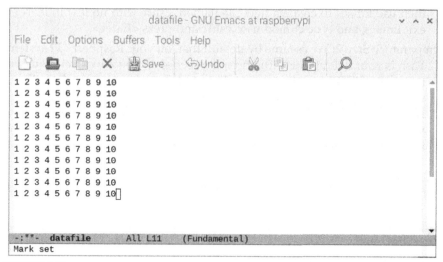

FIGURE 3.7
Datafile after editing and adding an 11th line.

3.12.2 How to Start, Save a File, and Exit in Graphical Emacs

As illustrated in Practice Session 3.5, GNU Emacs can give you a high degree of mouse/GUI command expediency. This method of working on a text file is most efficient for beginners, as well as experienced users. Note that, on the pull-down menu shown in Figure 3.6, keystroke commands also are shown for some of the menu choices. Clicking the menu choice button, or pressing the keyboard key combinations accomplish the same thing. This flexibility adds to the ease of your use of Emacs.

Of course, you still have to use the keyboard to enter text!

Practice Session 3.6 lets you edit the file **alien** that you created in Practice Session 3.2. That practice session allowed you to use Emacs to create a simple Bash shell script file of shell command aliases. You will now modify it so that it can be used to create aliases for the C shell. You will also modify the existing file **.cshrc** in your home directory so that when you are using the C shell, you have the aliased shell commands for the C shell in the file **alien3** available to you. Before you begin Practice Session 3.6, take the following preparatory steps to modify the **.cshrc** file in your home directory, and proceed through this practice session for the C shell rather than the Bash shell):

As with all of the previous Practice Sessions, we assume that you are working in an interactive shell terminal or console window. Also, the C shell is installed by default on your Raspberry Pi system.

Preparatory Step 1: Use the **ls -la** command to find out if you have a **.cshrc** file in your home directory. If you have no **.cshrc** file in your home directory, then use Emacs to create a new file named **.cshrc** with no text in it. Then exit Emacs, and type **chmod u+x .cshrc** and press **<Enter>**.

Preparatory Step 2: We assume by default that, on your Raspberry Pi system, Bash is your default shell. To find out which shell you are currently using, type **echo $SHELL** and pressing **<Enter>**. If you are using the C shell, the system will respond with /bin/csh. If you are using the Bash shell, the system will respond /bin/bash. To find out what shells are installed on your Raspberry Pi OS, and install the C shell if it's not installed, use the following commands:

```
bob@raspberrypi:~ $ cat /etc/shells
# /etc/shells: valid login shells
/bin/sh
/usr/bin/sh
/bin/bash
/usr/bin/bash
/bin/rbash
/usr/bin/rbash
/bin/dash
/usr/bin/dash
bob@raspberrypi:~ $ sudo apt install csh
Output truncated...
```

Practice Session 3.6

Step 1: At the C shell prompt %, type **emacs alien** and then press **<Enter>**. The file that you created in Practice Exercise 3.2 is loaded into the buffer, and the contents of the Emacs buffer looks like the one shown in Figure 3.2. Use the cursor and mouse for cursor positioning, and the keyboard keys for text entry and deleting, to modify the file so that it looks like this (the proper format of aliases for the C shell):

#DOS aliases for the C shell
alias del rm
alias dir='ls –la'
alias type more

Step 2: Position the cursor, using the mouse and left mouse button, to the right of the single-quote character (') at the end of the third line.

Step 3: Press **<Enter>** to open a blank line. The cursor will be at the beginning of the line.

Step 4: Type **alice dirw ls**.

Step 5: Position the cursor, using the mouse and left mouse button, at character a in alice.

Step 6: Hold down the left mouse button and move the mouse so that the word alice and the following space are highlighted. At the top of the screen, make the **Edit** pull-down menu choice **Cut** to cut the word alice from the buffer.

Step 7: Type **alias** . (with a space character after the s).

Step 8: Move the mouse so that the cursor is over the second a character in the word alias on that same line. Click the left mouse button.

Step 9: Press the **<Down>** arrow key on the keyboard twice. The cursor should now be at the beginning of the blank line below the line that reads **alias type more.**

Step 10: From the **Edit** pull-down menu, choose **Paste**. The cut word alice has been put back into the buffer at the start of the line.

Step 11: Use the mouse and left mouse button to position the cursor at the end of the word alice on that same line, in the space after the character e.

Step 12: Use the **<Delete>** or **<Backspace>** keys to delete the letters c and e from the word alice.

Step 13: Type **as copy cp.**

Step 14: Continue moving the cursor to the proper positions and add the necessary characters. Remember to remove the equal sign (=) in between the command **dir** and the string **'ls -la'.**

Step 15: From the pull down menu File, choose **Save As...**

Step 16: In the Write file: dialog box that opens on screen, save the file as **alien3** with the OK choice.

Step 17: From the File pull-down menu, make the choice **File>Open File**. In the Find file: dialog box that opens, put a check mark in the box that is for Show Hidden Files.

Locate and select the **.cshrc** file you created as an empty (no text in it) file in Preparatory Step 1 (which should be in your home directory), and make the **Open** choice. A new buffer opens on-screen containing the blank contents of the **.cshrc** file. Position the cursor anywhere on a blank line in the buffer for the file **.cshrc**.

Step 18: From the File pull-down menu, make the choice **File>Insert file...** In the dialog box that opens, choose **alien3** and insert it. The lines of text from **alien3**'s C shell aliases should now be inserted into the file **.cshrc** at the location you designated in Step 17.

Step 19: From the pull-down menu File, make the choice **File>Save (current buffer)**.

Step 20: Make the pull-down menu choice **File>Quit** to quit Emacs and return to the shell prompt.

Step 21: To test your new **.cshrc** file, do the following. Close and then reopen the terminal window to re-initiate the interactive Bash shell, run the C shell, and test the new aliases and note the results. For example, if you type **dir**, you should get the results of the **ls -la** command that is executed in the current working directory.

Step 22: Finally, to exit to Bash from the C shell, type **exit**.

3.13 Emacs Graphical Menus

Figures 3.8 and 3.9 show the contents of another two of the most important pull-down menus in a graphical Emacs: Files and Tools. To the right of each pull-down choice is the keystroke command equivalent, if there is one.

Visit New File...	C-x C-f
Open File...	
Open Directory...	C-x d
Insert File...	C-x i
Close	
Save	C-x C-s
Save As...	C-x C-w
Revert Buffer	
Recover Crashed Session	
New Window Below	C-x 2
New Window on Right	C-x 3
Remove Other Windows	C-x 1
New Frame	C-x 5 2
New Frame on Display...	
New Frame on Monitor...	
Delete Frame	C-x 5 0
New Tab	C-x t 2
Close Tab	C-x t 0
Print	>
Quit	C-x C-c

FIGURE 3.8
Files pull-down menu.

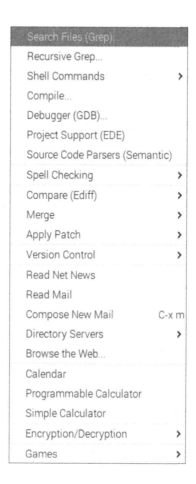

FIGURE 3.9
Tools pull-down menu.

3.14 Creating and Editing C Programs

Besides being a powerful text editor/word processor, Emacs can achieve many operations that are useful to a beginner, from within the Emacs program itself. Things such as composing e-mail, executing shell scripts, Internet work, and program development in C, C++, Python, HTML, and Java. Since the text for anything more than a trivial program must be generated in a text editor of some sort, it makes a lot of practical sense to use this editor to compile, link, debug, and keep a record of source code revisions, as well as execute the program code itself. This is easily done in Emacs using some of its built-in capabilities. These kinds of all-in-one capabilities are present, because in the days of character-only terminals and consoles, instead of leaving the editor to accomplish a chore outside of it, you could accomplish common tasks from within the editor. In a GUI-based Raspberry Pi system, we can now simply switch between windows and never leave the editor. But it is still very useful to be able to harness some of the multiple capabilities of the program, mainly for the sake of efficiency.

Practice Session 3.7 allows you to type in the source code of a C program, and use the special facilities of the editor to properly indent the text, compile and link the source code, and implement revisions according to compile-time errors. You can then execute the program in a terminal window to test it. The purpose of executing the program in Practice Session 3.7 is to allow the user to type in an integer, and then another integer, and the first integer will be raised to the power indicated by the second integer.

The source code for the program is as follows:

```
#include <stdio.h>
#include <math.h>

int main() {
    float x, y;

    printf("This program takes x and y values from stdin and displays x^y.\n");

    printf("Enter x: ");
    scanf("%f", &x);

    printf("Enter y: ");
    scanf("%f", &y);

    printf("x^y is: %6.3f\n", pow(x, y));

    return 0;
}
```

Practice Session 3.7

Step 1: At the shell prompt, type **emacs power.c**. Dismiss the startup screen. Above the minibuffer display, on the mode line, notice that the major mode for this new buffer is set to C/*l mode.

Step 2: Type in the program source code exactly as shown. Use the <Tab> key to produce the indentation shown in the C source code. Your Emacs screen display should look similar to Figure 3.10.

Step 3: From the pull-down menus, make the choice **File>Save**.

Step 4: From the pull-down menus, make the choice **Tools>Compile...** In the minibuffer, the prompt Compile command: **make -k** appears. Use the

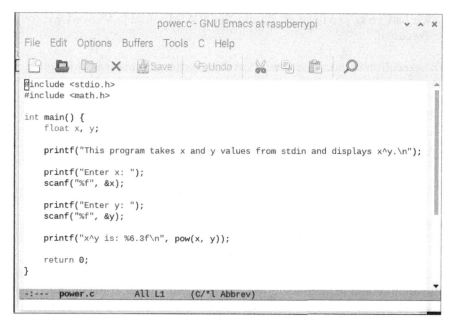

```
power.c - GNU Emacs at raspberrypi          v  ^  x
File  Edit  Options  Buffers  Tools  C  Help

  [ ]  [ ]  [ ]  X  [ ]Save  [ ]Undo  [ ]  [ ]  [ ]  [ ]

#include <stdio.h>
#include <math.h>

int main() {
    float x, y;

    printf("This program takes x and y values from stdin and displays x^y.\n");

    printf("Enter x: ");
    scanf("%f", &x);

    printf("Enter y: ");
    scanf("%f", &y);

    printf("x^y is: %6.3f\n", pow(x, y));

    return 0;
}
-:---   power.c        All L1      (C/*l Abbrev)
```

FIGURE 3.10
Display after step 2.

backspace key to erase make -k, and then, to replace it, type **gcc power.c -lm -o power**. A new buffer window appears in the Emacs frame, showing the progress of the compilation/linking process.

Step 5: From the pull-down menus, make the choice **Tools>Compile...** In the minibuffer, the prompt Compile command: **gcc power.c -lm -o power** should appear. Press **<Enter>** to accept this compile/link command.

If you made mistakes in typing the C code, repeat Steps 2 through 5 until you get no error messages that prevent compilation and linkage! The bottom buffer window showed *warning messages*, but not exceptions, that prevented compilation and linkage for us. How do you eliminate these?

Step 6: If all fatal syntax errors have been removed from the power.c source code, you get the message **Compilation finished**, and the date and time it did so, which indicates in the bottom buffer window that you have successfully compiled and linked power.c.

Step 7: You can now exit Emacs by making the **File>Quit** menu choice, and in a terminal window test the program by typing **./power** on the command line. Remember that the path must be set for the current shell so that executable programs in the directory the file power is in will run. On our Raspberry Pi system, the program **power** was in our home directory, and we had **rwxr** privilege on it, and the $PATH variable showed we could execute it.

The execution on our Raspberry Pi system command line was as follows:
bob@raspberrypi:~ $ **./power**
This program takes x and y values from stdin and displaysx^y.
Enter integer x: **3**
Enter integer y: **2**
x^y is: 9.000
bob@raspberrypi:~ $

3.15 Working in Multiple Buffers

As you saw in previous Practice Sessions, it is possible to insert one buffer into another and to open windows into different buffers, some of which may not even contain text you want to edit, at the same time. This capability is important when you want to compose the contents of one buffer or file with the contents of many other buffers or files that you have previously created. The following Practice Session shows you how to create, move between, and copy and paste between several buffers open within one Emacs frame.

Practice Session 3.8

Step 1: Create a subdirectory under your home directory named **multi**, and make that subdirectory the current working directory.

Step 2: At the shell prompt, type **emacs newfile**. You should now be editing the buffer **newfile** with a single window.

Step 3: In Emacs, make the pull-down menu choice **File>New Window Below**. The frame should now be split horizontally, so that you have two windows, one above the other, both showing the contents of **newfile**.

Step 4: Click with the mouse in the upper window, and then press **<Ctrl+X> 3**. The upper window from Step 3 should now be split vertically into two windows, showing you a total of three windows into the buffer **newfile**.

Step 5: Repeat Step 4 in the lower window of the frame. You should now have four windows showing the contents of the buffer **newfile**. Your screen display should look similar to Figure 3.11. If you did Steps 1–4 incorrectly, you can always use the **File>Remove Other Windows** pull-down menu choice to return you to a single window display, and then try again.

Step 6: Click the mouse in the upper-left window and type **1 2 3 4 5**. Then make the pull-down menu choice **File>Save As**. In the Write file: dialog

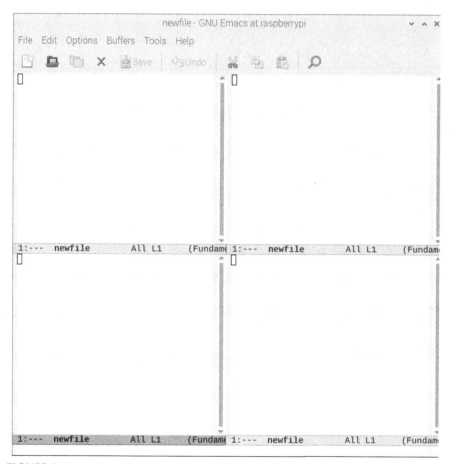

FIGURE 3.11
Display after step 5.

box that appears on screen, type **firstrow** in the Name: box, and then use the Name dialog pane and double left click on the folder **multi**. Then, make the choice **OK**. A new file named **firstrow** is created on disk in the directory named **multi**, and you are still seeing four windows into that buffer.

Step 7: Click the mouse in the upper-right window, position the cursor at the right after the 5, and use the **<Backspace>** or **<Delete>** keys to erase the numbers 1, 2, 3, 4, and 5. Then type **6 7 8 9 10**. Then make the pull-down menu choice **File>Save As**. In the Write file: dialog box that appears on screen, type **secondrow** in the Name: box. The file will be saved in the folder **multi**. Then make the choice **OK**.

FIGURE 3.12
Display after step 8.

Step 8: Click the mouse in the upper-left window. Make the pull-down menu choice **File>Open File**. In the Find file: dialog box that appears on screen, highlight the file **firstrow** in the Name dialog pane. Then make the choice **Open**. You now should have a screen display similar to Figure 3.12, with the upper-left window showing the contents of **firstrow**, and the remaining three windows showing the contents of **secondrow**.

Step 9: Click the mouse in the lower-left window, position the cursor to the right of the 0, erase 6, 7, 8, 9, and 10, and type **11 12 13 14 15**. Then make the pull-down menu choice **File>Save As**. In the Write file: dialog box that appears on screen, type **thirdrow** in the Name: box. Then make the choice **OK**.

Step 10: Click in the upper-right window and make the pull-down menu choice **File>Open File**. In the Find file: dialog box that appears on-screen, highlight the file **secondrow** in the Name dialog pane. Then, make the choice **Open**.

Step 11: Click in the lower-left window, and make the pull-down menu choice **File>Open File**. In the minibuffer, type **thirdrow**.

Step 12: Click the mouse in the lower-right window, and make the pull-down menu choice **File>Save As**. In the Write file: dialog box, type **fourthrow** in the Name: box. Make the choice **OK**. Click in the lower-left window, and make the pull-down menu choice **File>Open File**. In the Find file: dialog box that opens, highlight **thirdrow**, and open it.

Step 13: Continue the above procedures until your screen display should look similar to Figure 3.13.

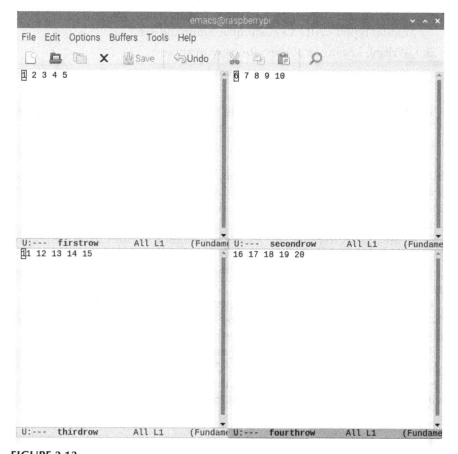

FIGURE 3.13
Display after step 13.

Step 14: Finally, with the lower-right window the current window, make the pull-down menu choice **File>Save As**. In the Write file: dialog box, in the Name box, type **fourthrow**. Overwrite the old buffer **fourthrow**. Then quit Emacs without saving any of the buffers.

3.16 Changing Emacs Behavior

This section describes the basic methods of customizing and modifying the behavior of GNU Emacs. This includes the following operations:

1. Using the Options menu to modify options.
2. Using Custom (a GUI-based interface) to change preferences and options, and in conjunction with that interface, also using the traditional typed **<Alt+X>** customize command set.
3. Writing keystroke abbreviations with abbrev.
4. Writing keystroke macro commands.
5. Redefining keyboard keys.
6. Writing Emacs Lisp (elisp) code to customize the behavior of Emacs, and entering that code directly into your **~/.emacs** startup configuration file.

All of these operations can make changes to your **~/.emacs** startup configuration file to give you a more customized and personalized Emacs session, one customized to your particular needs and methods of entering text for a particular application.

Be aware that by default, an ~/.emacs configuration file on the Raspberry Pi OS does not initially exist. But once you begin the procedures for customizing Emacs in the sections that follow, that file will be created by Emacs.

Also, as will be seen, elisp code is generated by what operations you do. But you don't really need to know any of the details of how to program in elisp to actually achieve all of these operations!

The following subsections describe and give examples of all of the given operations. In addition, Tables 3.5 and 3.6 give a summary of the important keystrokes that implement **<Alt+X>** customization, keystroke abbreviations with **abbrev**, and writing keystroke macros.

TABLE 3.5

Ways to Change Emacs Behavior

Customization Action	Keystrokes
Abbrevs	
Add global abbrev	**<Ctrl+X> a g**
Add mode-local abbrev	**<Ctrl+X> a l**
Add global expansion for this abbrev	**<Ctrl+X> a i g**
Add mode-local expansion for this abbrev	**<Ctrl+X> a i l**
Explicitly expand abbrev	**<Ctrl+X> a e**
Expand previous word dynamically	**<Alt+/>**
Macros	
Start defining a keyboard macro	**<Ctrl+X> (or <F3>**
End keyboard macro definition	**<Ctrl+X>) or <F4>**
Execute last-defined keyboard macro	**<Ctrl+X> e or <F4>**
Append to last keyboard macro	**<Ctrl+U> <Ctrl+X> (**
Name last keyboard macro	**<Alt+X> name-last-kbd-macro**
Insert Lisp definition in buffer	**<Alt+X> insert-kbd-macro**
Customize variables and faces	**<Alt+X> customize**
Simple customization with <Alt+X> customize	
(global-set-key (kbd "<Ctrl+C> g") 'search-forward)	
(global-set-key (kbd "<Alt+#>") 'query-replace-regexp)	

TABLE 3.6

Keystroke Macros

Keystrokes	Command Name	Action
<Ctrl+X> (	kmacro-startmacro	Start macro definition.
<F3>	kmacro-startmacro-or-insertcounter	Start macro definition. If pressed while defining a macro, insert a counter.
<Ctrl+X>)	kmacro-end-macro	End macro definition.
<F4>	kmacro-end-orcall-macro	End macro definition (if definition is in progress) or invoke last keyboard macro.
<Ctrl+X> e	kmacro-end-andcall-macro	Execute last keyboard macro defined. Can type e to repeat macro.
<Ctrl+X> <Ctrl+K> n	name-last-kbdmacro	Name the last macro you created (before saving it).
(none)	insert-kbd-macro	Insert the macro you named into a file.
(none)	macroname	Execute a named keyboard macro.
<Ctrl+X> q	kbd-macro-query	Insert a query in a macro definition.

(continued)

TABLE 3.6 (Continued)

Keystroke Macros

Keystrokes	Command Name	Action
<Ctrl+u> <Ctrl+X> q	(none)	Insert a recursive edit in a macro definition.
<Ctrl+Alt+C>	exit-recursive-edit	Exit a recursive edit.
<Ctrl+X> <Ctrl+K> b	kmacro-bind-tokey	Bind a macro to a key (<Ctrl+X> <Ctrl+K> 0-9 and A-Z are reserved for macro bindings). Lasts for current session only.
<Ctrl+X> <Ctrl+K> Space	kmacro-step-editmacro	Edit a macro while stepping through it.
<Ctrl+X> <Ctrl+K> l	kmacro-editlossage	Turn the last 100 keystrokes into a keyboard macro.
<Ctrl+X> <Ctrl+K> e	edit-kbd-macro	Edit a keyboard macro by typing <Ctrl+X> e for the last keyboard macro defined, <Alt+X> for a named macro, <Ctrl+H> l for lossage, or keystrokes for a macro bound to a key.
<Ctrl+X> <Ctrl+K> Enter	kmacro-editmacro	Edit the last keyboard macro.
<Ctrl+X> <Ctrl+K> <Ctrl+E>	kmacro-editmacro-repeat	Edit the last keyboard macro again.
<Ctrl+X> <Ctrl+K> <Ctrl+T>	kmacro-swap-ring	Transpose last keyboard macro with previous keyboard macro.
<Ctrl+X> <Ctrl+K> <Ctrl+D>	kmacro-deletering-head	Delete last keyboard macro from the macro ring.
<Ctrl+X> <Ctrl+K> <Ctrl+P>	kmacro-cycle-ringprevious	Move to the previous macro in the macro ring.
<Ctrl+X> <Ctrl+K> <Ctrl+N>	kmacro-cycle-ringnext	Move to the next macro in the macro ring.
<Ctrl+X> <Ctrl+K> <Ctrl+R>	apply-macro-toregion-lines	Apply this macro to each line in a region.

3.16.1 Using the Options Menu

The easiest and quickest way to customize the behavior of Emacs is by using the GNU Emacs pull-down menu choices under Options, which is shown in Figure 3.14. For example, with a check mark placed next to **Highlight Matching Parentheses** (a default choice), all matching left and right parentheses in the buffer will be highlighted as you type them.

The additional checkmarks you place will only be true for the current session of Emacs. For example, if you add a checkmark next to the option Enter Debugger on Error, and you want to retain that option for all future sessions of Emacs, make the Options menu choice **Save Options**. The first time you make this Options menu choice, the following valid line of *elisp* will automatically be written to your **~/.emacs** file, under the custom-set-variables group, as seen in the following .emacs file created:

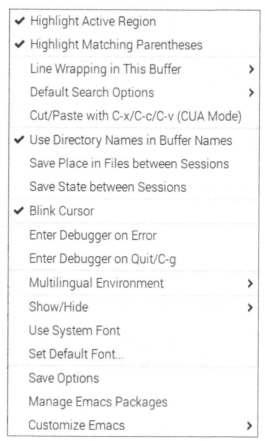

FIGURE 3.14
Options menu choices.

(custom-set-variables
  ;; custom-set-variables was added by Custom.
  ;; If you edit it by hand, you could mess it up, so be careful.
  ;; Your init file should contain only one such instance.
  ;; If there is more than one, they won't work right.
  '(debug-on-error t))
(custom-set-faces
  ;; custom-set-faces was added by Custom.
  ;; If you edit it by hand, you could mess it up, so be careful.
  ;; Your init file should contain only one such instance.
  ;; If there is more than one, they won't work right.
)

In-Chapter Exercise

3.13   Show the Emacs Help facility keystroke sequence you would use to find out what the option show-paren-mode is. Then, list the first few lines of how the Help facility describes the show-paren-mode option.

You can also customize by group from the **Options** menu, if you make the **Customize Emacs** choice, and then make any of the sub-choices below that. For example, if you make the **Options>Customize Emacs>Top-Level Customization Group** choice, a new buffer opens on screen, and allows you to select from all of the subgroups of custom variables.

The next section shows how to achieve this kind of customization as a typed command.

3.16.2 Changing Emacs Variables with Custom and the **<Alt+X> customize** Command

Emacs has many settings that you can change. Most settings are customizable via affecting the settings of *variables*, which are also called *user options*. There are a huge number of user options, controlling numerous aspects of Emacs behavior. A separate class of settings, which we do not cover here, are the *faces*, which determine the fonts, colors, and other attributes of text.

To browse and alter settings (both variables and faces), at the Emacs command prompt type **<Alt+Shift+X> customize**. This creates a customization buffer, which lets you navigate through a logically organized list of settings, edit and set their values, and save them permanently.

Customization settings are organized into *customization groups*. These groups are collected into bigger groups, all the way up to a master group called Emacs, shown near the top of the buffer in Figure 3.15.

<Alt+Shift+X> customize creates a *customization buffer* that looks similar to Figure 3.15.

If you are interested in customizing a particular setting, or customization group that you already know the name of, you can go straight there with the commands **<Alt+X> customize-option, <Alt+X> customize-face**, or **<Alt+X> customize-group**.

The main part of the buffer in Figure 3.15 shows the "Emacs" customization group, which contains several other subgroups ("Editing", "Convenience", etc.). The contents of those subgroups are shown in the single line of description for each group.

The *state* of the group indicates whether the settings in that group have been edited, set, or saved.

Most of the customization buffer cannot be changed, but it includes many editable fields. For example, at the top of the customization buffer is an

FIGURE 3.15
Emacs customization groups.

editable field for searching for settings, with a Search button next to it. There are also buttons and links that you can activate by either clicking with the mouse, or moving the point there and then pressing **<Enter>**. For example, group names like "[Editing]" are links; activating one of these links brings up another customization buffer for that group.

In any particular customization buffer, you can type **<Tab>** (**widget-forward**) to move forward to the next button or editable field. **<Shift+Tab>** (**widget-backward**) moves back to the previous button or editable field-

3.16.2.1 Browsing and Searching for Settings

From the top-level customization buffer created by **<Alt+X>** customize, you can follow the links to the subgroups of the "Emacs" customization group.

These subgroups may contain settings for you to customize; they may also contain further subgroups, dealing with yet more specialized subsystems of Emacs. As you graphically navigate the hierarchy of customization groups, you will find some settings that you want to customize according to your own personal preferences, and according to the nature of the text documents that you are efficiently trying to edit.

3.16.2.2 Changing a Variable

Here is an example of what a variable, or user option, looks like in a specific customization buffer. This variable is accessed by descending down from the top Emacs group through the groups **Editing>Killing**, and then left-clicking on the small diamond shape pointing towards the text **Kill Ring Max**:

Kill Ring Max: 60
[State]: STANDARD.

Maximum length of kill ring before oldest elements are thrown away.
   The first line shows that the variable is named kill-ring-max, formatted as Kill Ring Max for easier viewing. Its value is 60. On our graphical display, the line after the variable name indicates the customization state of the variable: in this example, STANDARD means you have not changed the variable, so its value is the default one. The [State] button gives a menu of operations for customizing the variable.
   Below the customization state is the documentation for the variable. To enter a new value for Kill Ring Max, just click to the right of the value and edit it. As you begin to alter the text, the [State] line will change to:
   [State]: EDITED, shown value does not take effect until you set or save it.
   Editing the value does not make it take effect right away. To do that, you must set the variable by left-clicking on the [State] button and choosing **Set for Current Session**. Then the variable's state becomes:
   [State]: SET for current session only.
   At this point, you could have made the menu choice **Save for Future Sessions**.
   Also, you don't have to worry about specifying a value that is not valid; the **Set for Current Session** operation checks for validity and will not install an unacceptable value.
   When you set a variable, the new value takes effect only in the current Emacs session. To save the value for future sessions, use the [State] button and select the **Save for Future Sessions** operation. Saving custom settings works by writing elisp code to a file, in this case your ~/**.emacs** file. Future Emacs sessions automatically read this file at startup, which invokes and establishes the customizations again.

You can also restore the variable to its standard value by using the [State] button and selecting the **Erase Customization** menu choice. There are four reset operations as follows:

- Undo edits: If you have modified but not yet set the variable, this restores the text in the customization buffer to match the actual value.
- Reset to saved: This restores the value of the variable to the last saved value, and updates the text accordingly.
- Erase customization: This sets the variable to its standard value. Any saved value that you have is also erased.
- Set to backup value: This sets the variable to a previous value that was set in the customization buffer in this session. If you customize a variable and then reset it, which discards the customized value, you can get the discarded value back again with this operation.

Sometimes it is useful to record a comment about a specific customization. Use the Add Comment item from the [State] menu to create a field for entering the comment.

3.16.2.3 Globally Saving Customizations for a Group

Near the top of any group's customization buffer, you can save all customization settings shown in that group buffer by choosing either the [Apply] or [Apply and Save] buttons. [Apply] only saves for the current session, and [Apply and Save] saves for future sessions by modifying the ~/.**Emacs** file accordingly by putting elisp code in the ~/.**Emacs** file.

3.16.2.4 More about Emacs Variables

A *variable* is an elisp symbol that has a value. The symbol's name is the *variable name*. A variable name can contain any characters that can appear in a file, but most variable names consist of ordinary words separated by hyphens.

The name of the variable is descriptive of its role in the Emacs environment. Most variables also have a documentation string, which describes what the variable's purpose is, what kind of value it should have, and how the value will be used.

You can view the documentation for a variable, such as **somevariablename**, using the help command **<Ctrl+H> v** *Describe variable:* **somevariablename** in the minibuffer. To use this facility, type in the command **<Ctrl+H> v**; the system prompts you in the minibuffer with *Describe variable:*; then type in the variable name, such as **somevariablename**, and press **<Enter>**.

Elisp uses variables for internal record keeping, but as noted earlier, the most interesting variables for a user who will not be writing elisp programs per se are those meant for users to change—these are called *customizable variables* or *user options*.

Elisp allows any variable (with a few exceptions) to have any kind of value. However, many variables are meaningful only if assigned values of a certain type. Only numbers are meaningful values for kill-ring-max, which specifies the maximum length of the kill ring; if you assign kill-ring-max a text string as a value, commands such as **<Ctrl+Y> (yank)** will signal an error. On the other hand, some variables don't care about what kind or type of value you assign them; for instance, if a variable has one effect for nil values and another effect for non-nil values, then any value that is not the symbol nil induces the second effect, regardless of its type (by convention, we usually use the value t—a symbol that stands for "true"—to specify a non-nil value). If you set a variable using the customization buffer, you need not worry about giving it an invalid type: the customization buffer usually only allows you to enter meaningful values. When in doubt, use **<Ctrl+H> v** *Describe variable:* **somevariablename** to check the variable's documentation string to see the kind of value it expects.

3.16.2.5 Examining and Setting Variables

The following are some examples of how to examine and set the values of user options. The first general form of this syntax is:

<Ctrl+H> v variablename <Enter>

This general form uses Emacs help function with the v option and displays the value and documentation for variable variablename.
The second general form achieves the change in the variables value:

<Alt+X> set-variable <ENTER> var <ENTER> value <ENTER>

This changes the value of variable var to value.
It reads a variable name that you supply by typing in the minibuffer, with completion, and displays both the value and the documentation of the variable. For example:

<Ctrl+H> v fill-column <ENTER>

A new buffer opens and displays the following:

    fill-column is a variable defined in 'C source code'.
    Its value is 70

    Automatically becomes buffer-local when set.
    This variable is safe as a file local variable if its value
    satisfies the predicate 'integerp'.

Documentation:
Column beyond which automatic line-wrapping should happen.
Interactively, you can set the local value with <Ctrl+X> f

You can customize this variable.

Click on the underlined text customize and you can use a buffer to change the value of this variable.

The most convenient keystroke method to set a specific customizable variable is by typing **<Alt+X>** set-variable. This reads the variable name with the minibuffer (with completion), and then reads an elisp expression for the new value that you type in the minibuffer a second time (you can insert the old value into the minibuffer for editing via **<Alt+N>**). For example:

<Alt+X> set-variable <ENTER> fill-column <ENTER> 75 <ENTER>

sets fill-column to 75.

<Alt+X> set-variable is limited to user options, customizable variables, but you can set any variable with an elisp expression like this:

(setq fill-column 75)

To execute such an expression, type <Alt+:> (eval-expression) and enter the expression in the minibuffer. Alternatively, go to the *scratch* buffer, type in the expression, and then type <Ctrl+J>.

Setting variables this way affects only the current Emacs session. The only way to alter the variable for future sessions is to put the alteration as a Lisp statement in your initialization file.

3.16.3 Init File elisp Syntax

Your GNU Emacs system's *init* file, *~/.emacs*, contains elisp expressions. Each elisp expression consists of a function name followed by arguments, all surrounded by parentheses. For example:

(setq fill-column 60)

calls the function setq to set the variable fill-column to 60.

You can set any Lisp variable with setq, but with certain variables setq won't work.

The second argument to setq is an expression for the new value of the variable. This can be a constant, a variable, or a function call expression. In your

~/.emacs file, constants are used most of the time. They can be one any of the following:

*   Numbers: Numbers are written in decimal, with an optional initial minus sign.
*   Strings: Lisp string syntax is the same as C string syntax with a few extra features. Use a double-quote character (") to begin and end a string constant.
*   Characters: Lisp character constant syntax consists of a? followed by either a character or an escape sequence starting with\.
*   True: t stands for "true".
*   False: nil stands for "false".
*   Other Lisp objects: Write a single quote (') followed by the Lisp object you want.

3.16.4 Keystroke Abbreviations or Abbrevs

Similar to ordinary language abbreviation, an *abbrev* is a word which expands when you insert it, into a pre-formatted expanded or enlarged string of text. Abbrevs are defined by the user to expand in specific ways. For example, you might define Bob as an abbrev expanding to Better off built. Then you could insert Better off built into the buffer by typing Bob <Space>.

A second kind of abbreviation facility, which we do not show examples of here, is called *dynamic abbrev expansion*. You use dynamic abbrev expansion with an explicit command to expand the letters in the buffer before the point by looking for other words in the buffer that start with those same letters.

Abbrevs expand only when *Abbrev mode*, a *buffer-local minor mode*, is enabled. Disabling Abbrev mode does not cause abbrev definitions to be forgotten, but they do not expand until Abbrev mode is enabled again. The command **<Alt+X> abbrev-mode** toggles Abbrev mode; using a numeric argument, it turns Abbrev mode on if the argument is positive, or turns it off otherwise.

You can define abbrevs interactively during the editing session, irrespective of whether Abbrev mode is enabled. You can also save lists of abbrev definitions in files, which you can then reload for use in later sessions.

3.16.5 Defining Abbrevs

The following are ways of defining and managing abbrevs:

<Ctrl+X> a g
Define an abbrev, using one or more words before point as its expansion (add-global-abbrev).

<Ctrl+X> a l
Similar, but define an abbrev specific to the current major mode (add-mode-abbrev).

<Ctrl+X> a i g
Define a word in the buffer as an abbrev (inverse-add-global-abbrev).

<Ctrl+X> a i l
Define a word in the buffer as a mode-specific abbrev (inverse-add-mode-abbrev).

<Alt+X> define-global-abbrev <Enter> abbrev <Enter> expression <Enter>
Define abbrev as an abbrev expanding into an expression.

<Alt+X> define-mode-abbrev <Enter> abbrev <Enter> expression <Enter>
Define abbrev as a mode-specific abbrev expanding into an expression.

<Alt+X> kill-all-abbrevs
Discard all abbrev definitions, leaving a blank slate.

The usual way to define an abbrev is to enter the text you want the abbrev to expand to, position the point after it, and type **<Ctrl+X> a g**. This reads the abbrev itself using the minibuffer, and then defines it as an abbrev for one or more words before the point. As with many other Emacs commands, you can use a numeric digit argument to specify how many words before the point should be taken as the expansion. For example, to define the abbrev Bob, insert the text Better off built and then type **<Ctrl+U> 3 <Ctrl+X> a g Bob <Enter>**.

An argument of zero to **<Ctrl+X> a g** means to use the contents of the region as the expansion of the abbrev being defined.

To remove an abbrev definition, give a negative argument to the abbrev definition command, as in one of the following ways:

<Ctrl+U> - <Ctrl+X> a g
<Ctrl+U> - <Ctrl+X> a l

The first way removes a global definition, while the second way removes a mode-specific definition.

   <Alt+X> kill-all-abbrevs removes all abbrev definitions, both global and local.

3.16.6 Controlling Abbrev Expansion

When Abbrev mode is enabled, an abbrev expands whenever it is present in the buffer just before the point and when you type a self-inserting whitespace or punctuation character like **<Space>** or a comma, etc. More precisely, any character that is not a word constituent expands an abbrev, and any word constituent character can be part of an abbrev. The most common way to use an abbrev is to insert it and then insert a punctuation or whitespace character to expand it.

These commands are used to control abbrev expansion:
<Alt+'>

Separate a prefix from a following abbrev to be expanded (abbrev-prefixmark).
<Ctrl+X> a e

Expand the abbrev before the point (expand-abbrev). This is effective even when Abbrev mode is not enabled.
<Alt+X> expand-region-abbrevs

Expand some or all abbrevs found in the region.
If you expand an abbrev by mistake, you can undo the expansion by typing C-/ (undo). This undoes the insertion of the abbrev expansion and brings back the abbrev text. You can also use the command **<Alt+X> unexpand-abbrev** to cancel the last expansion without deleting the terminating character.

3.16.7 Listing and Editing Abbrevs

<Alt+X> list-abbrevs

Display a list of all abbrev definitions. With a numeric argument, list only local abbrevs.
<Alt+X> edit-abbrevs allows you to add, change, or kill abbrev definitions by editing a list of them in an Emacs buffer. The buffer of abbrevs is called ***Abbrevs***, and is in **Edit>Abbrevs mode**. Type **<Ctrl+C> <Ctrl+C>** in this buffer to install the abbrev definitions as specified in the buffer, and delete any abbrev definitions not listed.

The commands **edit-abbrevs** and **list-abbrevs** are the same except they display the listing in a window and a buffer, respectively.

3.16.8 Saving Abbrevs

These commands allow you to keep abbrev definitions between editing sessions:

<Alt+X> write-abbrev-file <Enter> filename <Enter>
Save to filename describing all defined abbrevs.

<Alt+X> read-abbrev-file <Enter> filename <Enter>
Read from **filename** and define abbrevs as specified in that file.

<Alt+X> define-abbrevs
Define abbrevs from definitions in current buffer.

<Alt+X> insert-abbrevs
Insert all abbrevs and their expansions into current buffer.

<Alt+X> write-abbrev-file reads a file name using the minibuffer and then writes a description of all current abbrev definitions into that file. This is used to save abbrev definitions for use in a later session. The text stored in the file is a series of Lisp expressions that, when executed, define the same abbrevs that you currently have.

<Alt+X> read-abbrev-file reads a file name using the minibuffer and then reads the file, defining abbrevs according to the contents of the file. The function quietly-read-abbrev-file is similar except that it does not display a message in the echo area; you cannot invoke it interactively, and it is used primarily in your init file. If either of these functions is called with nil as the argument, it uses the file given by the variable abbrev-file-name, which is ~/.Emacs.d/ **abbrev_defs** by default. This is your standard abbrev definition file, and Emacs loads abbrevs from it automatically when it starts up.

Emacs will offer to save abbrevs automatically if you have changed any of them, whenever it offers to save all files (for **<Ctrl+X> s** or **<Ctrl+X> <Ctrl+ C >**). It saves them in the file specified by abbrev-file-name. This feature can be inhibited by setting the variable save-abbrevs to nil.

The commands **<Alt+X> insert-abbrevs** and **<Alt+X> define-abbrevs** are similar to the previous commands but work on text in an Emacs buffer. **<Alt+X> insert-abbrevs** inserts text into the current buffer after the point, describing all current abbrev definitions; **<Alt+X> define-abbrevs** interprets the entire current buffer, and defines abbrevs accordingly.

3.16.9 Keystroke Macro Commands

In this section we more fully describe how to record, save, edit, and list a sequence of commands in a *macro*, so you can repeat it conveniently later. A keyboard macro is a command defined by an Emacs user that represents, in a shortened form, a sequence of keys. For example, if you discover that you are about to type three different keystroke combinations 400 times, you can speed your work by defining a much shorter keyboard macro to do those three different keystroke combinations, and then execute it 399 more times.

You define a keyboard macro by executing and recording the commands which are its definition. As you define a keyboard macro, the definition is being executed for the first time. When you close the definition, the keyboard macro is defined and also has been executed once. You can then repeat the commands by invoking the macro as many times as you like.

3.16.9.1 Keystroke Macros: Basic Use

These are the basic operations in defining and using keystroke macros:

<F3>
Start defining a keyboard macro (kmacro-start-macro-or-insert-counter).

<F4>
Dual-purpose function key. If a keyboard macro is being defined, end the definition; otherwise, execute the most recent keyboard macro (kmacro-end-or-call-macro).

<Ctrl+U> <F3>
Re-execute last keyboard macro, then append keys to its definition.

<Ctrl+U> <Ctrl+U> <F3>
Append keys to the last keyboard macro without re-executing it.

<Ctrl+X> <Ctrl+K> r
Run the last keyboard macro on each line that begins in the region (apply-macro-to-region-lines).

To start defining a keyboard macro, type **<F3>**. From then on, your keys continue to be executed, but also become part of the definition of the macro. Def appears in the mode line. When you are finished, type **<F4>** (kmacro-end-or-call-macro) to terminate the definition. For example:

<F3> <Alt+F> Bob <F4>

defines a macro to move forward a word and then insert Bob at the point. **<F3>** and **<F4>** do not become part of the macro.

After defining the macro, it is the most recently defined keyboard macro, and you can call it with **<F4>**. In the example, this has the same effect as typing **<Alt+F> Bob** again.

The two roles of the **<F4>** command: it ends the macro if you are in the process of defining one, or calls the last macro otherwise.

You can also supply **<F4>** with a numeric prefix argument n, which means to invoke the macro n times. An argument of zero repeats the macro indefinitely, until it gets an error or you type **<Ctrl+G>** to terminate it.

After ending the definition of a keyboard macro, you can append more keystrokes to its definition by typing **<Ctrl+U> <F3>**. This is equivalent to plain **<F3>** followed by retyping the whole definition so far. As a consequence, it re-executes the macro as previously defined. If you change the variable kmacro-execute-before-append to nil, the existing macro will not be re-executed before appending to it (the default is t). You can also add to the end of the definition of the last keyboard macro without re-executing it by typing **<Ctrl+U> <Ctrl+U> <F3>**.

When a command reads an argument with the minibuffer, your minibuffer input becomes part of the macro along with the command. So when you replay the macro, the command gets the same argument as when you entered the macro. For example:

<F3> <Ctrl+A> <Ctrl+K> <Ctrl+X> b Bob <Enter> <Ctrl+Y> <Ctrl+X> b <Enter> <F4>

defines a macro that kills the current line, yanks it into the buffer **Bob**, then returns to the original buffer. The command **<Ctrl+X> <Ctrl+K>** r (apply-macro-to-region-lines) repeats the last defined keyboard macro on each line that begins in the region. It does this line by line, by moving the point to the beginning of the line and then executing the macro.

All defined keyboard macros are recorded in the *keyboard macro ring*. There is only one keyboard macro ring, shared by all buffers. The basic keyboard macro ring operations are:

<Ctrl+X> <Ctrl+K> <Ctrl+K>
Execute the keyboard macro at the head of the ring (kmacro-end-or-callmacro-repeat).
<Ctrl+X> <Ctrl+K> <Ctrl+N>
Rotate the keyboard macro ring to the next macro (defined earlier) (kmacrocycle-ring-next).
<Ctrl+X> <Ctrl+K> <Ctrl+P>
Rotate the keyboard macro ring to the previous macro (defined later) (kmacrocycle-ring-previous).

Note
The maximum number of macros stored in the keyboard macro ring is determined by the customizable variable kmacro-ring-max.

3.16.9.2 Naming, Saving, and Invoking or Using Keyboard Macros

The following are the ways to name, save, and invoke or use keyboard macros, particularly with regard to retaining them in your ~/.emacs so that they will be available in all future sessions of Emacs (anything below enclosed in [] is optional).

1. <Ctrl+X> <Ctrl+K> n <Enter> macroname <Enter>
Gives a command name (for the duration of the current Emacs session only) to the most recently defined keyboard macro (kmacro-name-last-macro). If you wish to save a keyboard macro for later use, you can give it a name using this syntax. This sequence reads a name as an argument, by prompting for the name in the minibuffer, and uses the minibuffer-supplied name and defines that name so that you can execute the last keyboard macro, in its current form, using that name. The macro name is an elisp symbol, and defining it in this way makes it a valid command name for invoking or using it with <Alt+ X>, or for binding a key to it with global-set-key. If you specify a name that has a prior definition other than a keyboard macro, you get an error.

2. <Ctrl+X> <Ctrl+K> b <Enter> key <Enter>
Binds the most recently defined keyboard macro to a key sequence (for the duration of the current Emacs session only) (kmacro-bind-to-key).

3. <Alt+X> insert-kbd-macro <Enter> [macroname <Enter>]
Inserts in the current buffer a keyboard macro's definition as elisp code. If you do not supply an already-defined macroname, the last keyboard macro defined is inserted as elisp code.

4. <Alt+X> macroname <Enter>
Invokes macroname in the current buffer.

5. Pressing the function key <F4> invokes the last defined keyboard macro.

3.16.9.3 Saving Keyboard Macros for Future Sessions

Once a keyboard macro has a name, you can save its definition in a file, and particularly in the ~/.emacs file or other initialization file that you may use to initialize Emacs at startup. By taking the following steps, it can be used in all future editing sessions.

The steps to accomplish this are as follows:

1. Visit the file you want to save the definition in, which becomes the current buffer. This is usually ~/.emacs.

2. Use the command <Alt+X> insert-kbd-macro <Enter> macroname <Enter>

   This uses the macroname you already have previously defined, and inserts equivalent elisp code that the keyboard macro represents, into the current buffer.

3. Save the current buffer. If the file you save in is your initialization file ~/.emacs, then the macro will be defined for all future sessions of Emacs.

The sections below describe key bindings, which map keys to commands, and keymaps, which record key bindings. They also explain how to customize key bindings, which is done by editing your Emacs init file.

3.16.10 Keys, Commands, and Variables

Emacs does not assign meanings to keys directly. Instead, Emacs assigns meanings to labeled commands, and then gives keys their meanings by *binding* them to commands. As you have seen in the previous sections, every command has a name, which is usually made up of a few words separated by hyphens—for example, **insert-kbd-macro** or **abbrev-file-name**. Internally, each command is an Emacs form of a Lisp function, and the actions associated with the command are performed by running the function.

The bindings, or mappings, between keys and commands are recorded in tables called *keymaps*.

The effect of "<Ctrl+N> moves point down vertically one line" is that the vertical movement of the command next-line is bound to the key sequence <Ctrl+N>. If you rebind <Ctrl+N> to the command forward-word, <Ctrl+N> will move forward one word instead. The key is bound to a command.

A *variable* is a name used to store a value. The variables we described in Section 3.16.2 are intended to be customized: some commands or mechanisms in Emacs examine the variable and behave according to the value that you assign to the variable when and if you customize it.

3.16.10.1 Keymaps

Emacs commands are elisp functions whose definition instances interactive use. Like every elisp function, a command has a function name, which usually consists of lowercase letters and hyphens. A keystroke (*key* for short) sequence is a sequence of input events that have a meaning as a unit. Input events include characters, function keys, and mouse buttons—all the inputs that you can send to the computer. A key sequence gets its meaning from its binding, which dictates what command it runs.

The bindings between key sequences and command functions are recorded in data structures called *keymaps*. Emacs has many of these, each used on particular occasions.

The global keymap is the most important keymap because it is always in effect. The *global keymap* defines keys for *Fundamental mode*; most of these definitions are common to most or all major modes. Each major or minor mode can have its own keymap which overrides the global definitions of some keys.

For example, a self-inserting character such as **g** is self-inserting because the global keymap binds it to the command **self-insert-command**. The standard Emacs editing characters such as **<Ctrl+A>** also get their standard meanings from the global keymap. Commands to rebind keys, such as **<Alt+X> global-set-key**, work by storing the new binding in the proper place in the global map.

Most modern keyboards have function keys as well as character keys. Function keys send input events just as character keys do, and keymaps can have bindings for them. Key sequences can mix function keys and characters. For example, if your keyboard has a **<Home>** function key, Emacs can recognize key sequences like **<Ctrl+X> <Home>**. You can even mix mouse events with keyboard events, such as **S-down-mouse-1**.

On text terminals, typing a function key actually sends the computer a sequence of characters; the precise details of the sequence depends on the function key and on the terminal type. (Often the sequence starts with **ESC [**.) If Emacs understands your terminal type properly, it automatically handles such sequences as single input events.

3.16.10.2 *Prefix Keymaps*

Emacs stores only single events in each keymap. Interpreting a key sequence of multiple events involves a chain of keymaps: the first keymap gives a definition for the first event, which is another keymap that is used to look up the second event in the sequence, and so on. A *prefix key* such as **<Ctrl+X>** or **<Esc>** has its own keymap, which holds the definition for the event that immediately follows that prefix.

A prefix key is usually the keymap to use for looking up the following event. The definition can also be an elisp symbol whose function definition is the following keymap; the effect is the same, but it provides a command name for the prefix key that can be used as a description of what the prefix key is for. Thus, the binding of **<Ctrl+X>** is the symbol **Control-X-prefix**, whose function definition is the keymap for **<Ctrl+X>** commands. The definitions of **<Ctrl+C>**, **<Ctrl+X>**, **<Ctrl+H>**, and **<Esc>** as prefix keys appear in the global map, so these prefix keys are always available.

Some prefix keymaps are stored in variables with names:

_ **ctl-x-map** is the variable name for the map used for characters that follow **<Ctrl+X>**.

_ **help-map** is for characters that follow **<Ctrl+H>**.

_ **esc-map** is for characters that follow **<Esc>**. Thus, all metacharacters are actually defined by this map.

_ **ctl-x-4-map** is for characters that follow **<Ctrl+X> 4**.

_ **mode-specific-map** is for characters that follow **<Ctrl+C>**.

3.16.10.3 Local Keymaps

So far, we have explained the details of the global map. Major modes customize Emacs by providing their own key bindings in *local keymaps*. For example, C mode overrides <Tab> to make it indent the current line for C code. Minor modes can also have local keymaps; whenever a minor mode is in effect, the definitions in its keymap override both the major mode's local keymap and the global keymap. In addition, portions of text in the buffer can specify their own keymaps, which override all other keymaps.

A local keymap can redefine a key as a prefix key by defining it as a prefix keymap. If the key is also defined globally as a prefix, its local and global definitions (both keymaps) effectively are combined: both definitions are used to look up the event that follows the prefix key. For example, if a local keymap defines <Ctrl+C> as a prefix keymap, and that keymap defines <Ctrl+Z> as a command, this provides a local meaning for <Ctrl+C> <Ctrl+Z>. This does not affect other sequences that start with <Ctrl+C>; if those sequences don't have their own local bindings, their global bindings remain in effect.

Another way to think of this is that Emacs handles a multievent key sequence by looking in several keymaps, one by one, for a binding of the whole key sequence. First it checks the minor mode keymaps for minor modes that are enabled, then it checks the major mode's keymap, and then it checks the global keymap.

3.16.10.4 Changing Key Bindings Interactively

The way to redefine an Emacs key is to change its entry in a keymap. You can change the global keymap, in which case the change is effective in all major modes (except those that have their own overriding local bindings for the same key), or you can change a local keymap, which affects all buffers using the same major mode.

The following describes how to rebind keys for the current Emacs session (see Section 3.16.10.5 for a description of how to make key rebindings affect future Emacs sessions by putting them in your ~/.emacs file):

1. **<Alt+X> global-set-key <Enter> key command <Enter>**
Defines key globally to run command.

2. **<Alt+X> local-set-key <Enter> key command <Enter>**
Defines key locally (in the major mode now in effect) to run command.

3. **<Alt+X> global-unset-key <Enter> key**
Makes key undefined in the global map.

4. **<Alt+X> local-unset-key <Enter> key**
Makes key undefined locally (in the major mode now in effect).

For example, the following binds **<Ctrl+Z>** to the shell command, replacing the normal global definition of **<Ctrl+Z>**:

<Alt+X> global-set-key <Enter> <Ctrl+Z> shell <Enter>

The global-set-key command reads the command name after the key. After you press the key, a message like this appears so that you can confirm that you are binding the key you want:

Set key <Ctrl+Z> to command:

You can redefine function keys and mouse events in the same way; just type the function key or click the mouse when it's time to specify the key to rebind. You can rebind a key that contains more than one event in the same way. Emacs keeps reading the key to rebind until it is a complete key (that is, not a prefix key). Thus, if you type **<Ctrl+F>** for the key, that's the end; it enters the minibuffer immediately to read the command. But if you type **<Ctrl+X>**, since that's a prefix, it reads another character; if that is **4**, another prefix character, it reads one more character, and so on. For example:

<Alt+X> global-set-key <Enter> <Ctrl+X> 4 $ spell-other-window <Enter>

redefines **<Ctrl+X> 4 $** to run the (fictitious) command spell-other-window.

You can remove the global definition of a key with global-unset-key. This makes the key undefined; if you type it, Emacs will just beep. Similarly, local-unset-key makes a key undefined in the current major mode keymap, which makes the global definition (or lack of one) come back into effect in that major mode.

If you have redefined (or undefined) a key and you subsequently wish to retract the change, undefining the key will not do the job; you need to redefine the key with its standard definition.

To find the name of the standard definition of a key, go to a Fundamental mode buffer in an Emacs session that you have not done any key remappings in, and type **<Ctrl+H> c**. So, if you want to prevent yourself from invoking a command by mistake, it is better to disable the command than to undefine the key!

3.16.10.5 Rebinding Keys in Your Init File

If you have a set of key bindings that you like to use all the time, you can specify them in your initialization file by writing elisp code. There are several ways to write a key binding using elisp. The simplest is to use the kbd function, which converts a text representation of a key sequence, similar to how we have written key sequences up to this point, into a form that can be passed as an argument to global-set-key. For example, here's how to bind **<Ctrl+Z>** to the shell command.

(global-set-key (kbd "C-z") 'shell)

The single-quote (') before the shell command name designates it as a constant symbol rather than a variable. If you omit the quote, Emacs tries to evaluate shell as a variable.

3.16.10.6 Examples

Here are some additional examples, including binding function keys and mouse events:

(global-set-key (kbd "<Ctrl+C> y") 'clipboard-yank)

(global-set-key (kbd "<Ctrl ><Alt+Q>") 'query-replace)

(global-set-key (kbd "<f5>") 'flyspell-mode)

(global-set-key (kbd "<Ctrl ><f5>") 'linum-mode)

(global-set-key (kbd "<Ctrl ><right>") 'forward-sentence)

(global-set-key (kbd "<mouse-2>") 'mouse-save-then-kill)

In-Chapter Exercises

3.14 (a) Use the Emacs Help function, via keyboard keystrokes only, to find out what the commands that are being bound to each of the keys sequences in the six examples in Section 3.16.10.6 accomplish. So, for **forward-sentence**, what explanation does Help supply? Make a list of the answers that the Help function supplies.

(b) What are the default key sequence bindings, if any, for the commands in the six examples? Make a list of the default key sequence bindings for commands that have them.

3.15 Place all six examples of key sequences bound to commands in your ~/.emacs file, and test them according to your findings in In-Chapter Exercise 3.14.

3.17 Summary

This chapter explained the general, and detailed utility, of editing text files on a Raspberry Pi system. It showed the basic capabilities of the GNU Emacs editor, illustrated some of the important ways of customizing this editor, and covered the commands and primitives **cp, emacs, ls, pwd, sh**, and **who**. A complete summary of Emacs commands is given in Table 3.7.

TABLE 3.7

Command Summary

Emacs Commands	
Command	**Action**
\<Ctrl+X> \<Ctrl+F>	Visit a file (find-file).
\<Ctrl+X> \<Ctrl+R>	Visit a file for viewing, without allowing changes to it (find-file-read-only).
\<Ctrl+X> \<Ctrl+V>	Visit a different file instead of the one visited last (find-alternate-file).
\<Ctrl+X> \<Ctrl+S>	Save the current buffer to its file (save-buffer).
\<Ctrl+X> s	Save any or all buffers to their files (save-some-buffers).
\<Alt+~>	Forget that the current buffer has been changed (not-modified).
\<Ctrl+X> \<Ctrl+W>	Save the current buffer with a specified file name (write-file).
\<Ctrl+H>	Display a help message about these options.
\<Ctrl+X> \<Ctrl+C>	Exits Emacs.
\<Ctrl+X> \<Ctrl+Z>	Suspends Emacs and exits to the shell.

Emacs Help Command	
\<Ctrl+H> a topics \<Enter>	Display a list of commands whose names match topics (apropos-command).
\<Ctrl+H> b	Display all active key bindings—minor mode bindings first, then those of the major mode, then global bindings (describe-bindings).
\<Ctrl+H> c key	Show the name of the command that the key sequence key is bound to (describe-key-briefly). Here c stands for "character". For more extensive information on key, use \<Ctrl+H> k.
\<Ctrl+H> d topics \<Enter>	Display the commands and variables whose documentation matches topics (apropos-documentation).
\<Ctrl+H> e	Display the *Messages* buffer (view-echo-area-messages).
\<Ctrl+H> f function \<Enter>	Display documentation on the Lisp function named function (describe-function). Since commands are Lisp functions, this works for commands too.
\<Ctrl+H> r	Display the Emacs manual in Info (info-Emacs-manual).
\<Ctrl+H> s	Display the contents of the current syntax table (describe-syntax). The syntax table says which characters are opening delimiters, which are parts of words, and so on.
\<Ctrl+H> t	Enter the Emacs interactive tutorial (help-with-tutorial).
\<Ctrl+H> K key	Enter Info and go to the node that documents the key sequence key (Info-goto-Emacs-key-command-node).
\<Ctrl+H>	Display the help message for a special text area, if the point is in one (display-local-help). (These include, for example, links in *Help* buffers.)

Emacs Cursor Movement		
Entity to Move Over	**Backward**	**Forward**
Character	\<Ctrl+B>	\<Ctrl+F>
Word	\<Alt+B>	\<Alt+F>
Line	\<Ctrl+P>	\<Ctrl+N>
Go to line beginning (or end)	\<Ctrl+A>	\<Ctrl+E>
Sentence	\<Alt+A>	\<Alt+E>
Paragraph	\<Alt+{>	\<Alt+}>
Page	\<Ctrl+X> [	\<Ctrl+X>]

TABLE 3.7 (Continued)

Command Summary

Emacs Commands

Entity to Kill		Backward	Forward
Character (delete, not kill)		\<Del>	\<Ctrl+D>
Word		\<Alt+Del>	\<Alt+D>
Line (to end of)		\<Alt+0> \<Ctrl+K>	\<Ctrl+K>
Sentence		\<Ctrl+X> DEL	\<Alt+K>
Kill region	\<Ctrl+W>		
Copy region to kill ring	\<Alt+W>		
Yank back last thing killed	\<Ctrl+Y>		

Emacs Interactive Search and Replace

Search and Replace Action	Keystrokes
Search forward	\<Ctrl+S>
Search backward	\<Ctrl+R>
Regular expression search	\<Ctrl+Alt+S>
Reverse regular expression search	\<Ctrl+Alt+R>
Select previous search string	\<Alt+P>
Select next later search string	\<Alt+N>
Exit incremental search	\<Enter>
Undo effect of last character	\<Del>
Abort current search	\<Ctrl+G>
Interactively replace a text string	\<Alt+%>
Using regular expressions	\<Alt+X> query-replace-regexp
Replace this one, go on to next	\<Space> or y
Replace this one, don't move	,
Skip to next without replacing	\<Del> or n
Replace all remaining matches	!
Back up to the previous match	^
Exit query-replace	\<Enter>
Enter recursive edit (**\<Ctrl+Alt+C>** to exit)	\<Ctrl+R>

Changing Emacs Behavior

Customization Action	Keystrokes
Abbrevs	
add global abbrev	\<Ctrl+X> a g
add mode-local abbrev	\<Ctrl+X> a l
add global expansion for this abbrev	\<Ctrl+X> a i g
add mode-local expansion for this abbrev	\<Ctrl+X> a i l
explicitly expand abbrev	\<Ctrl+X> a e
expand previous word dynamically	\<Alt+/>
Macros	
Start defining a keyboard macro	\<Ctrl+X> (or \<F3>)
End keyboard macro definition	\<Ctrl+X>) or \<F4>
Execute last-defined keyboard macro	\<Ctrl+X> e or \<F4>
Append to last keyboard macro	\<Ctrl+U> \<Ctrl+X> (
Name last keyboard macro	\<Alt+X> name-last-kbd-macro
Insert Lisp definition in buffer	\<Alt+X> insert-kbd-macro
Customize variables and faces	\<Alt+X> customize

Questions, Problems, and Projects

Chapter 0

0.1 Create a directory called Raspberry in your home directory. What command line did you use to do this?

0.2 Give a command line for displaying the files **lab1**, **lab2**, **lab3**, and **lab4**. Can you give two more command lines that do the same thing? What is the command line for displaying the files **lab1.c**, **lab2.c**, **lab3.c**, and **lab4.c**? (Hint: use shell metacharacters.)

0.3 Give a command line for printing all the files in your home directory that start with the string memo and end with **.ps** on a printer called **upmpr**. What command line did you use to do this?

0.4 Give the command line for nicknaming the command **who -H** as **W**. Give both Bash and C shell versions. Where would you put it if you want it to execute every time you start a new shell?

0.5 Type the command **man ls > ~/Raspberry/ls.man** on your system. This command will put the man page for the **ls** command in the **ls. man** file in your Raspberry directory (the one you created in Problem 1). Give the command for printing two copies of this file on a printer in your lab. What command line would you use to achieve this printing?

0.6 What is the **mesg** value set to for your environment? If it is on, how would you turn it off for your current session? How would you set it off for every login?

0.7 What does the command **lpr -Pqpr [0–9]*.jpg** do? Explain your answer.

0.8 Use the **passwd** command to change your password. If you are on a network, be aware that you might have to use the **yppasswd** command to modify your network login password. Also, make sure you abide by the rules set up by your system administrator for coming up with good passwords!

0.9 Using the correct terminology (e.g., command, option, option argument, and command argument), identify the constituent parts of the following Raspberry Pi OS single commands.

ls -la *.exe

lpr -Pwpr file27

chmod g+rwx *.*

0.10 View the man pages for each of the useful commands listed in Table A.1. Which part of the man pages is most descriptive for you? Which of the options shown on each of the man pages is the most useful for beginners? Explain.

0.11 How many users are logged on to your system at this time? What command did you use to discover this?

0.12 Determine the name of the operating system that your computer runs. What command did you use to discover this?

0.13 Give the command line for displaying manual pages for the socket, read, and connect system calls on your system.

TABLE A.1

Useful Commands for the Beginner

Command	What It Does
\<Ctrl+D\>	Terminates a process or command
alias	Allows you to create pseudonyms for commands
biff	Notifies you of new e-mail
cal	Displays a calendar on screen
cat	Allows joining of files
cd	Allows you to change the current working directory
cp	Allows you to copy files
exit	Ends a shell that you have started
hostname	Displays the name of the host computer that you are logged on to
login	Allows you to log on to the computer with a valid username/password pair
lpr or lp	Allows printing of text files
ls	Allows you to display names of files and directories in the current working directory
man	Allows you to view a manual page for a command or topic
mesg	Allows or disallows writing messages to the screen
mkdir	Allows you to create a new directory
more	Allows viewing of the contents of a file one screen at a time
mv	Allows you to move the path location of, or rename, files
passwd	Allows you to change your password on the computer
pg	Solaris command that displays one screen of a file at a time
pwd	Allows you to see the name of the current working directory
rm	Allows you to delete a file from the file structure
rmdir	Allows deletion of directories
talk	Allows you to send real-time messages to other users
telnet	Allows you to log on to a computer on a network or the Internet
unalias	Allows you to undefine pseudonyms for commands
uname	Displays information about the operating system running the computer
whatis	Allows you to view a brief description of a command
whereis	Displays the path(s) to commands and utilities in certain key directories
who	Allows you to find out login names of users currently on the system
whoami	Displays your username
write	Allows real-time messaging between users on the system

Advanced Questions and Problems

0.14 Following is a typical /etc/profile configuration file, this particular one is from a default installation on our Raspberry Pi OS system:

```
# /etc/profile: system-wide .profile file for the Bourne shell (sh(1))
# and Bourne compatible shells (bash(1), ksh(1), ash(1), ...).

if [ "$(id -u)" -eq 0 ]; then
  PATH="/usr/local/sbin:/usr/local/bin:/usr/sbin:/usr/bin:/sbin:/bin"
else
  PATH="/usr/local/sbin:/usr/local/bin:/usr/sbin:/usr/bin:/sbin:/bin:/usr/\
  local/games:/usr/games"
fi
export PATH

if [ "${PS1-}" ]; then
  if [ "${BASH-}" ] && [ "$BASH" != "/bin/sh" ]; then
    # The file bash.bashrc already sets the default PS1.
    # PS1='\h:\w\$ '
    if [ -f /etc/bash.bashrc ]; then
      . /etc/bash.bashrc
    fi
  else
    if [ "$(id -u)" -eq 0 ]; then
      PS1='# '
    else
      PS1='$ '
    fi
  fi
fi
if [ -d /etc/profile.d ]; then
  for i in /etc/profile.d/*.sh; do
    if [ -r $i ]; then
      . $i
    fi
  done
  unset i
fi
```

Write an explanatory sentence in your own words describing exactly what you consider important lines in the file accomplish, including the comments (the lines that begin with the pound sign #). Examine this file on your Raspberry Pi OS. How does it compare, line-for-line, with the one above? We assume here that, by default, Bash is both the interactive and login shell on your system.

0.15 What is the default umask setting in an ordinary, non-privileged account on your Raspberry Pi OS, from both a login and non-login shell? Describe in your own words what the umask setting is, and how it is applied to newly created directories and files. Is the umask set in /etc/profile on your Raspberry Pi OS system? If not, where can the umask be set most effectively on a persistent basis, for a particular single user, both in a login and non-login shell?

0.16 Assume that all users, when they log into your Raspberry Pi OS, have Bash as their default shell. What file sets the shell prompt for them on your Raspberry Pi OS? Is it the file illustrated in Problem 14? Describe the lines in the file that actually specify the shell prompt, and give a short description of the components of those lines. Experiment to find out which file accomplishes the actual shell prompt setting for ordinary users (for both interactive or login shells), and write an explicit description of what you have discovered.

Additionally, set the shell prompt for yourself in the current interactive shell, so that it contains the following:

A display of just the date/time.
A display of the date and time, hostname, and current directory.
A display where the entire prompt is in red text, along with hostname and current directory.

Then make those changes persistent for yourself in both login and interactive shells. Finally, undo the persistent changes.

As a follow-up, design your own shell prompt so that it contains the information you want in a useful display given your use case(s), and make that designed prompt persistent for yourself on your Raspberry Pi OS.

0.17 Give a sequential list of the exact commands you would use to make the TC shell the default login shell for your user account on your Raspberry Pi OS. Is the TC shell installed by default on your Raspberry Pi OS? If not, how would you install it on a Debian-family or CentOS? Give the exact commands for installation of not only the TC shell, but any of the other four major Raspberry Pi OS shells available.

0.18 Execute all of the compound command Examples provided at the web link https://explainshell.com/, and then use the output shown to explain all of them in your own words. Try executing the Examples with meaningful arguments on your Raspberry Pi OS, if possible.

Project 1

After completing Problems 14 through 16, gather your findings together in a summary report that details the default settings (within the scope of the files you have examined, and in the context of those problems) of the Bash environment on your Raspberry Pi OS. For example, which actual file takes precedence by default, and what components of the Bash environment are set in that file? What are the critical default settings in the Bash environment, and what actual files on your Raspberry Pi OS effect them?

Chapter 1

1.1 Is it possible to create a zpool using only a single slice (commonly referred to as a *partition*) on a vdev, and if so, what would the advantages and disadvantages of doing this be? Does your answer reflect the fact that only one file system can exist on that slice?

To follow up on this question, is it possible to create a *volume* with a ZFS file system on it? What would be the advantage of doing this?

1.2 List the advantages and disadvantages that ZFS has for your use case on your Raspberry Pi system.

1.3 Give a brief description of the **zdb** command.

1.4 Similar to Example 1.3, create a mirrored zpool using two files that simulate disk drives, and are 256 MB in size each. Name the files **disk1** and **disk2**. Then answer the following questions:

    a. What is the pathname to the default filesystem that's created when you create the zpool?

    b. If you create a 32 MB file in your zpool, but put nothing in it, what size increase do you see in the files **disk1** and **disk2**? How did you find this out?

    c. How much free space is now in the zpool?

1.5 Define the following terms in ZFS, in your own words:

Scrubbing, resilvering, slicing, mirroring, zpool, vdev.

1.6 If you create a zpool named **pool1**, and a file system on that zpool named **bobsfiles** with the **zfs** command, what is the entire and full pathname to a file named **data27** in that file system? What is the exact syntax of the command you used to create the file system?

1.7 List eight of the basic **zfs** sub-commands that allow you to do file and file system backups and archiving.

1.8 Do the following:

   a. Use the **zfs** command to create a dataset named **usbdrive** on a zpool named **test3** which is on a USB flashdrive. The name of the dataset would be **test3/usbdrive**.

   b. Type the command **zfs set copies=2 test3/usbdrive**

   c. What you have achieved with this command is a signature validation of using ZFS and creating a zpool on the USB flashdrive. The USB flashdrive is a redundant device to the extent shown. But more importantly, by setting the property of **copies=2** on this dataset, you have made the USB flashdrive redundant to itself, because ZFS now keeps two copies of everything. And you can use ZFS facilities to ensure integrity of the data to the bit level on the USB flashdrive. Given how inexpensive USB flashdrives are, even in larger capacities, having two automatically created copies of your files on this flashdrive is not prohibitive.

   d. Copy a number of important user files into this new dataset from your Raspberry Pi system's boot/system medium, using either the **cp** or **rsync** commands.

   e. Retain the zpool and dataset you have created on the flashdrive, and use it as a backup drive for your important files. You can periodically use **rsync** to keep the backup files synchronized to the important files on your hard drive. You may even decide that the important files you want to back up to the flashdrive are in a single directory or multiple directories. You can then use rsync to copy directories over to the flashdrive.

   f. To remove the USB flashdrive temporarily at any time, use the **zfs unmount** command. Then you can remove it from the computer. Remember to use the **zfs mount** command when you want to reinsert the USB flashdrive and archive or backup files to it.

1.9 Repeat Example 1.4, using two Raspberry Pi systems on your intranet, or LAN, using directories of your choice.

1.10 How would you create a script file, like the **Example_1_6.sh** Bourne shell script file, that takes snapshots that are retained any number of times between two systems? In other words, each time that you run it, the previous time's snapshot is retained on the destination Raspberry Pi, and the one from the time before, and the time before that, etc. The interval does not have to be one calendar day. Provide the code for the complete Bourne shell script as your answer.

Projects

1. Using the techniques shown in the six examples of Section 1.2.2, create a mirrored pair of USB flashdrives on your single Raspberry Pi system. A single dataset on the mirrored pair is automatically created, and named with the same name as the zpool name. We used the following command to give the user bob permissions on the zpool, named dest, thus created:

   sudo chown bob:bob -R /dest

   Do the same thing, so that an ordinary user other than root can place files in the filesystem on the zpool. Finally, using the following Bash shell script, backup an important data file directory in your home directory, in tar format, to the dataset on the mirrored-pair of USB flashdrives. Substitute your pathnames, on your Raspberry Pi system, for source and destination directories shown for our system.

   Code **proj1.bash**, Bash Backup to a Mirrored Pair

```
# !/bin/bash
# A time stamp variable for logging
TIMESTAMP=$(date +"%Y%m%d.%H%M")
# Destination directory location on the mirrored pair as a variable
DEST_DIR="/dest"
# Source directory as a variable
SRC_DIR="/home/bob/Desktop/raspberry_linux"
# Variable for the backup file name file
FNAME="MyBackup"
# Variable for a log file, in an already created sub-directory in your home
# directory, and name the log file with the file name and time stamp
LOG="/home/bob/log/$FNAME-$TIMESTAMP.log"
# Message that the backup is started
echo -e "Starting backup of $SRC_DIR directory" >> ${LOG}
# Compress the source directory and files, copy the tar.gz file to
# your destination directory
tar -vczf ${DEST_DIR}/${FNAME}-${TIMESTAMP}.tar.gz ${SRC_DIR} >>\
${LOG}
# Message that the backup has ended, and append to log file
echo -e "Ending backup of $SRC_DIR" >> ${LOG}
```

2. Exchange a pair of ZFS mirrored USB flashdrives, that have some useful data on them, with a friend that has a Raspberry Pi, and have

them utilize the flashdrives on their system. How would you do this? Use the hint we provided In-Chapter Exercise 1.13.

3. Use the procedures and Bourne shell script of Example 1.6 to send incremental backup snapshots of an important user dataset, over a LAN to another system that can accommodate mirrored vdevs in higher RAID-Z configurations of your choice.

4. Create a zpool on a file as was done in Example 1.2, include some nano-edited text files in it, and then take a snapshot of it. What procedures would you have to execute to then reedit the snapshot, and the nano-created text files in the snapshot? Explain in detail. Then rollback the snapshot onto the original file system and zpool.

Chapter 2

2.1 Give definitions, in your own words, for the following terms as they relate to the X Window System: window system, window manager, desktop manager, client, server, focus, iconify, maximize, minimize, xterm, application user interface, management interface.

2.2 Which Window System window manager is used on your computer system? How can you identify and recognize which window manager you are using by default?

2.3 Which command allows another user to have their windows displayed on your screen under the X Window System? What would be the advantages of doing this? What would be the disadvantages of doing this? Explain why this is even possible at all under the X Window System.

2.4 Identify the xterm options that are set on your computer system. What is the default size of an xterm window? What is the default background color for an xterm window? What do you think are the most useful xterm options for you? How did you find all of the previous things out?

2.5 a. When you hold down the left-most mouse button when the screen cursor is in the root window of your Window System display, what appears on your screen? What appears when you hold down the middle mouse button? What appears when you hold down the right-most mouse button?

   b. What controls the appearance and content of the menus that are presented to you when you take these actions?

2.6 Do all windows launched on your Window System display have the same components—that is, scroll bars, iconify button, title bar, and resize handles? What facility controls the look and feel of these components? How do these components compare in function and operation to what you might be familiar with from another GUI—for example, when using OS X or Windows?

2.7 Use your favorite Web browser to explore the site www.X.org. What are the objectives of this organization? What is another good source of information on the X Window System?

2.8 Use your favorite Web browser to explore the site https://wayfire.org. What are the objectives of this organization? What is another good source of information on the Wayfire compositor?

2.9 Use your favorite Web browser to explore the site https://wayland. freedesktop.org/docs/html/ . What are the objectives of this organization? What is another good source of information on Wayland?

2.10 Install and use Gimp on your Raspberry Pi system to design a bit-mapped image for use as an icon in a pull-down menu. For example, if you were going to design a menu choice for reading from a file, your bitmapped image might look like a book that is open for reading.

2.11 After completing Problem 10, find an X-based application on your network that allows you to customize menu items. Then, design icon images for use with the application using Gimp and install them for use with the application.

2.12 What is a session manager, and how is it different from a desktop management system, or a window manager?

2.13 Why would someone want to do a nonintegrated installation of the Raspberry Pi OS, such as the "lite" version—that is, without a GUI (with only a text-based interface to the system)?

2.14 Why are server-class installations of Linux done without a GUI? What's the advantage of that, in terms of utilization of system resources? How is that achieved with systemd, for example, when you're running in a graphical.target state?

2.15 The primary task, and biggest challenge, of programming a client application in the X Window System is connecting the output of code that generates or actually is data—such as numbers, text strings, files, file structures, and so on—to a user UI implemented by one of the toolkits we show in this chapter. Of course, if the only objective of the UI of a client application program is to produce output graphics, then it is advisable to partition the client application into a data generation part (if there is one) and a graphics production part. Separating these two parts out is helpful and useful when the code for each needs to be modified, maintained in the future, or documented and understood by other developers or team programming members, and the connectivity between the two discrete parts must remain the same.

Examine all of the program examples we provide for Xlib, XCB, and Qt, and make a brief list of where the data in each program are generated, so that each of the toolkits can make graphics out of it. Also describe how those data are passed to the toolkit that uses the data, either as literal arguments, or as data structure mechanisms.

For example, since Xlib uses mostly a procedural paradigm to pass the data-generating components to the UI components, an entry in your answer tableau for the program example Xlib test1.c should appear like this:

Xlib test1.c	XFillRectangle(...,20, 20, 10, 10), XDrawString(..., msg, ...)	Integers, string

2.16 Modify client application program test1.c so that it draws three other types of graphics primitives in a single window opened on screen. Make sure the window is appropriately enlarged so that the primitives, whose geometry you customize by selecting coordinates of your choice, will be adequately framed.

2.17 Combine programs test1.c and test4.c so that you draw an unfilled rectangle and text strings into the same window opened on screen. Additionally, modify the GC of the window so that it provides different attributes for both the rectangle graphics primitive and the text drawn at each mouse click location.

2.18 Write a description of the Xlib API as you formulate it from the documentation available, both on-line and in printed media. Be sure to include details of how Xlib uses the C language data structure capabilities to accomplish its interactions between a) the client application code, b) the Xlib API, c) the X Window System Protocol, and d) lower-level graphics systems such as OpenGL and Mesa.

2.19 Modify the client application program 2ndxcbdraw.c so that the resulting program draws at least three of the primitives (with numerical parameters of your choice) found in the following table. You may also change the attributes of the primitives drawn by varying the GC.

Function	Description
xcb_poly_point (xcb_connection_t *conn, uint8_t coord_mode, xcb_drawable_t window, xcb_gcontext_t context_id, uint32_t num_points, const xcb_point_t *points)	Draws points

Function	Description
xcb_poly_line (xcb_connection_t *conn, uint8_t coord_mode, xcb_drawable_t window, xcb_gcontext_t context_id, uint32_t num_points, const xcb_point_t *points)	Draws lines between points
xcb_poly_segment (xcb_connection_t *conn, xcb_drawable_t window, xcb_gcontext_t context_id, uint32_t num_segments, const xcb_segment_t *segments)	Draws separate line segments
xcb_poly_arc (xcb_connection_t *conn, xcb_drawable_t window, xcb_gcontext_t context_id, uint32_t num_arcs, const xcb_segment_t *arcs)	Draws elliptical arcs
xcb_fill_poly (xcb_connection_t *conn, xcb_drawable_t window, xcb_gcontext_t context_id, uint8_t shape, uint8_t coord_mode, uint32_t num_points const xcb_point_t *points)	Draws a filled polygon polygon
xcb_poly_fill_rectangle (xcb_connection_t *conn, xcb_drawable_t window, xcb_gcontext_t context_id, uint32_t num_rects, const xcb_rectangle_t *rects)	Draws filled rectangles
xcb_poly_fill_arc (xcb_connection_t *conn, xcb_drawable_t window, xcb_gcontext_t context_id, uint32_t num_arcs, const xcb_arc_t *arcs)	Draws filled elliptical arcs

2.20 Modify client application program simple_xcb.c so that it draws at least one of the primitives shown in the table for Problem 1.

2.21 Modify program xcb_events.c so that it only reports mouse button presses and releases, and the coordinates at those points.

2.22 Use the Xlib program simple1.c to create a window display. Then, using the hex display ID number for that window, in gnuplot interactive mode, plot sin(x) in that Xlib-created window.

2.23 Use the XCB program xcb_simple.c, to create a window display.

Then, using the hex display ID number for that window, in gnuplot interactive mode, create plots of sin(x), cos(x), and tan(x) simultaneously in that XCB-created window.

2.24 A large set of demo plots is available on the web page www.gnuplot.info/demo/.

Be sure to go to a demo page that has demos for your version of the software, and supports the type(s) of terminals that you actually have available! Use the code shown in the demos to plot a variety of examples that interest you, in either the specified terminal type, or in an X11 window created by Xlib or XCB.

2.25 Find a simple example of a C program online that implements a window, and drawing, in Wayfire. How does it compare, in terms of complexity and ease of use, to Xlib, XCB, GTK4, or QT5 programs that do a similar thing? How do you compile it?

Chapter 3

3.1 This problem assumes that:

You can interactively start up a new non-login shell, the Bourne Again shell, or *bash*, which is already installed by default on that system. To do this, at the Bash shell prompt just type **bash** and press <Enter>. If a ~/.bashrc exists, before you begin, be sure to back up your existing ~/.bashrc file by using the **cp** command. To do so, type- **cp .bashrc .bashrc_bak** and then press <Enter>. If for any reason you destroy the contents of the ~/.bashrc file while doing this problem, you can restore the original by typing **cp .bashrc_bak .bashrc** and then pressing <Enter>.

If there is no .bashrc file in your home directory, use Emacs to create one and save it in your home directory as an empty file (with nothing in it). Also, in order for you to have permissions on that file, type:

chmod u+x .bashrc and press <Enter>.

Use Emacs to edit the ~/.bashrc file in your home directory, and then use the **<Ctrl-X>I** command to insert the file alien3 that you created in Practice Session 3.6 into the buffer. Save the buffer, exit Emacs, and log off your computer system. Log on to your computer system again, start up a new bash shell interactively by typing **bash** at the command line (so that the new ~/.bashrc is in effect), and test each of the DOS aliases that are in alien3 by typing them at the shell prompt, with their proper arguments (if necessary). They should give you the same results as when you ran the Bourne shell aliases in Step 21 of Practice Session 3.6.

What other way can you invoke the ~/.bashrc file immediately in this interactive session without logging off the system?

3.2 As you saw in the Practice Sessions, you can be editing more than one file at a time in Emacs, where each of the files' contents are being held in different buffers. Experiment by first using the **cp** command at the shell prompt to make a copy of the file datafile that you created in Practice Session 3.5. Name this copy datafile2. Use Emacs to open both files, datafile and datafile2, with the command **<Ctrl-X><Ctrl-F>**. You can switch between buffers with **<Ctrl-X B>**. Then edit both of them at the same time and cut and paste three or four lines of each between the two, using **<Ctrl-@>**, **<Ctrl-W>**, and **<Ctrl-Y>**.

Don't save your changes to the file named datafile!

3.3 Write a keyboard macro, as described in Section 3.16.4, to do everything shown in Steps 10–16 of Practice Session 3.4.

3.4 Try working with Emacs in a text-only window, and use only keystroke commands.

To do this, you will have to launch Emacs from a console or terminal window by typing **Emacs -nw newfile** The **-nw** option specifies that Emacs will run in a nongraphical mode. Then, in the console or terminal window, a non-graphical Emacs will open on the buffer newfile. Remember that you can still gain access to the Menu Bar menus at the top of the Emacs screen by pressing the escape **<Esc>** key on the keyboard and then pressing the single backquote (`) key. You can then descend through the menu bar choices by pressing the letter key of the menu choice you want to make. For example, pressing the **F** key on the keyboard gives you access to the File pull-down menu choices, and then pressing the **S** key on the keyboard allows you to save the current buffer.

3.5 To compare keystroke to graphical Emacs, repeat Problem 4, using purely graphical Emacs—that is, with no keystroke commands allowed. This time, make two copies of datafile named datafilex and datafilexx at the UNIX shell prompt with the **cp** command. Open all three files and, using the multiple-buffer and multiple window capability of the graphical form of Emacs, cut and paste among the files using only the mouse. Again, as in Problem 4, don't save your changes to the file datafile.

3.6 Use Emacs' capability of sending e-mail while you're in Emacs. Send an e-mail message to one of your friends, composing the message body and sending from within Emacs.

3.7 Use the **<Alt-x> customize** facility in Emacs to find the values of the following: Global Mark Ring Max, Tab Width, Fill Column, Standard Indent, Undo Limit, and provide a list of the values you find for each.

3.8 What Emacs command toggles Abbrev mode? What Emacs command removes all abbrev definitions, including global ones?

3.9 Define the following abbreviation as global abbreviations in Emacs with Abbrev using the word on the left of the equal sign (=) as the abbreviation, and list the command and keystrokes you used to create the abbreviations, and invoke them:

> **now = Now is the time for all good women to come to the aid of their country.**

3.10 Define a GNU Emacs keyboard macro that, when invoked, automatically enters all 26 lower-case letters of the alphabet, with a single space between each letter, at point. Name the macro **le** and bind it to the key **1** (the numeric number 1) for use only during this session of Emacs. Give the exact steps, commands, and typed-input you use to accomplish defining this macro and invoking it.

3.11 Define a GNU Emacs keyboard macro that, when invoked, automatically enters the integers 1 through 10, with a single space in between each number, at point. Name that macro **row** and bind it to the key **r** so that both the name and the key binding can be used in every subsequent Emacs session. Give the exact steps, commands, and typed-input you use to accomplish defining this macro and invoking it.

3.12 Define a line of elisp code and place it in your ~/.emacs file, that will designate the second mouse button on your mouse to issue a command to split the current buffer window horizontally.

Advanced GNU Emacs

3.13 Using **Emacs**, type in a paragraph of text from one of your favorite books, but without altering the size or shape of the **Emacs** frame or using the Enter key, use the word wrap feature of **Emacs** to format it exactly the way that it is printed in the book. Print the file at your Linux system line printer.

3.14 Define an **Emacs** keyboard macro that accomplishes a common editing task for you.

3.15 Create, edit, compile, link and execute a short C program of your choice in **Emacs**.

3.16 zenity is a graphical GTK+ dialog box program that allows you to create interactive dialog boxes using Bash script files. It is installed by default on our Raspberry Pi system. In this problem, you will use Emacs to create a zenity Bash script file.

a. Use Emacs to create and save the following bash script file, named zen1, in your home directory:

```
#!/bin/bash
zenity --forms --title="newusers Command" --text="Add batch new
user" \
  --add-entry="Username" \
  --add-password="Password" \
  --add-entry="User Number UID" \
  --add-entry="Group Number GID" \
  --add-entry="GECOS Entry" \
  --add-entry="Default Home Directory" \
  --add-entry="Default Shell" \
>> zen_out
sed -i -e 's/|/:/g' /home/bob/zen_out
```

b. On the command line, use the command **chmod u+x zen1**, then type ./zen1

A zenity dialog box will open on-screen, as seen in Figure A.1.
In the GUI dialog box you will create the seven fields needed to be supplied to the **newusers** command, to create new users from a "batch file" on your Raspberry Pi system. The seven inputs you supply to the dialog box will be written to a file named zen_out.

The seven fields, separated by the colon character (:), are the new user accounts name, password, UID, GID, GECOS commentary, default home directory, and default shell.

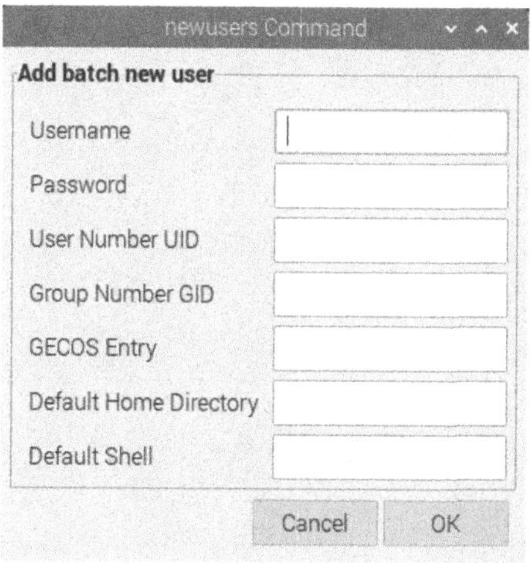

FIGURE A.1
Zenity dialog box.

For example:

bob:QQQ:2001:2001:CFO of Accounting:/home/bob:/bin/bash

    c.   Use zen1 to create a file of several new users you want to put on your system.

Index

Printed in the United States
by Baker & Taylor Publisher Services